D0574846

5

THEORIES
of the
MIND

———

THEORIES
of the
MIND

—

Stephen Priest

HOUGHTON MIFFLIN COMPANY

Boston   New York   London

Copyright © 1991 by Stephen Priest

All rights reserved

The moral right of the author has been asserted.

For information about permission to reproduce
selections from this book, write to Permissions, Viking Penguin,
375 Hudson Street, New York, New York 10014.

Library of Congress Cataloging-in-Publication Data
Priest, Stephen.
Theories of the mind / Stephen Priest.
p.   cm.
Includes index.
ISBN 0-395-62338-3
1. Philosophy of mind.   I. Title.
BD418.3.P75   1991
128´.2 — dc20   91-48100
CIP

Printed in the United States of America

AGM   10   9   8   7   6   5   4   3   2   1

To my mother, Peggy Priest

CONTENTS

PREFACE

Are you just a complicated physical object? If not, are you a mind? If so, what are minds? What exactly is the relationship between the mind and the body? Are you a mind with a body or a body with a mind? You are looking out of your body now. Does that mean you are your body or does it mean you are inside your body, or neither? Could we be immaterial souls which survive our bodily death, or has that been ruled out by modern science? Are you your brain? How, if at all, is grey matter connected to our innermost thoughts and emotions?

It is one of our peculiarities that we do not know what we are. The most fundamental problem we face in finding out what we are is the mind–body problem: the problem of stating correctly what the relation is between mental and physical, or between the mind and the body. Philosophy is the attempt to solve philosophical problems and this book is about what certain outstanding philosophers of the Western intellectual tradition have said in order to try to solve the mind–body problem.

The book is divided into eight chapters, each dealing with a different solution to the mind–body problem. Some philosophers think that you and I are just complicated physical objects. Some philosophers think you and I are immortal souls. Some think we have both mental and physical characteristics. Others again think we are fundamentally neither mental nor physical. Some philosophers are inspired by religion, others by the natural sciences, others again by sheer puzzlement about ourselves and the universe.

Necessarily, a book of this kind is selective. I have set aside issues in philosophy of mind, philosophy of psychology, cognitive science and artificial intelligence which do not bear directly on the mind–body problem. Instead I concentrate on the attempts of philosophers to solve the metaphysical question of whether human beings, such as you and I, are just highly complicated physical objects or something more. Also, if space had permitted I would have discussed the views of many more philosophers than those presented here. However, all the main solutions to the mind–body problem in the Western philosophical tradition are portrayed, and in the last chapter I offer a new one.

The word 'theories' in the title of the book is used broadly, to denote any answer to the questions of the nature of the mind and its relation to the body that may be sustained by argument. While I may suggest criticisms of the theories as I explain them, I mainly reserve judgement until the final chapter. I shall be well satisfied if the reader finds plausibility in theories that are incompatible with his or her own assumptions. Part of the value of philosophy lies in the discovery that world-pictures radically different from one's own are eminently plausible.

I am grateful to my colleagues in the Department of Philosophy, in the University of Edinburgh for providing such an intellectually . stimulating work-place, and I thank in particular Willie Charlton, Vincent Hope, Peter Lewis, Geoffrey Madell and Stig Rasmussen for useful conversations. Versions of the last chapter were read to philosophical audiences at the University of Edinburgh and at Fort Lewis College, Colorado. I thank them for their responses. I have discussed the mind–body problem with many people in Scotland and the United States but I thank in particular Graham Bird, William Coe, Dugald Owen, Reyes García, Byron Dare, Joanna Swanson and John Thomas. None of them is necessarily to be taken as agreeing with the theses of this book.

I thank Jonathan Riley and Roger Wells of Penguin Books Ltd for their friendly efficiency. That the book exists as a physical object and not just a mental one is due in part to Peggy Priest and Lynn Evans.

Stephen Priest
Department of Philosophy
David Hume Tower
University of Edinburgh
October 1990

THEORIES
of the
MIND

1

DUALISM

Dualism is the theory that two and only two kinds of substance exist: minds and physical objects. A mind is a purely mental, non-material or spiritual substance, and a physical object is a purely material, non-mental, spatially extended substance. It logically follows that no mind is a physical object and no physical object is a mind. A person, on the dualist account, comprises both a mind and a body, but most dualists maintain that a person is *essentially* his or her mind but only *contingently* his or her body or, to put it another way, a person *is* his or her mind but a person *has* or *owns* his or her body. It follows that if a person's body should cease to exist it is logically possible that that person should continue to exist; but if a person's mind should cease to exist, then that person necessarily ceases to exist. In principle, minds may exist without bodies and bodies may exist without minds.

Mind–body dualism of this kind has been advocated repeatedly in the history of Western philosophy, and in this chapter we shall concentrate on two of its clearest and most celebrated exponents: Plato, the Athenian philosopher who lived and wrote in the fourth century BC and who arguably did most to initiate the problems and concerns of the Western intellectual tradition, and René Descartes, the seventeenth-century French philosopher and mathematician whose work is part of the transition from the theocentric world-picture of the Middle Ages to the more scientific ways of thinking of modern Europe.

The fact that I have chosen to examine the arguments of two figures drawn from the history of philosophy should not be taken to suggeset that dualism is in some way out of date. It would, for example, be a serious mistake to think that the progress of modern science has disproved the existence of the mind or the soul. On the contrary, some of our most sophisticated scientific and philosophical thinkers are mind–body dualists who take the reality of the mental most seriously. I have in mind in particular the Nobel Prize-winning neurobiologist Sir John Eccles, the philosopher of science Sir Karl Popper, and the Oxford philosopher of science and religion Richard Swinburne.

Nor should we be misled by the relation between dualism and religious, especially Christian, belief. The two are logically quite independent. Dualism might be true even if it is false that God exists, and God might exist even if dualism is false. In other words, the conjunction of dualism and atheism is not inconsistent, nor is the conjunction of the rejection of dualism with theism. It is true that Eccles and Swinburne are Christians, but Popper is an agnostic. Descartes was a Christian, but Plato's writings predate the life of Christ by four hundred years. Indeed, it is important historically to note that the immortality of the soul formed no part of Christianity before Paul and was only fully introduced into that religion by St Augustine of Hippo in the fourth century AD. The doctrine that an immaterial mind survives death was not part of Christ's teaching. He taught the resurrection of the body. It follows that mind–body dualism and orthodox Christianity are not only logically independent, they are incompatible.

There is a large variety of mind–body dualisms. Different taxonomies of dualisms may be generated, for example, by asking the following two questions: what are minds? and what is the relation between minds and bodies?

In their answers to the first question, all dualists agree that minds are both numerically and qualitatively distinct from those solid, spatio-temporally extended, publicly observable entities composed of matter called 'physical objects'. However, dualists disagree among themselves as to what minds are. For example, in their book The Self and Its Brain, Popper and Eccles argue that there exists a 'self-conscious mind', the states of which are not identical with any brain states, nor indeed with any sum of mental states.

There is nothing 'other-worldly' about their self-conscious mind. It is what you are, at least from when you wake up in the morning until you go to sleep at night. For Plato, Descartes and

Swinburne, however, the mind is identical with the immortal soul. In the writings of the fourth-century Greek philosopher-scientist, Aristotle, the soul is the 'form' of the body and so does not survive death. Nevertheless Aristotle holds that the mind, in the sense of 'intellect', is immortal. The Aristotelian philosopher-theologian St Thomas Aquinas holds that each person's immaterial soul survives that person's bodily death. However, a person does not thereby survive death because the person that one is is necessarily embodied. These points about surviving death bear closely on dualism because, if it may be proved that the mind is the soul and also proved that the soul is immortal, then it is proved that the mind is something distinct from the body because the body is mortal.

It is clear then that there are several dualist concepts of mind. They range from the commonsensical notion of the centre of conscious awareness which each of us seems to be, to the immaterial soul. It is important to note this variety because it is sometimes assumed that the claim, that consciousness exists, implies that immaterial minds exist. However, on the face of it it might be true that consciousness exists but false that immaterial minds exist. Both claims need argument.

The second way of classifying dualisms is according to the relations which allegedly hold between mind and body. Some dualists think causal relations hold between mind and body; other dualists deny this. Some dualists hold that events in minds are simultaneous with events in bodies; other dualists deny this. There is one relation which all dualists agree is not the relation between mind and body, and that is identity. Clearly, if the mind is identical with the body, or with any part of the body, dualism is false.

Descartes, Popper and Eccles maintain that events in minds cause events in bodies and events in bodies cause events in minds. So, on their dualistic theories there may be mental causes with physical effects and physical causes with mental effects. This view, that causal relations between mind and body are two-way, is known as 'psycho-physical interactionism' or just 'interactionism'.

Incompatible with that view is 'epiphenomenalism', the theory that there are physical causes of mental events but no mental causes of physical events. The mental is thus causally dependent on the physical. It is an 'epiphenomenon' of the physical just as, in T. H. Huxley's memorable image, the smoke above the factory is causally dependent upon the workings of machinery. It is often mistakenly said that epiphenomenalism is a kind of materialism. When some people are asked whether dualism is true, they reply: no, of course mental states are caused by states of the brain, or some such. A widespread confusion needs to be dispelled here. Suppose it is true, as it might well be, that mental states are caused by physical states of the brain. That fact, if it is a fact, by no means refutes dualism. A non-material mind could pre-date and post-date the states it is caused to be in by a brain. Also, if A and B are causally related then it logically follows that A and B are numerically distinct entities: A is not B and B is not A. If that is right, then if mental events causally depend upon physical events, that confirms dualism and does not refute it. Causal relations obtain only between distinct entities so if mental and physical are causally related, as epiphenomenalism has it, mental and physical are distinct entities. Mental events are not physical events: they are their mental effects.

Yet a different claim is that mental events are properties of physical events, or properties of physical objects. Even then, we still have a dualism of kinds: a dualism of physical objects and their mental properties. This sort of dualism is inconsistent with epiphenomenalism so long as it is impossible for something to be the cause of its properties.

Several dualists maintain the view that there are no causal relations between minds and bodies. The seventeenth-century French philosopher Nicolas de Malebranche, for example, believed that bodies cannot affect minds and minds cannot affect bodies, yet both minds and bodies exist and no body is a mind and no mind is a body. It is his view that the mind is not in the body and the body is not in the mind, but that both exist only in God. It is God who causes and sustains a parallel conjunction of mental and physical events. Notice that it is not necessary to accept the thesis that only God causes mental and physical events in order to accept the thesis that mental and physical events do not interact causally. Indeed, there is some intuitive or pre-philosophical plausibility in the view that there cannot be mental causes of physical effects or physical causes of mental effects. Consider the fact that the brain, as a physical object, is only a collection of atoms in motion. No matter how extraordinarily numerous and no matter how tremendously complex the motions of the atoms of the brain, it is hard to see how they could cause events like hopes, fears, regrets, depressions, memories of yesterday and images in the mind's eye. Indeed this fact, if it is a fact, also makes it hard to see how mental events could be identical with physical events in the brain, as the materialist wishes to argue.

The dualist is struck by the intense qualitative differences between the occurrences in one's consciousness and mere matter in motion which, however complex, is mere matter in motion. Dualists agree that minds and physical objects are qualitatively so different that the mental could not possibly be physical. Some dualists, for example Malebranche, conclude from this that mental and physical cannot causally interact. Other dualists, Descartes and Popper for example, do not conclude this even though they agree that nothing is both mental and physical.

The theory, that minds and bodies do not causally interact but that mental events and physical events in a person are correlated, is called 'psycho-physical parallelism' or sometimes just 'parallelism'. Apart from Malebranche, this has been maintained by another seventeenth-century philosopher: the German, G. W. Leibniz. Leibniz accepts that mental events may have mental effects and physical events may have physical effects but denies that mental events may have physical effects or physical events may have mental effects. Leibniz invites us to compare the operations of the mind and the operations of the body to two clocks, each of which keeps perfect time. God has initiated the causal chain which is the mental events in the mind and God has initiated the causal chain which is the physical events in the body by a 'pre-established harmony'. This ensures an orderliness in mental and physical events which may lead us to believe that the two kinds of event are causally related. (As with Malebranche's view we may, if we wish, disagree that God causes mental and physical chains of events and yet affirm that mental and physical do not interact causally.) The difference between Malebranche's parallelism and Leibniz's is this: Leibniz thinks that God initiates the two causal chains but does not subsequently intervene;

Malebranche thinks that God both initiates the two causal chains and intervenes as the real cause of every effect. The events which appear to us humans as genuine causes are only apparent causes or the 'occasions' for divine interventions. Hence Malebranche's particular brand of psycho-physical parallelism is sometimes known as 'occasionalism'. Leibniz and Malebranche may be thought of as trying to solve a problem bequeathed by Descartes: suppose dualism is true, how do mental and physical substance interact causally? Their solution is that they do not interact at all.

The dualisms of Descartes, Malebranche and Leibniz are consistent with the view that each mental event happens at the same time as some physical event with which (for Descartes) it may be causally related, and with which (for Malebranche and Leibniz) it may be caused by God to be simultaneous with. (I leave aside here the trivial point that if there are mental and physical events, and many of them, then it is likely that some events of each kind will happen simultaneously.) Eccles, by contrast, concludes from his neurological investigations that it is false that a given mental event is simultaneous with any physical (brain) event with which it is putatively identical or by which it is putatively caused. On the contrary, mental events may pre-date and/or post-date such brain events. It is in any case difficult to correlate mental events with brain events in order to establish either identities or causal dependencies because similar mental states are associated with qualitatively dissimilar neural patterns in different brains and in the same brain at different times. Eccles thinks the point about time is important for dualism. In this he might be right, because if A is B then A and B exist at all and only the same time, and if A wholly or partially pre-dates B or if B wholly or partially pre-dates A then it logically follows that A is not B. If mental events do not happen at the same time as physical events, then those mental events are not physical events and dualism is true.

Those, then, are the main sorts of dualism. I hope I have said enough to show that the truth or falsity of dualism does not depend upon the existence or non-existence of God, even if many dualists are also theists. Our starting point for discussion should be, so far as this is possible, some shared set of assumptions about mental and physical. We may wish to reject these assumptions later but, pre-philosophically, clods of earth that you turn over in digging the garden are physical but moods and emotions are mental. Lumps of metal are physical but images in the mind's eye are mental. Telephones, motor cars and houses are physical but perceptions of telephones and memories of motor cars are mental. The house is physical but as you stand and look at it your conscious awareness of it is mental.

To give some initial plausibility to dualism, or to show that on the face of it there is a distinction between mental and physical, consider the Battle of Waterloo first described just physically and then with a mental description added. In the purely physical description the trajectory and velocity of cannon balls and musket balls are mentioned, their striking human bodies or the earth. Sound waves make contact with the auditory nerves in these bodies and light waves with the retinas. Electro-chemical activity in those physical objects called 'brains' causes the movement of human bodies to and fro across the spatio-temporal region described. When a metal ball with a certain mass and velocity comes into contact with a human body, that body is damaged and gravity pulls it to the earth.

What is missing from this description? Many things, no doubt, but in particular everything mental is missing. There is no terror, desperate hope or deep-felt relief. There are no audible shouts of command, no fearful sights of masses of soldiers, no colours, no crash of musketry, no boom of cannon. There is no imagination of imminent death or injury, no prayers or pleas for survival, no acrid stench of blood and smoke; only silent, invisible matter in motion.

The point is this: no matter how complex and no matter how detailed the physical description, it does not capture what is mentioned in the mental description. No mental facts about the world logically follow from any list of purely physical facts, no matter how long. If that is right then the mental cannot be 'reduced' to the physical. The mental cannot be 'explained away'. The mental is all too real. The difference between the two Battles of Waterloo is that one is only physical and the other is both physical and mental. For the dualist it amounts to this: the Battle of Waterloo as fought by complicated robots, and the Battle of Waterloo with conscious minds participating. Physical objects seem to be spatio-temporal, publicly observable, tangible, solid and objective. Minds seem to be non-spatial, private to the owner, intangible, ethereal and subjective.

We may turn now to some of the arguments for mind–body dualism presented by Plato and Descartes.

PLATO

As is well known, Plato wrote philosophy in the form of dialogues. These take place between Socrates, Plato's great partial contemporary in Athens, and a series of interlocutors. So far as we know, Socrates never wrote any philosophy but questioned people he met about philosophical problems. Plato wrote down the ensuing dialogues and produced the most outstanding works of Western philosophy. I shall not enter here into the vexed historical questions as to whether Plato's Socrates is the historical Socrates, or the extent to which Plato's dialogues are expressions of Plato's philosophy rather than Socrates'. We just need to extract the mind–body dualism from Plato's work, decide exactly what it is and see whether it might be true. It finds its most sustained expression in the dialogue called the *Phaedo*.

The Cyclical Argument

The topic of the *Phaedo* is Socrates' arguments for the immortality of the soul, and his defence of them against the criticisms of his two philosophical friends, Cebes and Semmias. The issue has an especially poignant importance because it supposedly takes place while Socrates is awaiting execution for allegedly corrupting the youth of Athens by talking philosophy with them. The first argument he deploys concerns the coming to be and ceasing to be into and out of opposites. For this reason the argument is usually known as the Cyclical Argument. Socrates next asks Cebes whether he thinks living has an opposite and Cebes naturally replies that it has: being dead. Applying the general principle that opposites arise out of each other, Socrates concludes that living comes to be out of that which is dead and being dead comes to be out of that which is living: 'living people are born from the dead no less than dead people from the living' (*Phaedo*, 18).

Socrates takes this conclusion as evidence for reincarnation. As he puts it: 'the souls of the dead must exist somewhere whence they are born again' (*Phaedo*, 18), and the possibility of reincarnation clearly implies mind–body dualism. If one wished to question the soundness of this argument, two criticisms might be made. It seems relatively uncontroversial that, if something grows, then, it is larger than it was, or that, if something increases in strength, it was weaker than it is. But death might just be the cessation of life and that is all. It does not follow that being dead is a state in some ways rather like being alive but in other ways very different. Being dead might be not being at all. Secondly, it might be objected that the relevant opposite of 'alive' is not 'dead' but 'not alive' or 'inanimate'. Then, if a person is alive, what he has 'come to be out of' might be merely some inanimate matter and not some pre-natal, non-physical realm. It would seem to require further argument to show that if a person is not alive then he or she still exists, but as a non-material soul.

The Recollection Argument

However, Socrates deploys a second argument designed to show just that. The so-called Recollection Argument has as its conclusion that our souls existed before we were born. This thesis also clearly implies dualism because, if one's soul existed before one's body, then clearly one's soul cannot be identical with one's body. The argument appears in many places in Plato's dialogues, most notably in the *Meno*. There Socrates teaches some geometry to Meno's slave boy, but the tuition has a peculiar form. It consists in eliciting from the slave boy what he already knows but has forgotten. Socrates questions him about the mathematical properties of certain geometrical figures and receives true replies which the slave boy had not been taught. It is concluded on this basis that the knowledge we have is in fact all recollection. It was not acquired in the physical world we currently experience, so it must have been acquired in some non-physical world which we previously experienced. In the *Phaedo* this conclusion is used directly to maintain that the soul is immortal. Socrates asserts that 'our learning is nothing but recollection' (*Phaedo*, 19), and that this would be impossible unless the soul existed previously, independently of the human body, so the conclusion is: 'the soul is something immortal' (*Phaedo*, 19).

Cebes and Simmias present a fairly obvious objection to this

argument. It seems to prove that our souls existed before we
were born but fails to prove that they will continue to exist after
we die. Socrates' reply is that the Cyclical Argument and the
Recollection Argument have to be combined in order to obtain
the whole truth about reincarnation. This is that the living and
the dead 'come to be from each other' (*Phaedo*, 17) that there is a
'perpetual reciprocity in coming to be', and that we should think
of this process as 'revolving in a circle' (*Phaedo*, 18).

The Soul and the Forms

Mind–body dualism and the doctrine that knowledge is recollection are fully consistent with Plato's theory of Forms, as outlined
in the *Republic* and other dialogues. Plato thinks that the ordinary
physical objects with which we are acquainted through sense
perception are instances or exemplifications of perfect, quasi-
mathematical, non-spatio-temporal, general ideas called 'forms', in
which they 'participate'. The empirical world we perceive is supposedly less real than the perfect realm which makes it possible,
and it is only through a strict philosophical training, an ethically
disciplined life-style and a rational exercise of the intellect that
we may obtain knowledge of the Forms – knowledge of the true
nature of reality. It is Plato's view that before birth our souls
were in fact in direct contact or communion with the Forms. We
were appraised of the nature of goodness, justice, courage, knowledge, the state and so on by knowing the corresponding form.
At birth our souls are plunged into a forgetful ignorance by
confrontation with the objects of the senses, and sensuous
pleasures distract our spiritual natures from achieving true
wisdom. At death, however, the soul is restored to its previous
status, and once again we may know the Good and all the other
Forms.

This metaphysical picture clearly requires the truth of mind–
body dualism, because being alive consists in being temporarily
connected to a body. It is not essential to one's existence that
one's body should exist, but it is essential that one's soul should
exist. Similarly, if we seem to be acquiring knowledge while we
are embodied – as for example Meno's slave boy seemed to be –
then what is in fact happening is that the soul is recollecting its
direct acquaintance with the Forms before birth. I mention the

doctrine of Forms here because it is possibly part of Plato's philosophical motivation in arguing for dualism in the *Phaedo*.

The Affinity Argument

Socrates deploys yet a third argument for the immortality of the soul in the *Phaedo* because he observes that Simmias and Cebes are still not completely persuaded of that conclusion. He says that 'you seem afraid, like children, that as the soul goes out from the body, the wind may literally blow it apart and disperse it' (*Phaedo*, 26). Cebes replies with honesty: 'maybe there is a child inside us who has fears of that sort' (*Phaedo*, 26).

The problem is whether the soul is destructible or indestructible. If the mind or soul can be proved to be indestructible, then we may take it that mind–body dualism is true, so long as the body is destructible – which is an eminently plausible assumption to make. There is a general principle at work here which is of considerable importance in the philosophy of mind. If we want to know whether something is the same thing as something else or is something entirely distinct from it, one criterion to invoke is the following: suppose x has properties A, B and C but not D, E and F, but suppose y has properties D, E and F but not A, B and C; then it follows that x is not y. If x and y are to turn out to be one and the same, then x and y must share all and only each other's properties. If x has properties y lacks or if y has properties x lacks, then x is not y. The principle is known as 'Leibniz's Law'.

We shall encounter this criterion in Chapter 4, but it is worth mentioning here because it is tacitly at work in Socrates' present argument. If it turns out that the soul has properties which the body lacks or that the body has properties which the soul lacks, then it must be the case that the soul is something distinct from the body.

Socrates' strategy is to ask what sorts of things are liable to dispersal, or destruction, and which things are not so liable. It is decided that composite things, things made up of other parts, are destructible but that non-composite things are indestructible. The thinking here seems to be that a composite thing may be broken along the points of composition but a non-composite thing has no such points of vulnerability. Dispersal or destruction is in this sense the opposite of composition, so perhaps the thought also is that what was once composed may be dispersed, but what was never composed may not be dispersed. In any case, Socrates' conclusion about dispersal is 'If there be anything incomposite, it alone is liable, if anything, to escape this' (*Phaedo*, 27).

The next premiss is the suggestion that incomposite entities are those which are 'constant and unvarying' (*Phaedo*, 27) and that they tend also to be invisible and intangible. By contrast, composite items never remain the same and are visible and tangible. At work at this stage of the argument is Plato's distinction between the universal perfect Forms, which are indeed invisible and unchanging, and the physical objects we perceive about us, which constantly undergo change. As examples of things which do not change Socrates gives 'being itself', 'the beautiful itself' and 'the equal itself'. The word 'itself' is often an indication that the Form of the phenomenon in question is being referred to.

All that remains for Socrates to do in order to obtain his desired conclusion is to decide to which category the soul belongs, the composite or the non-composite, and to which category the body. Perhaps predictably, at this point of the dialogue Socrates distinguishes soul and body thus: 'Soul is most similar to what is divine, immortal, intelligible, uniform, indissoluble, unvarying and constant in relation to itself' (*Phaedo*, 29) and 'Body ... is most similar to what is human, mortal, uniform, non-intelligible, dissoluble, and never constant in relation to itself' (*Phaedo*, 29). If Socrates has shown that soul and body have different properties, and if Leibniz's Law is true, then Plato has proved mind–body dualism. But how persuasive should we find his argument? One problem for using it to prove dualism is that the truth of dualism seems to be assumed as a premiss, in the sense that, in order for it to make sense to talk of body and soul possessing distinct properties, it has to be assumed that in some sense we have both bodies and souls. Indeed, this assumption is made explicit when Socrates invites Cebes to agree that 'We ourselves are part body and part soul' (*Phaedo*, 28). This would seem to make the Affinity Argument, as an argument for dualism, blatantly circular. Socrates' position could be defended against this objection if we weaken the premiss so that it becomes the claim that people have both physical and mental aspects. This in itself is relatively non-controversial: we talk about a person thinking and perceiving and so on, but also as being located in a particular place, as weighing so many kilograms, and so on. Nor would this plausible assumption prejudice any argument towards a conclusion claiming the truth of a particular theory of the mind. It would, however, leave room for emphasizing the differences between the mental and the physical in the way Socrates wishes.

A perhaps more serious objection is to the tacit role of Leibniz's Law. It is perhaps true that, if two seemingly different entities are to turn out to be one and the same, then they must share all and only each other's properties. What Socrates needs to show is that soul and body are such that they cannot share the properties crucial to the characterization of each. It seems possible at first glance that one and the same entity could possess both psychological and physical properties (a sensation?) or divine and physical properties (Jesus Christ?). If the reply to this is that the soul lasts longer than the body and so is not any part of the body, then an independent argument is required for just that reply; otherwise the argument is open to a new charge of circularity. It becomes essential to prove that the soul outlives the body in order to prove dualism, because it is that alleged characteristic which could not possibly be possessed by the body.

In fairness to Socrates, it is likely that he intends to persuade us only that it is very probable that the soul survives the death of the body. He notes that the body does not disintegrate immediately after death, and so, given their respective natures, it is most likely that the soul endures longer than the body. In that case this conclusion is intended as possessing only a high degree of certainty: 'With that kind of nature, surely, Simmias and Cebes, there is no danger of its [the soul's] fearing that on separation from the body it may be rent apart, blown away by the winds, go flying off, and exist no longer anywhere at all' (Phaedo, 34). Simmias' response to this conclusion is that 'In these matters certain knowledge is either impossible or very hard to come by in this life' (Phaedo, 35), but both he and Cebes proceed to bring an objection to Socrates' dualism.

Simmias' objection takes the form of an analogy. The tuning of a lyre is something invisible and non-physical, and the musical instrument itself is both physical and destructible. Nevertheless, we do not conclude on this basis that the tuning of a lyre could outlast the destruction of that lyre. Similarly, from the fact that the soul is invisible and non-physical it does not follow that it will outlast the body. The implied lesson for the dualist is that the mental and the physical may well have different properties, but it does not follow from that that the existence of the mental is not dependent upon the existence of the physical.

Cebes also thinks that the Affinity Argument does not prove that the soul is immortal. His objection is that, from the fact that the soul lasts longer than the body, it does not follow that it lasts for ever. He too deploys an analogy: a man's cloak may last longer than he does, but we do not accept that as a reason for believing that cloaks are immortal.

Socrates has three rebuttals to Simmias. He points out that the attunement analogy's holding good is incompatible with the Recollection Argument. The tuning of the lyre does not pre-date the lyre, but if the soul does not pre-date the body then knowledge cannot possibly be the soul's recollection of its contact with the Forms before birth. It follows that Simmias is forced to choose between his lyre analogy and the recollection doctrine. He chooses the recollection doctrine and concedes to Socrates: 'I must allow neither myself nor anyone else to say that the soul is attunement' (*Phaedo*, 43).

The second rebuttal is more complex. Socrates obtains Simmias' agreement that tuning is a state of the elements of the musical instrument and that the physical parts of the lyre act on the tuning but that the tuning does not affect the physical parts of the lyre. But then Socrates points out that this is not at all the same as the relation between soul and body; for example, the soul frequently manages to act against bodily feelings by mastering and disciplining them. In the case of the lyre, the causal relation operates only one way, from physical to non-physical or, to follow the analogy through, from physical to mental. But in the case of people, the causal relation seems to operate both ways, from mental to physical as well as from physical to mental. There is some intuitive plausibility in this because we do commonsensically recognize that our thoughts or emotions may influence our physical movements and that our bodily sensations may affect our thoughts and desires. It remains an open question whether this fact of two-way causal interaction supports mind–body dualism or hinders it.

Finally, Socrates points out yet another disanalogy between attunement and the soul: attunements vary. Being in tune is arguably a matter of degree, and one lyre can be more in tune than another. But 'no soul is more or less a soul than another' (Phaedo, 44). Being or having a soul does not admit of degrees. It is an all-or-nothing matter.

The Argument from Opposites

Socrates' reply to Cebes is the final argument for the immortality of the soul in the Phaedo. As in the Cyclical Argument, Socrates makes use of the concept of an opposite, but in a rather different way. His claim is that opposites exclude one another; for example, if a number is odd then it is impossible for that number to be even; if something is just then it cannot in exactly that respect be unjust; if something is musical then it is not unmusical, and so on. This has to be the case, Socrates argues, because 'an opposite will never be opposite to itself' (Phaedo, 56). He draws on the theory of Forms to substantiate this thesis, but in fact the point is a logical one. It amounts to the truth that, if something is true of a thing, it is logically impossible for it in just that respect not to be true of that thing. To put it another way, it is impossible for something both to possess and to lack a certain property in exactly the same respect.

Having established the mutual exclusivity of opposites, Socrates invites Cebes to decide: in virtue of the presence of what exactly is a body living? Cebes replies that it is the soul. But death is the opposite of life, so life and death are opposites. If the soul gives rise to life, it can no more admit of death than an odd number can be even, and so, Socrates concludes, it must be immortal: 'When death attacks a man, his mortal part, it seems, dies; whereas the immortal part gets out of the way of death, departs, and goes away intact and undestroyed' (Phaedo, 61).

If this argument is sound, then Socrates has refuted Cebes' objection and shown that the soul not only outlasts the body but is immortal. If either of these conclusions is true, then mind–body dualism is true.

DESCARTES

Descartes is perhaps best known as the philosopher who

systematically called into question his most fundamental beliefs in order to place knowledge on secure, indubitable foundations. In the history of modern philosophy he is a pivotal figure in the transition from the theocentric and Aristotelian world-picture of the Middle Ages to the rationalist and scientific methods which emerged in the seventeenth century. Much of Descartes' philosophy may be read as an attempt to reconcile the merits which he perceived in orthodox Christianity with the explanatory power of the new sciences. In particular he wished to substitute proof and observation for scholastic authority, yet repudiate scepticism concerning the existence of God and the soul. His conviction was that, if some item of knowledge could not be doubted, then that item was absolutely certain, and the rest of knowledge could be reinstated using that certain knowledge as first premiss. Notoriously, he doubted in turn the evidence of the five senses, the existence of physical objects, the truths of the various sciences, the existence of God, the claims of mathematics and geometry, and indeed all the various kinds of truth he had previously taken for granted. This procedure culminated in his being unable to cast doubt on just one belief – the belief in his own existence. He concluded that, just so long as he doubted, he had to exist in order to do the doubting. Doubting is a kind of thinking, so he felt entitled to affirm his famous principle *cogito ergo sum* – 'I think therefore I am' – as the sought-for foundation of knowledge.

We do not need to explore all the philosophical merits and demerits of Descartes' doubting procedure in order to decide what his mind–body dualism is and whether it may be true. Nor need we concern ourselves with his various arguments reinstating science, mathematics, God and common sense, but we do need to address Descartes' treatment of a question that arises naturally out of his proof of his own existence. He takes himself to have proved the truth of this belief: I exist; but then he goes on to ask a quite new question: what am I? The way in which Descartes tries to answer this question leads us straight to his dualism because the answer he eventually offers is that he is essentially a thing that thinks. This in itself does not commit him to mind–body dualism, but he goes on to argue that he is essentially or really a mind or a soul and that, if his body ceased to exist, he could still continue to exist, and this is manifestly dualist.

The argument that he is essentially a thing that thinks is to be found in the second *Meditation*, and the argument that there is a real distinction between mind and body is in the sixth *Meditation*. I shall treat each of these in turn and, where appropriate, draw on arguments from the *Discourse on Method*.

Existence and Essence

Descartes says that 'I exist' is necessarily true so long as he expresses or thinks it. We could understand this in various ways. If a sentence is necessarily true, then not only is it true but it could not be false. We do not want to make it a necessary truth in this unqualified sense that Descartes – or, indeed, anyone – exists because it is plausible to assume that no one might have existed. The necessity of 'I exist' arises from its first-person form. We could say that 'I exist' is necessarily true while it is thought or spoken as a sentence, or, to put it another way, its truth is a condition of its being produced. 'I exist' is a premiss in the arguments for Descartes' dualism, so we need to bear in mind its status in what follows. Descartes notes that, although he has proved the truth of 'I am', he does not know clearly enough the answer to the question as to what he is. He uses the same method of doubt he has employed so far in order to answer this new question. But what does the question mean? The shift is from a question about existence to a question about essence. Existence questions have the form: Is it? or Am I?, and so on. Essence questions have the form: What is it? or What am I? and so on. The distinction was popular during the Middle Ages and dates back at least as far as Aristotle; and Descartes inherits it from this tradition, despite his reluctance to regard Aristotle as an authority on most matters. Something's essence is what that thing really is. The idea is that there is a set of attributes such that if something possesses those attributes then that thing exists as a specific sort of thing, but if it lacks those attributes it does not exist as that sort of thing. Descartes wants to know what his essence is.

He says: 'I who am certain that I am do not yet know clearly enough what I am' (*Meditations*, 103). The first answer he entertains is the Aristotelian one that he is a rational animal. He rejects this solution abruptly on the grounds that it would give rise to a regress of definitions: he would have to decide what was meant by 'animal' and what was meant by 'rational', and then define the terms used to define those terms, and so on. Rather than rely on Aristotle as an authority for his own nature, he decides to examine himself. As he puts it: 'I applied myself to a consideration of my being' (*Meditations*, 104). His technique is to perceive himself and think about himself and decide what characteristics he commonsensically seems to have. On the face of it he seems to have both physical and mental characteristics:

I considered myself, firstly, as having a face, hands, arms, and the whole machine made up of flesh and bones such as appears in a corpse and which I designated by the name of body. I thought, furthermore, that I ate, walked, had feelings, and thought, and I referred all these actions to the soul. (*Meditations*, 104)

It is clear from this passage that Descartes shares the pre-philosophical assumption that in some sense each of us has both a mind and a body, but he wants a much stronger conclusion than this. He argues that he is essentially his mind or soul. He considers in turn each of the main features he seems to possess – eating, walking, sensing and so on – and doubts the existence of each in turn. He finds he is able to doubt even the existence of his own body; after all, he doubts the evidence of the senses in general and so doubts the existence of all physical objects. If the existence of physical objects is dubitable, then it logically follows that the existence of one's own body is dubitable because one's own body is a physical object. He finds he can conceive of himself as existing in the absence of all the common-sense characteristics of a person except one:

Another attribute is thinking, and here I discover an attribute which does belong to me; this alone cannot be detached from me. I am, I exist; this is certain; but for how long? For as long as I think, for it might perhaps happen, if I ceased to think, that I would at the same time cease to be or to exist. I now admit nothing which is not necessarily true: I am therefore, precisely speaking, only a thing which thinks, that is to say, a mind, understanding or reason. (*Meditations*, 105)

Earlier he had concluded that he exists because he thinks, now he adds that thinking is the attribute which is essential to his being what he is. The premiss which facilitates this transition is the claim that thinking cannot be 'detached from' him. By 'detached from' him, he means conceived or imagined not to pertain to him, or doubted so to pertain. So Descartes is claiming that he cannot doubt that he is thinking so long as he exists. But is that correct? We have to distinguish these two issues: whether one can doubt that one thinks so long as one exists, and whether one can doubt that one thinks so long as one is thinking. On the first of these, it is quite possible to imagine oneself existing but not thinking; I can imagine myself being unconscious, for example. As to the second, it seems difficult to believe that one is not thinking now if one is thinking now. That is at least psychologically awkward, if not incoherent. Descartes is aware of this distinction, so he reaches a cautious conclusion. He says that, if he ceased thinking, it is possible that he would cease to exist. He feels entitled to affirm his existence only at those times when he is thinking. The reason for this is the status of *cogito ergo sum*. Although this means 'I think therefore I am', a more cautious claim is 'I am thinking now therefore I exist now'. This second interpretation is suggested by Descartes' belief that he can be sure that he exists only so long as he thinks.

Is Descartes correct to conclude that thinking is his essential attribute on the basis of this argument? He can doubt all his other attributes, but he cannot doubt that he is thinking, so thinking really belongs to him. Two problems emerge here. From the fact that he cannot imagine that he is not thinking so long as he thinks, it does not seem to follow that thinking is his essential attribute. As he admits, it is possible that he could exist without thinking. In that case he would exist, and exist as the sort of being he is, without thinking, so thinking would not be his essential attribute.

Secondly, from the fact that it can be doubted whether certain attributes are essential to him, it does not seem to follow that they are in fact inessential. Suppose it is true that he could not exist without a body, and could not be the sort of being he is without a body. Then, even if he can imagine not having a body, it does not follow that his body is inessential to him. The difficulty is with Descartes' method. He assumes that if it can be doubted that something is part of him then it is really not part of him, and if it cannot be doubted that something is part of him then it is really part of him. But perhaps what we can doubt includes what is really the case, and perhaps what we cannot doubt includes what is really not the case.

Descartes' cautious claim is that he is sure that he exists just so long as he continues to think, so thinking is his essential attribute. But what is he? He thinks he is being equally cautious when he says he is precisely a 'thing that thinks': 'I am ... a real thing, and really existing; but what thing? I have already said it: a thing which thinks' (*Meditations*, 105) and he has already defined 'a thing which thinks' as 'a mind, understanding or reason'. We need to decide now whether Descartes has any good grounds for two steps which are vital to his attempt to prove dualism. He argues that he is a thing, and he argues that the thing that he is is a mind. On both these points it might be objected that his doubting has not been thorough enough. We may agree that 'I exist' is in some sense true if 'I am thinking' is true, but it may be doubted whether there has to be a thinker to do the thinking. After all, perhaps the 'I' in 'I exist' just refers to the thinking itself. Then 'I think therefore I am' would amount to no more than 'I think therefore thinking exists' or even 'thinking exists therefore thinking exists'. It is no doubt part of common sense that there cannot be thinking going on without an 'I' to do the thinking, but many tenets of common sense have been subjected to Cartesian doubt, and there seems to be no special argument to guarantee immunity to the I.

Suppose however we concede to Descartes the assumption that there cannot be thinking without a thing which thinks. The question now is whether this thing, this I, has to be a Cartesian mind; might it not be something else — for example, a physical object such as a brain? Descartes says: 'I am not this assemblage of limbs called the human body' (*Meditations*, 105). Again, the argument is that he can doubt the existence of his body but he cannot doubt that he is thinking, so he is not essentially his body. He is essentially a thing which thinks. However, it might be the case that the thing which thinks is the body — especially perhaps the brain — even if he can doubt the body's existence. It might even be suggested that the idea of a mind or soul is a kind of imagined residue left by imagining away the body but still thinking of what thinks, as though, because the thinker is not a physical object, the thinker must be some strange non-physical object.

In defence of Descartes, there is something peculiar about saying, I am a physical object. Physical objects are objective and are not normally thought of as having subjective mental properties. Also, Descartes is trying to admit nothing that does not seem to him to be indubitably true, so when it is objected that he should have said only 'there is thinking', he could reply that the idea of the self is missing here. This is perhaps captured by 'I am however a real thing and really existing' (*Meditations*, 105). Perhaps the truth of this is self-evident to consciousness even when the body is imagined not to exist. Perhaps being a mind or soul makes the various activities of thinking into activities of one and the same self.

Two Substances

Descartes presents a similar argument in the *Discourse on Method*, and this is worth examining because it places greater emphasis on the point that he is not his body. It is worth quoting in full:

Examining attentively what I was, and seeing that I could pretend that I had no body and that there was no world or place that I was in, but that I could not for all that pretend that I did not exist, and that on the contrary, from the very fact that I thought of doubting the truth of other things, it followed very evidently and very certainly that I existed: while on the other hand, if I had only ceased to think, although the rest of what I had ever imagined had been true, I would have had no reason to believe that I existed; I thereby concluded that I was a substance of which the whole essence or nature consists in thinking, and which, in order to exist, needs no place and depends upon no material thing; so that this I, that is to say the mind, by which I am what I am, is entirely distinct from the body, and even that it is easier to know than the body, and moreover, that even if the body were not, it would not cease to be all that it is. (*Discourse on Method*, 54)

The first part of this quotation is a reiteration of the argument that he can doubt whether he has a body but he cannot doubt that he exists; but on the other hand he can doubt whether he would continue to exist if he ceased to think. These are his main reasons for holding that he is essentially a thing that thinks but not a physical object. To appreciate the full force of this conclusion, we need to understand what Descartes means by 'substance'. He says that he is a substance whose whole essence or nature consists in thinking. The concept of substance is, again, one that was popular in the Middle Ages and really originates with Aristotle. It can be defined in two main ways. Something is a substance if it is the bearer or holder of properties or characteristics but is not itself a property or characteristic; also, something is a substance if it does not depend upon the existence of anything else for its own existence – if it can exist independently. Descartes thinks there are two and only two sorts of substance: mental and physical. A mind or soul is a mental substance because it has its various thoughts as properties or characteristics. It is not identical with those thoughts, it is what has them. A physical object is a physical substance because it has the various characteristics of size or shape. It is not identical with these characteristics, it is what has them. Nor are minds and physical objects properties or characteristics of anything else. Descartes also thinks they can exist independently of one another. However, Descartes has one important reservation about the second definition of 'substance'. Strictly speaking, God is the only substance in the sense of that which depends on nothing else for its own existence. Minds and physical objects depend on God for their existence because God created them all and God could, in principle, annihilate them all. So minds and physical objects are substances in the sense that they depend upon nothing for their existence except God.

In the passage just quoted, Descartes claims that he is a substance: one of the mental substances or minds. He needs an argument for this conclusion because prima facie there seem to be two plausible alternatives. He might be a physical thinking object, or he might be just the thinking itself. His argument that he is a non-physical substance consists in the fact that he can doubt the existence of his body, and indeed of the whole physical world where he normally thinks of himself as located. He assumes that if it can be doubted that the physical world exists then it is logically possible that the physical world should not exist. Normally, when we say something is logically possible, we mean there is no contradiction in supposing it to be so. So, even if it would be false to assert that there is no physical world, someone who affirmed this would not have produced a contradiction. Descartes uses the power of God as a criterion to determine what is or is not logically possible, so that if, for example, it is logically possible that there should be no physical world, what this means for Descartes is that God might not have created a physical world, and perhaps could destroy this one. Now if it is logically possible that he, Descartes, could exist as a thinker even if there were no physical world, then it follows that he is not essentially a physical object. It also follows that he is a non-physical substance in the sense that he could still exist even if nothing else (except God) existed. This is in fact precisely what Descartes asserts when he claims in the passage quoted above that 'in order to exist' he 'needs no place and depends on no material thing' (*Meditations*, 54). The only plausible candidates for substances that exist are mental substances and physical substances. He is not a physical substance, but he exists. Therefore he must be a mental substance: a mind or a soul.

Identity and Difference

Two lines of objection might be brought against this argument. First, is it really possible to suppose one has no body? Secondly, even if this is conceivable, does it follow that one could exist without one's body? As regards the first of these, people's powers of imagination vary greatly, but it seems to me not impossible to imagine oneself as disembodied. It is perhaps difficult to believe oneself disembodied if one is embodied, but not contradictory to assert that one has no body. One might wish to identify oneself, for example, with the train of one's thoughts and emotions, or just think of oneself as a kind of unified consciousness.

The second objection perhaps presents Descartes with a more serious difficulty. From the fact that we can imagine that certain things are possible it does not in fact follow that they are possible; they may be or they may not be. Indeed, from the fact that something is logically possible it does not follow that it is in fact possible. So the fact that one can imagine oneself existing without one's body does not prove that one could exist without one's body. Even if the fact that one can imagine oneself existing without one's body shows that it is logically possible that one could exist without one's body, it does not show that one's existence is not causally or otherwise dependent upon the existence of one's body. The question would seem to be open.

Or is it? Descartes can advance at least two replies. Suppose we accept Descartes' thesis that God can make happen anything that is logically possible – anything which is not contradictory to describe. Suppose we accept further his view that from the fact that it can be imagined that something is possible then it is logically possible. Then if I can imagine myself disembodied then it is logically possible that I could exist disembodied, and, if that is so, God could bring it about that I exist disembodied. Then it would in fact be true that I could exist disembodied. This argument makes dualism rest on theological premisses – premisses about the existence and power of God. It takes us outside the scope of this book to investigate the plausibility of these premisses – out of the philosophy of mind and into the philosophy of religion – so we may just bear in mind here that one of the arguments for dualism is made more plausible if theism is true, that is, if God exists.

The second reply does not rely on theological premisses. It employs instead a version of Leibniz's Law, which we met in the discussion of Plato. If two seemingly distinct things are to turn out to be one and the same thing, then they must share all and only each other's properties. Suppose for example Dr Jekyll is to turn out to be one and the same person as Mr Hyde, then all the things that are true of that person who is Dr Jekyll must turn out to be in fact true of Mr Hyde, and vice versa. This is a condition of their being one and the same person. Conversely, if there are things that turn out to be true of Mr Hyde that are not true of Dr Jekyll, then they cannot be the same person. We need to apply this principle now to the case of mind and body. If it should turn out that there are things true of the body but not true of the mind, then mind and body must be distinct. But if anything true of the mind is true of the body and vice versa, then they are one and the same. I borrow this analogy from Anthony Kenny's book *Descartes*.

Descartes' view is that he can doubt the existence of his body, but he cannot doubt that he is a thinking thing or mind. It follows that something is true of the body but false of the mind. The body's existence can be doubted but the mind's cannot. By Leibniz's Law it would seem to follow that the mind is not the body, that mind and body are distinct. It would seem to follow that dualism is true.

The difficulty with this argument is that Leibniz's Law admits of exceptions. Consider the Jekyll and Hyde case. We might believe that Dr Jekyll did something but disbelieve that Mr Hyde did that very thing. We might doubt whether Dr Jekyll did something but be in no doubt as to whether Mr Hyde did that very thing. Then, in a sense, things would be true of the one which were not true of the other. But it would be fallacious to conclude from this that Dr Jekyll is not one and the same person as Mr Hyde. In the story, they turn out to be one and the same man.

In a parallel way, the fact that Descartes is able to doubt the existence of his body but unable to doubt the existence of his mind does not prove that mind and body could turn out to be distinct. Nor does it follow that Descartes is his mind rather than his body. He can imagine that his body does not exist but he cannot imagine that he does not exist (while he thinks), but that does not prove that he is not his body. Verbs like 'imagine', 'believe', 'doubt' and 'hope' are among those which generate exceptions to Leibniz's Law. Philosophers call the linguistic contexts which they produce 'referentially opaque'.

Making dubitability the distinction between body and mind leaves Descartes open to these objections. But Descartes thinks there are more important distinctions between the mental and the physical. Physical things are extended, that is, they have size; but it does not seem to make sense to talk about minds or consciousnesses having size. We can ask how broad a person is across the shoulders but only metaphorically inquire how broad his mind is. Bodies can be measured in feet and inches or metres and centimetres, but it would be absurd to attempt this with consciousnesses. For this reason Descartes thinks that extension is the defining characteristic or essential attribute of physical substance, and consciousness or thinking is the defining characteristic of mental substance.

In addition, according to Descartes, physical objects exist in both time and space, but minds exist only in time. They have no spatial characteristics. The first claim is relatively uncontroversial, but the view that minds exist only in time needs some argument. Intuitively or commonsensically, the thought seems to be as follows. If you are thinking, for example thinking about a piece of philosophy, then your thought seems to take time. It has a beginning, a duration and an end. You could even time it with a watch. On the other hand, were someone to inspect the contents of your skull while you were thinking, they would not come across those philosophical thoughts, or at least they would not observe them in the same way as you think them. No matter how closely we scrutinize someone's brain – and, it seems, no matter how much neurology we do – we cannot isolate the various thoughts, moods and emotions experienced by the person whose brain we are inspecting. If we take these points together, they suggest that minds are temporal but not spatial. If minds were located in space, it ought to be possible to encounter them in the public space we all share. Descartes thinks this marks an important and clear distinction between the mental and the physical.

Another difference between the mental and the physical on the Cartesian view is that one's knowledge of one's mental states is peculiarly incorrigible, but one's knowledge of physical objects is corrigible. This means that, if you believe you are in a mental state, then that belief cannot be mistaken; but if you are perceiving or thinking about a physical object, there is room for error – you might misidentify it or ascribe to it some characteristic it lacks. So, Descartes maintains, our beliefs about physical objects are corrigible: it is possible for them to be corrected; but our beliefs about the existence and nature of our own mental states are incorrigible. There is no room for them to be corrected because, if we have them, then they are true. Descartes also holds that minds are in a sense transparent to themselves. It is not possible to think without knowing that you think and what you are thinking. Also the thinker is always the best authority on what he is thinking, because, if a person is in a mental state, then they know they are in that state.

Notice that the transparency thesis and the incorrigibility thesis are logically related. If it is true that, if I am in a mental state, then I know I am in that state, then it is true that the belief I thereby have about that state is true. If it is true that, if I believe I am in a mental state, then that belief is true, then the belief I have in knowing I am in a mental state, if I am in that state, cannot be false. However, the incorrigibility thesis and the transparency thesis are not the same thesis. It is consistent with the truth of the thesis, if I believe I am in a mental state, then that belief is true that it be false that, if I am in a mental state, then I know I am in that state. This is because the incorrigibility thesis does not preclude the possibility of a mind being in a mental state it does not know it is in: an unconscious mental state. Descartes, however, thinks there are no unconscious mental states. Indeed, he believes the notion to be contradictory.

This is related to the final distinction between the mental and the physical. Physical objects are public in the sense that they may be publicly observed by more than one person; but minds, according to Descartes, are private to their owners. He means that the various mental processes which take place in a mind may be directly experienced only by that mind itself. They are intimately private to that mind and cannot be perceived by another person.

If we amass these various Cartesian distinctions between the mental and the physical, then Descartes seems to have ample grounds for arguing that minds and physical objects are quite distinct, if we assume Leibniz's Law. Minds are non-extended, merely temporal, known incorrigibly, and private; but none of these things is true of physical objects. Physical objects are extended, spatio-temporal, known only corrigibly, and public; but none of these things is true of minds. But if minds and bodies are not distinct they must share all and only each other's properties. They do not share all and only each other's properties. Therefore they are distinct.

If this argument is sound, then mind–body dualism is true. Minds and physical objects are entirely different sorts of things. No mind is a physical object and no physical object is a mind. For example, no brain can be a mind and no mind can be a brain. Our brains cannot be what we use to think with. We must think with our minds, and these are immaterial substances.

I postpone criticism of this argument until the discussion of materialism in Chapter 4. For the moment, we may note that from the fact that we have separate vocabularies, one mental and one physical, it does not logically follow that there are two separate substances, one mental and one physical. It makes sense to talk about a brain tumour but not about a mind tumour, but that does not seem conclusive proof that one's mind is something entirely distinct from one's brain. Perhaps, in order to speak accurately, we need to alter the way we use our language.

It should also be noted that Descartes is committed to the view that some of the things true of minds are true of physical objects and vice versa; for example, both exist, both are substances, both are temporal, both may be created and destroyed by God, both have attributes and each has an 'essence'. If we accept that there exist the following contrasts between mental and physical: temporality/spatio-temporality, incorrigibility/corrigibility and private/public, but we wish to deny that there exist two substances, one mental and one physical, then the onus is on us to show how these seemingly mutually exclusive properties could in fact turn out to be properties of one and the same single substance. In other words, we would have to prove monism against Descartes' dualism, in the face of these contrasting properties.

Clear and Distinct Ideas

We may now turn to the argument for the distinction between mind and body in the sixth *Meditation*. In essentials it is similar to the arguments we have met so far, but there is one all-important difference. The new argument depends upon the Cartesian doctrine of clear and distinct ideas. Descartes thinks that if something can be conceived very clearly and distinctly, then it is true. He does not mean by this that we may imagine clearly what we wish, and that what we imagine will then be the case. What he means is that, for example, it clearly and distinctly follows from I think that I exist. If you conceive something clearly and distinctly in your mind, you cannot doubt it. It is psychologically impossible to disbelieve it because its self-evident nature is such as to make it compelling to the intellect.

He uses this concept as a premiss in his new argument for dualism: 'It is sufficient for me to be able to conceive clearly and distinctly one thing without another to be certain that the one is distinct or different from the other' (*Meditations*, 156). So, if you can form a clear conception of what something is without having to have recourse to thinking of a second thing, those two things are distinct. What does Descartes mean by 'distinct' here? He means at least this: if A and B are distinct, then they are not the same thing; A is not B and B is not A. He also often means that A and B are not the same sort of thing: not only is A not B and B not A, but A is not like B and B is not like A. Also, if A and B are distinct, then this frequently carries the connotation that A and B do not depend upon each other for their existence. For example, if A and B are distinct sorts of substance, then A could exist without B and B could exist without A. As he puts it, 'they can be placed in existence separately, at least by the omnipotence of God' (*Meditations*, 156).

Descartes applies this principle directly to the case of mind and body:

Although perhaps ... I have a body to which I am very closely united, nevertheless, because on the one hand I have a clear and distinct idea of myself in so far as I am only a thinking and unextended thing, and because on the other hand I have a distinct idea of the body in so far as it is only an extended thing which does not think it is certain that I, that is to say my mind, by which I am what I am, is entirely and truly distinct from my body and may exist without it. (*Meditations*, 156)

In order to form a clear and distinct idea of himself he does not have to think of his body, and to form a clear and distinct idea of his body he does not have to think of himself; therefore his mind and body are distinct.

Is this argument sound? If we allow that one may conceive of oneself existing without one's body, and that one may conceive of one's body without conceiving of oneself existing, then the only questionable premiss is the claim that, if mind and body may be clearly and distinctly conceived to be distinct, then they are distinct. This premiss would seem in fact to be false. I can frame a clear and distinct idea of Dr Jekyll without framing a clear and distinct idea of Mr Hyde, but it does not follow that Dr Jekyll and Mr Hyde are distinct; they are in fact one and the same person. The general principle, that if a clear and distinct idea of A may be formed without a clear and distinct idea of B then A is not one and the same thing as B, would seem to be false. The truth or the falsity of 'A is B' is logically consistent with the clear and distinct conceivability of A and B as distinct; so, from the fact that mind and body may be clearly and distinctly conceived as distinct, it does not logically follow that they are distinct. Clearly it does not follow that they are not distinct either, so the appeal to clear and distinct ideas does not settle the issue either way.

Even if it is true that Descartes can frame a clear and distinct idea of his thinking as being his essential property, it does not follow that he has thereby framed an idea of his only essential property. It does not seem impossible that he should possess essential properties of which he is wholly ignorant or of which at least he may not frame clear and distinct ideas. If that is right, then it is possible that he cannot frame a clear and distinct idea of his whole essence but only of a part of it. From the fact that he can clearly and distinctly conceive an essential property of himself it does not follow that he can clearly and distinctly conceive all the essential properties of himself. Indeed, the possibility does not seem to be ruled out that some of his essential properties are physical – if we accept that, from the fact that one may clearly and distinctly conceive of oneself without physical properties, it does not follow that all of those properties are inessential to one's existence.

If these objections hold good against Descartes then the doctrine of clear and distinct ideas does not rescue the argument from the dubitability of the body from criticism. The problem is the general one about Descartes' method that from the fact that something may be doubted it does not follow that it is false, and that from the fact that something may be clearly and distinctly conceived it does not follow that it is true.

Descartes thinks the veracity of clear and distinct ideas is guaranteed by God; for example, if we may clearly and distinctly conceive A without B or B without A, part of what this means is that God may cause A and B to exist independently of each other. Once again, however, theological premises are invoked to strengthen a dualist argument. We would have to accept at least that God exists and that God has certain powers and that God would not grossly deceive human beings into accepting such premises if false. These claims about the existence, omnipotence and benevolence of God require separate argument, but again that would take us out of the philosophy of mind and into the philosophy of religion.

So, how plausible is Descartes' dualism? His strongest arguments for the distinction between mind and body are those which do not produce opaque contexts and therefore exceptions to Leibniz's Law. There is at least strong *prima facie* reason to suppose that mental and physical are in some sense different. The mental is private, subjective and not obviously spatial. The physical is public, objective, and obviously spatial. The problem remains of whether Descartes has really adduced compelling grounds for holding that mind and body are really two different substances, with the logical consequence that minds could exist without bodies and bodies without minds.

Interaction

I now turn from Descartes' arguments for dualism to the question of the relationship which might hold between mind and body if mind–body dualism is true. To appreciate this issue we have to assume that mind and body are in fact two distinct substances, and ask whether there then may be causal relations between them. Descartes thinks this is possible and does happen: minds cause things to happen in bodies and bodies cause things to happen in minds. There is some intuitive or pre-philosophical plausibility in this view. On the face of it there are physical causes of mental events and mental causes of physical events. For example, a mental event such as a decision or a desire may be a cause of a physical event such as an arm movement; and a physical event such as a bodily injury may be a cause of a mental event such as a pain or an emotion. The question is whether this two-way causal interaction is possible if mind and body are two different substances.

Minds and bodies are not only different entities but radically different sorts of entity. Descartes is quite emphatic about this. He says, 'the soul is nothing but a thing which thinks' (*Philosophical Letters*, p. 106), and 'it is a spiritual substance' (*Philosophical Letters*, p. 107), and 'it is not corporeal' (*Philosophical Letters*, p. 109). 'I', 'soul' and 'mind' are different names for one and the same entity and 'this I which is thinking is an immaterial substance with no bodily element' (*Philosophical Letters*, p. 84). Given this theory of the mind, are its operations capable of being either the causes or the effects of occurrences in physical substance as Descartes defines it in the second Meditation?

By body, I understand all that can be terminated by some figure; that can be contained in some place and fill a space in such a way that any other body is excluded from it; that can be perceived, either by touch, sight, hearing, taste or smell; that can be moved in many ways, not of itself but by something foreign to it by which it is touched, and from which it receives the impulse. (*Meditations*, p. 104).

Seventeenth- and eighteenth-century philosophers frequently use 'body' to mean 'matter' or 'physical substance', so Descartes is defining 'matter' as that which has shape ('figure'), is located in some place, occupies space, excludes other physical objects, can be detected by the five senses, can be moved by contact with another thing, and cannot move of its own accord. None of these is a characteristic of a mind or soul. Indeed, these are not just properties minds happen to lack. Descartes thinks it does not make sense to ascribe such characteristics to minds. It is equally senseless in Descartes' view to talk about matter thinking. It is not just that physical objects happen not to think. It is meaningless to suppose that they do. Indeed, we cannot even conceive of what it would be like for a physical thing to think.

It follows that within the Cartesian picture it is impossible for psycho-physical causal interaction to take place either by matter thinking or by mind being in motion. The real difficulty is how a non-spatial item, a mind, may cause effects in a spatial item, a body, or how a spatial body may cause effects in a non-spatial mind. Descartes thinks that causal interaction between mind and body takes place in a particular part of the brain – the pineal gland. This claim, however, does not help us resolve the causal problem. Philosophically, it is irrelevant. If the mind is not physical then it cannot possibly contact the pineal gland or any other part of the body. Once we drop the mental image of the mind or soul as a kind of see-through intangible object and restrict our thinking to just those properties Descartes says minds have, it becomes very difficult to imagine how minds could influence physical objects. Perhaps the nearest we could come to this is just to reflect upon our own experience. You decide, for example, to reach out for something and then you do so: the mental causes the physical. Our difficulty is perhaps that we mistakenly think of mind–body causal interaction on the model of one physical object causing another to move. Nevertheless, it is not the uncontroversial common-sense picture we are trying to understand. We are trying to make sense of the idea of causal interaction between a mental and a physical substance.

Descartes used to correspond with Princess Elizabeth, the daughter of Frederick, the Elector of the Palatinate, and he wrote to her that we have three central ideas about mind and body. We may conceive of the mind without the body. We may conceive of the body without the mind. Or, we may conceive of the union of the two. In the end he had to confess to Princess Elizabeth that he did not know how causal interaction between mind and body takes place, he only knew that it did. Even so, perhaps it is possible to make more sense of Descartes' idea of a union between mind and body than Descartes himself did.

Union

Clearly this union cannot be a logical one because it is logically possible that there should be minds without bodies and bodies without minds. That is largely what Descartes means by their being two different substances. We have seen that Descartes thinks that he is essentially his mind: he is a thing that thinks – an immortal soul – but what is his relation to his body? Descartes equivocates between two positions. He sometimes talks as though he is not his body, as though his body is just something he has. This means that his body is just something he is uniquely associated with and interacts with causally in a peculiarly intimate and direct way. But sometimes he says he is his body but not essentially his body. This means that a certain body is a part of what the person Descartes is, but not an essential part. Both of these views are consistent with his belief that if his body ceased to exist then he could continue to exist.

In a famous passage near the end of the sixth *Meditation* Descartes says: 'I am not only lodged in my body like a pilot in his ship but, besides ... I am joined to it very closely and, indeed, so compounded and intermingled with my body that I form, as it were, a single whole with it' (*Meditations*, 159). If the mind did not have this relation to the body, he says, it would be aware of injuries to the body only at a distance. The soul would understand them as a pilot perceives damage to his ship.

But what sense are we to make of the idea that I, as a mind or soul, am compounded or intermingled with my body? If souls are not spatial, it is hard to see how they could have any spatial relationship to a body – like a pilot in a ship or not like a pilot in a ship. The image of the pilot suggests that the soul is located in the brain, or perhaps behind one's eyes. Am I what looks through my eyes? The idea of the soul's not just being thus located suggests its pervading the whole body. Do I pervade my body?

In the sixth *Meditation* Descartes uses the word 'union' to denote the relation between mind and body (*Meditations*, 159). Being a soul is what my existence essentially consists in; but I am, at least at present, united with this particular body. I think perhaps the best way to make sense of this is to think of one's own body in objective, third-person terms – to think that there should be a functioning human body, just like one's own, which is different from one's own in just one respect: it is not yours. Now think of one's consciousness as existing in this world, and of this body thereby being your body. This body is then no longer just one body among others. It is, for example, the one you look out of and the one you are, in some peculiar sense, co-extensive with. This is an interpretation of what Descartes means by 'union' which takes seriously his couching his argument in first-person-singular terms.

Ever since Descartes wrote, the relationship between mind and body has been thought the least satisfactory aspect of his dualism. As we have seen, even Descartes himself did not think this relation could be made fully intelligible. Some philosophers – idealists, materialists and others – have thought the problem fatal to the plausibility of dualism. It seems to me that the problem may not be insuperable and is perhaps part of a wider question about the self. There is a deep sense in which, ironically, we do not know what we are, and this is an area for further philosophical investigation. A large part of Descartes' greatness as a philosopher lies in his contributions to that area and we may learn from his insights and arguments, even if in the end we should wish to repudiate his strict mind–body dualism.

2

LOGICAL BEHAVIOURISM

Logical behaviourism is the theory that being in a mental state is being in a behavioural state. Thinking, hoping, perceiving, remembering and so on are all to be understood as either behaving or else possessing a complex disposition or propensity to behave. The mind is nothing over and above behaviour, whereby 'behaviour' is meant publicly observable bodily behaviour. This reduction of the mental to the behavioural is advocated by the logical behaviourist as a linguistic thesis: a thesis about how it is possible for psychological concepts like 'image', 'perception', 'thought' or 'memory' to have a use in our language. This is possible, according to the logical behaviourist, because any sentence or set of sentences about minds may be translated, without loss of meaning, into a sentence or set of sentences about publicly observable behaviour. This is the essence of logical behaviourism. Unless our psychological vocabulary referred to overt behaviour, it could not be meaningful. Logical behaviourists differ among themselves as to why this should be so. Some maintain that there would be no way of deciding the truth or falsity of psychological claims unless these were behavioural claims. Others hold that psychological concepts could not have a role in our public language unless there exist publicly available criteria for their use. All logical behaviourists are agreed that, unless our psychological language is about behaviour, it is about nothing.

Logical behaviourism needs to be carefully distinguished from behaviourism in psychology. Behaviourism in psychology is a method for studying human beings. It is not a doctrine about the meanings of psychological concepts, nor a putative solution to the mind–body problem. It is the view common to the American psychologists J. B. Watson and B. F. Skinner that all human behaviour can be explained as a set of responses to stimuli to which a person is subjected. Neurological facts are not invoked by behaviourists any more than the findings of introspection. It is maintained that knowing the causes of human behaviour – which stimuli cause which responses – is sufficient for explaining that behaviour. It is certainly true that the psychological behaviourists sometimes make pronouncements of a quasi-philosophical kind: Watson, for example, thinks that consciousness does not exist. These pronouncements, however, are no part of their behavioural method. That is the attempt to predict and control human behaviour through the study of its environmental causes.

Indeed, the merits and demerits of behaviourism as a method in psychology are logically independent of putative solutions to the mind–body problem. I mean, for example, that even if mind–body dualism is true, behaviourism might be the best method for explaining behaviour and, even if materialism is true, behaviourism might not be the best method for explaining behaviour.

Even though psychological behaviourism and logical behaviourism are quite distinct, and even though the practice of psychological behaviourism is logically consistent with various ontologies of the mental, logical behaviourism may be construed as a philosophical legitimation of psychological behaviourism. This is because, if all meaningful psychological language is really behavioural language, then behavioural psychology is the only meaningful kind of psychology. Putative rivals to behavioural psychology may then be ruled out a priori. Also, logical behaviourism may partly justify psychological behaviourism's claim to be genuinely scientific. Watson and Skinner think one of the hallmarks of genuine science is the study of some publicly observable subject matter. If the subject matter of psychology is private and subjective, psychology's being scientific in that sense is impossible. But if it may be proved, as the logical behaviourists argue, that the mental is really behavioural then psychology is guaranteed a publicly observable subject matter. Logical behaviourism seems to open the way for a scientific psychology.

The two logical behaviourists I have selected for examination in this chapter are the North American philosopher of science, Carl Hempel, and the English philosopher, Gilbert Ryle. Each is

an important exponent of a movement in twentieth-century philosophy: Hempel is a logical positivist and Ryle is a linguistic philosopher. These two philosophies are mutually distinct. Logical
positivism is essentially the view that every genuine problem may
be solved scientifically and that putative non-scientific ways of
finding out about the universe are literally meaningless. Linguistic
philosophy is the view that philosophical problems like the
mind–body problem arise from the misuse of our ordinary non-
scientific language. I shall say something more about logical positivism and linguistic philosophy in the sections on Hempel and
Ryle, below.

I also include a discussion of some of the massively influential
work of the later Wittgenstein. Wittgenstein cannot correctly be
called a 'logical behaviourist' in any clear or straightforward
sense; his thoughts are too complex and subtle for such an easy
taxonomy. However, his anti-Cartesianism bears a closer resemblance to logical behaviourism than any of the other views discussed in this book.

HEMPEL

To understand what logical behaviourism is, it is useful to compare it with two other important developments in modern philosophy. Logical behaviourism grew out of and, in a sense, is a
philosophical extrapolation of logical positivism; and in its strategy it bears a relationship to certain remarks made by the Austrian philosopher, Wittgenstein, in his later work. I shall say
something about logical positivism now but postpone discussion
of Wittgenstein until the end of this chapter.

The Vienna Circle

Positivism is the doctrine that any phenomenon may in principle
be explained using the techniques of the natural sciences. The
logical positivists who met in Vienna in the 1930s to form the so-
called 'Vienna Circle' tried to reformulate philosophical problems
so that they could be solved scientifically. To achieve this, they
employed a specific criterion for what was to count as meaningful,
and any sentence in philosophy which did not meet this criterion
was categorized as meaningless. This criterion for distinguishing

the meaningful from the meaningless was called the 'Verification Principle'. The Verification Principle implied that a sentence is meaningful if and only if there is or could be some procedure to determine its truth or falsity. So, a sentence is meaningful only if it is at least in principle possible to prove or disprove it. Clearly, on this criterion, many traditional philosophical suggestions – about the origin of the universe, about the existence of God, or the soul – were in fact devoid of meaning. Notice, the logical positivists do not claim that such claims are false, but that they are utterly nonsensical. They further believed that there are two and only two broad ways of determining the truth or falsity of sentences, and so two and only two broad sorts of sentence which may be determined to be true or false. The first sort are the tautologies of mathematics and logic and, indeed, all definitions. The second sort are the scientific and commonsensical sentences which may be confirmed or refuted by observation. These latter are empirical sentences. Clearly, a large number of philosophical sentences did not fall straightforwardly into either category. At best these could be of emotional significance to the people who utter them.

By applying the Verification Principle to philosophical language, the logical positivists hoped to solve all genuine philosophical problems scientifically. The meaningless residue of 'pseudo-problems' could be safely disregarded.

Hempel's logical behaviourism is an extrapolation of this project because he wishes to dispel any qualitative difference between psychology and the natural sciences; in fact, he wants psychology to be another natural science. His reasons for this are that he shares with the logical positivists an ideal of the unity of science – sciences should form a mutually supporting whole to explain the natural world – and he recognizes that the natural sciences possess a precision and an explanatory power that psychology and, for that matter, metaphysical philosophy do not. His technique is to reduce psychology to the physical sciences. One subject is 'reducible' to another if and only if it is possible to translate the theoretical content of one into the other. For example, biology may be reduced to chemistry if and only if, in principle, any sentence from biology may be translated without loss of meaning into a sentence or sentences of chemistry (even if such sentences of chemistry would have to be extremely long and complicated). Ideally, according to this view, all the sciences would in the last resort be reduced to physics.

The Translation Project

The essential step in this reduction of psychology according to Hempel is to translate the sentences of psychology into sentences about the physical behaviour of human beings. This is clearly fully congruent with the view of the Vienna Circle that, for a sentence to be meaningful it must be verifiable. It is notoriously difficult to verify claims about other people's mental states. Indeed, it is the philosophical problem of 'other minds' that one person cannot know what another person thinks, or even perhaps whether they think; or, at least, there is a problem about how we know whether and what other people think if we do know these things. Hempel hopes to leave this problem aside as a pseudo-problem, and provide psychology with a scientific content, that is, with sentences which may be confirmed or disconfirmed by observation. Obviously claims about a person's behaviour are of this sort.

Hempel is fully aware that the project is controversial. He realizes that many maintain there is an irreducibly subjective, private and experiential dimension to the mental which is available only to introspection. He also knows that several theorists – the nineteenth-century German philosopher Wilhelm Dilthey for example – believe mental states are inherently 'meaningful' and that these meanings can be appreciated only by an empathetic leap of the imagination called 'understanding' ('Verstehen'). In addition there are the claims that the mental is inherently culture-bound, and that it is impossible to understand the mentality of an individual without understanding the mentality of the group of which that individual is a part. Hempel also knows that if all these claims may be sustained then there exist insuperable barriers to psychology's inclusion within the set of natural sciences.

But Hempel's view is that these positions may not be sustained, because they are devoid of meaning. Hempel overtly invokes a version of the Verification Principle to eradicate the claims of introspective and Verstehen psychology as meaningless. He says 'the meaning of a statement is established by the conditions of its verification' ('The logical analysis of psychology', p. 17), but there are no conditions for the verification of sentences about allegedly private mental events, so any such apparent claims are really pseudo-claims, or nonsensical utterances. They fall into the category which Hempel defines in this way:

A statement for which one can indicate absolutely no conditions which would verify it, which is in principle incapable of confrontation with test conditions, is wholly devoid of content and without meaning. In such a case we have to do, not with a statement properly speaking, but with a 'pseudo-statement', that is to say, a sequence of words correctly constructed from the point of view of grammar, but without content. ('The logical analysis of psychology', p. 17)

It is not Hempel's view that the claim that a person thinks, or is in pain, or has certain emotions, is meaningless, but that its meaning is to be correctly given only in a specific way. The ·meanings of psychological claims are given by sentences which report the 'test conditions' for them. To make this clear, Hempel provides us with the example, 'Paul has a toothache' ('The logical analysis of psychology', p. 17). To understand the meaning of this sentence, we have to consider the circumstances which would make it true. We may then give the meaning in a set of sentences characterizing the truth conditions of 'Paul has a toothache' – or the conditions under which it could be verified. These are behavioural conditions. The person who has toothache perhaps cries and makes certain gestures, when questioned about the toothache he answers sincerely that he has it and, in addition, his tooth shows signs of decay, there are changes in his blood pressure and central nervous system. It is important to note that Hempel is not claiming that all these behavioural and physiological phenomena are just symptomatic of something else – the toothache – on the contrary, he is saying that this is what having a toothache consists in. Mentioning them is giving the meaning of the word 'toothache'. As he puts it: 'all the circumstances which verify this psychological statement are expressed by physical test sentences' ('The logical analysis of psychology', p. 17), and because the meaning of a sentence is ·its method of verification the psychological sentence means those test sentences. So the word 'pain' is really just a shorthand term for the fact that certain forms of behaviour are exhibited by the subject: 'The statement in question, which is about someone's "pain" is therefore ... simply an abbreviated expression of the fact that all its test conditions are verified' ('The logical analysis of psychology', p. 18). Hempel thinks similar analyses may be provided for all our psychological concepts.

If Hempel is right, then not only has he provided psychology with a subject matter which may be studied using the techniques of the natural sciences – controlled experiments, careful observation, the deployment of hypotheses, the subsumption of events under natural laws – but he has succeeded in 'reducing' psychology to physics. It is worth quoting Hempel's own summary of the position he has reached:

All psychological statements which are meaningful, that is to say, which are in principle verifiable, are translatable into statements which do not involve psychological concepts, but only the concepts of physics. The statements of psychology are consequently physicalist statements. Psychology is an integral part of physics. ('The logical analysis of psychology', p. 18)

By a 'physicalist statement' Hempel means a statement which may be translated into the vocabulary of physics without loss of meaning. If it is right that the meaning of a sentence consists in the method of verifying it, and if it is right that psychological claims may be verified only by the observation of public bodily behaviour, then he is entitled to the conclusion that psychology may indeed be reduced to physics, because it is undeniable that our bodily behaviour forms part of the natural physical world, which falls under the laws physicists operate with. If we disagree with this account, then the onus is on us to say what the meaning of psychological terms like 'thought', 'pain' or 'emotion' consists in. We would have to deny that there is no loss of content when a mental term is translated by some behavioural term, but we would also have to be able to specify what the lost content actually is.

A Pseudo-Problem

What is the bearing of logical behaviourism on dualism and idealism? Those two theories are solutions to the mind–body problem – the question of whether a person is wholly physical, wholly mental or both physical and mental. But Hempel is not concerned to produce yet another solution to this problem. His view is that the problem itself is in fact meaningless – a pseudo-problem. So, however closely Hempel's theory seems to drift towards materialism – the view that a person is nothing but a highly complicated physical object – we should remember that Hempel regards the whole debate, to which materialism is designed to be an answer, as being devoid of meaning. It seems to arise only because we do not understand the proper functioning of our psychological concepts. Once we have clarified them on logical behaviourist lines, the mind–body problem itself disappears. Once we see that words like 'mind' are shorthand terms for a person's bodily behaviour, there is simply no conceptual room to ask the question whether minds exist as well as bodies. Hempel draws an analogy with the running of a watch. To say that a watch is 'running' is just a shorthand way of saying that all its parts are functioning correctly and in particular that its hands are moving appropriately. It would be a conceptual error to suggest that the running of the watch was anything over and above this well-functioning or to suggest that the functioning of the watch was only a symptom or sign of something else called the watch's 'running' – it is what its 'running' actually means or consists in. So too would it be a mistake to wonder what had become of the running of the watch, once all observable parts had ceased to function. So too is it a mistake of the same conceptual kind to suggest that minds are anything over and above bodily behaviour, that that behaviour is a symptom or sign of mentality, or that there could be minds as a kind of residue once there had ceased to be any bodily behaviour. On Hempel's view, these claims are not false but are literally nonsensical because they are misuses of psychological concepts.

Hempel's position is thus a most radical one. If it may be coherently maintained, then he had succeeded in bypassing the very problem to which all the other theories in this book are attempted solutions. Using linguistic premisses – premisses about the correct use of our psychological vocabulary – he concludes that certain ontological claims (claims about what sorts of things exist) are thoroughly misplaced. Whether mental events are really physical, or whether physical events are really mental, or whether they are two separate classes of events and, if so, whether they are capable of causal interaction, for the logical behaviourist are all pseudo-questions. As Hempel puts his own version:

The time-worn problem of the relation between mental and physical events is ... based on this confusion concerning the logical function of psychological concepts. Our argument therefore enables us to see that the psycho-physical problem is a pseudo-problem the formulation of which is based on an inadmissible use of scientific concepts. ('The logical analysis of psychology', p. 20)

RYLE

The seminal work of the Oxford philosopher Gilbert Ryle is a systematic repudiation of Cartesian mind–body dualism. *The Concept of Mind* is written in a highly distinctive style, full of wit, picturesque metaphor and historical allusions, and it draws on a vast multiplicity of homely, everyday practices to illustrate its main thesis. Ryle permits us, with reservations, to think of the book as a theory of the mind and says it does not matter much if we call it 'behaviourist', but we should bear in mind that the originality and detail of the book belie any straightforward categorization of that sort. It would certainly be a crude mistake to think of Ryle as a materialist, despite his abusive and ridiculing attack on the idea of an immaterial mind. The reason for this is that he subscribes to the position described at the end of the last paragraph, that the very belief that there is a mind–body problem is the result of a series of deep conceptual muddles. Ryle sees the putative solutions to this supposed problem as oscillating incoherently between the views that the mental is really physical and that the physical is really mental. He does indeed wish to draw the historical debate to a close but not by adopting either of those positions: 'the hallowed contrast between mind and matter will be dissipated, but dissipated not by either of the equally hallowed absorptions of Mind by Matter or of Matter by Mind, but in a quite different way' (*The Concept of Mind*, p. 22).

What is this 'quite different way'? It certainly does not consist in giving any new information about minds. It is an important part of Ryle's argument that each of us is already possessed of a large body of information about the mental. We can without any philosophical reflection decide when a person is acting intelligently or stupidly, exercising some measure of self-control, being witty, careless, vain, observant, industrious, and many other things. We certainly do not need to have any recourse to the Cartesian distinction between a mental and a physical substance to make such judgements accurately and habitually in everyday life. Indeed, the concepts we use to understand and appraise people's performances typically do not fall sharply on either side of a distinction between 'mental' and 'physical'. A mind–body problem seems to arise only when people reflect philosophically, and that is because in such speculation our ordinary vocabulary is misused. Ryle traces this misuse back to early modern dualism – the specific theory of the mind proposed by Descartes in the seventeenth century and examined in the first chapter of this book. Ryle sets himself the task of showing how failing to understand the logic of our ordinary concepts leads us to mistakenly believe there is a problem about minds, and that dualism is the solution to it. This is what he means when he says his project is only to 'rectify the logical geography of the knowledge which we already possess' (The Concept of Mind, p. 7).

The Ghost in the Machine

Ryle calls Cartesian dualism the 'dogma of the Ghost in the Machine' (The Concept of Mind, pp. 15–16) and, because it has been so widely subscribed to, sometimes refers to it as 'The Official Doctrine' (ibid., p. 11). It is the theory that both minds and bodies exist, but that, while bodies are spatio-temporal, publicly observable and to be explained by mechanical laws, minds are merely temporal and their workings are private to that mind itself and explicable by mysterious non-mechanical laws. Minds are thought to be inside bodies, but this cannot be in any usual sense of 'inside' because minds themselves are not spatial. Arising within this picture of the mental are the problems of how one mind can ever know what is happening inside another mind, and how minds can affect bodies and how bodies can affect minds. Any such causal relations would seem not to belong to either category. On the dualist view, each of us has a privileged and unique access to the operations of our own mind, so our knowledge of our own mental states is of an especially certain kind: if a person is in a mental state then they know they are in that state, with the doubtful exception of unconscious thoughts and motivations. In particular, the mental words of our ordinary language refer to episodes in minds described in this way, so 'mind' refers to something peculiarly secret and occult.

The verdict Ryle pronounces on dualism is

that it is entirely false, and false not in detail but in principle. It is not merely an assemblage of particular mistakes. It is one big mistake and a mistake of a special kind. It is namely a category mistake. It represents the facts of mental life as if they belonged to one logical type or category (or range of types or categories), when they actually belong to another. (*The Concept of Mind,* p. 16)

Category Mistakes

We need now to understand Ryle's idea of a 'category mistake' because it is an essential part of his thesis that mind–body dualism is an illusion produced by the misuse of our ordinary language. Ryle usefully provides us with a number of examples of category mistakes, so if we examine these we should be able to discern exactly what sort of conceptual muddle he has in mind.

Ryle invites us to consider the case of a foreign visitor to Oxford or Cambridge who is shown various colleges, libraries, administration buildings and academic faculties. He sees where the various staff and students live and work and visits museums and scientific laboratories. But at the end of his tour he asks this question: 'Where is the university?' In asking this question, he was under the misapprehension that the essential element had been omitted from his tour. He assumed that, although he had seen the various colleges and offices with the people who work in them, he had not seen the university itself, as though the university were some additional or extra entity which existed over and above all that he had seen. In fact, of course, the university is not an extra thing like another college or another department; rather, the word 'university' is used to refer to all the colleges, all the departments and all their members operating together as a single, cohesive whole. So, although he did not realize this, the visitor was in fact already acquainted with the university – there was nothing extra to see. He just had not realized that the university does not fall into the same category as one of the colleges or laboratories.

Similarly, Ryle imagines a child watching the march past of an army division composed of the various sub-units of infantry battalions, artillery batteries and so on. After the parade, the child asks when the division is going to appear. Just as the visitor to Oxford or Cambridge thought that the university was something over and above the various colleges and departments, so the child wrongly assumed that a division is rather like another battalion, battery or squadron. In fact, however, in witnessing the march past of the various sub-units, the child has already seen the division. The division is just the sum of its parts in so far as these have a certain military co-ordination. In the same way, in a game of cricket the demonstration of 'team spirit' is not the deployment of an extra skill of the same sort as bowling, batting or fielding; rather, it is the keenness and dexterity with which such skills are exercised.

Why does Ryle think these category mistakes are conceptual muddles? His point is that the people led into error did not know how to use certain ordinary words properly. They did not know the correct uses of 'university', 'division' and 'team spirit'. This led them to suppose that in each case they were dealing with a puzzling new entity which existed over and above what they were already familiar with. Ryle thinks there are also category mistakes in our abstract thinking, so that a person might mistakenly think 'the British Constitution' some shadowy being which exists as well as or extra to the functioning of the cabinet, parliament and other institutions. Or they may believe the 'average taxpayer' to be some peculiarly ghostly additional taxpayer.

Ryle is not fond of this term, but 'ontology' is the branch of philosophy which tries to decide what exists. We can say that Ryle's view is that, by misunderstanding how our language functions in its ordinary everyday contexts, we are led into ontological mistakes. By misusing generic or abstract concepts, we tend to postulate as existing entities which in fact do not exist. When we think in this way our ideas are modelled on the things we are familiar with, so, because we know the extra entities are not physical objects, we think of them as strange, ghostly, non-physical objects. The purpose of *The Concept of Mind* is to correct this habit of our thinking and in particular to show that the word 'mind' is not the name of a strange, non-physical entity but refers to a complexity of skills and performance we are all familiar with, such as imagining, believing, knowing, problem solving, perceiving and desiring.

Ryle is concerned that he should not be misunderstood. He is not trying to deny the very obvious fact that each of us lives a fully fledged psychological life – that we all feel our pleasures and pains, have our thoughts and emotions, moods, interests and inclinations. He is saying that these well-known facts, and the fact that our psychological vocabulary is meaningful, should not lead us into Cartesian dualism.

I shall give some examples of Ryle's 'rectifying the logical geography' of our mental concepts later, but first we should note that his philosophical project is fundamentally a logical behaviourist one. It is his view that mental terms take on meaning by referring to overt bodily behaviour and public utterances, and not through any secret labelling of the findings of introspection. For example he claims that 'when we describe people as exercising qualities of mind, we are not referring to occult episodes of which their overt acts and utterances are effects; we are referring to those overt acts and utterances themselves' (*The Concept of Mind*, p. 25).

Dispositions

Let us consider, for example, Ryle's analysis of 'believe'. Someone might hold the view that beliefs are in fact private mental states, straightforwardly knowable to the believer but revealed only by speech and action to others. It might also be part of this view that beliefs are like ideas, perhaps episodes or occurrences in a non-physical medium called a 'mind'. Ryle utterly repudiates this view. He substitutes instead the idea that having beliefs actually consists in having a tendency to speak and behave in certain ways. He is not saying that our utterances and actions are symptomatic of something else that is peculiarly other-worldly; he is saying that our propensity to act and speak is what the belief actually is. To make this clearer I shall quote the example Ryle himself provides:

Certainly to believe that the ice is dangerously thin is to be unhesitant in telling oneself and others that it is thin, in acquiescing in other people's assertions to that effect, in objecting to statements to the contrary, in drawing consequences from the original proposition and so forth. But it is also to be prone to skate warily, to shudder, to dwell in imagination on possible disasters and to warn other skaters. (*The Concept of Mind*, pp. 134–5)

For Ryle it is a mistake to think of a belief as any kind of occurrence at all. Beliefs are dispositions. According to Ryle's account, a person has a disposition if he or she has a tendency or propensity to behave in a particular way. So, in the example above, a person's believing that the ice is thin is his or her disposition to tell others, to skate warily, and so on.

Several objections spring to mind when this account is presented, but I believe that Ryle does not think them fatal. For example, might not a person believe that the ice is thin but not tell others or skate warily – perhaps because that person is in a particular inconsiderate or reckless frame of mind? That would mean that behaving or speaking in a particular way is not a necessary condition for holding the belief. Conversely, might not some people tell others that the ice is thin, and skate warily, even though they do not hold the belief that the ice is thin – perhaps in the first case they are lying and in the second they have some other reason for skating warily? If so, then it seems that behaving or speaking in a certain way is not a sufficient condition for holding a certain belief. Ryle fully accepts that people may and do deceive one another and themselves, and he has an account of what pretending is. I think his reply here would be that there is a limit to the kind of scepticism I have brought against his example. He says elsewhere that there can be no counterfeit coins without genuine currency, and this is right. It does not make sense to talk about lying unless there also exists some truth telling, and there cannot be pretending without genuine behaviour. In particular, our psychological words like 'believe' take on their meanings – take on the use they have in ordinary language and everyday situations – in the sort of context which the skating example describes. Ryle is providing an account of how our concepts are used, not claiming that every profession of belief is genuine.

Ryle applies the dispositional analysis to a whole range of our psychological concepts. When we speak of a person as being 'polite', what we mean is that such a person passes the salt when it is asked for and does not ignore our request. If we ask whether a soldier scored a bull's eye by skill rather than luck, we mean that he could do it again and again, perhaps even if the wind condition and other variables were different. If we say someone is 'intelligent', that means the person has the ability to solve certain sorts of problem accurately and perhaps speedily. It does not mean that the problem solving was preceded by or accompanied by a parallel and purely mental series of intellectual steps. It is just not true, on Ryle's view, that every intelligent action is mentally rehearsed beforehand or done in duplicate, once mentally and once physically.

Nor is it true, according to his view, that actions performed voluntarily are preceded by or caused by purely mental items called 'volitions' or 'acts of will'. He agrees of course that there exists a genuine distinction between doing something voluntarily and being compelled to do it; but he denies that this distinction is properly made by saying that some actions are and some are not caused by mysterious mental tryings called 'volitions' occurring in an occult medium which shadows the actions themselves. On the contrary, to say that someone did something voluntarily is just to say that they were competent to do it, they were not impeded from doing it, and they did do it. It is because we witness people in situations of this sort that we are able to make the distinction between 'voluntary' and 'involuntary', and it is philosophers under the illusions of the 'dogma of the Ghost in the Machine' who misuse these concepts to pose the bogus problem of the freedom of the will.

There is doubtless much intuitive plausibility in the dispositional account Ryle offers. It seems to accord with common sense that, if a person knows that the solution to a piece of arithmetic is a certain number, then that person can write that number as the answer in an examination, or mention that number to us when we ask for the answer to the sum. Or if a person knows how to speak German or how to tie reef-knots, he ought to be able to speak some German or tie some reef-knots when asked to, other things being equal. But, the reader may wonder, could this account plausibly ever be extended to cover certain highly experiential features of the mental, such as having perceptions or other sensations? Indeed, could introspection and the exercise of the imagination by the having of mental images be explained in this way?

Occurrences

Ryle is aware of this issue and allows that not all psychological concepts admit of a dispositional analysis. Some mental terms refer to occurrences, not to dispositions; but, even then, these are not occurrences in a mind in any Cartesian sense.

To understand what Ryle means by an 'occurrence', we may contrast this notion with that of a disposition. To take one of Ryle's everyday examples, there is an important difference between claiming that someone is a cigarette-smoker and claiming that a person is smoking a cigarette. The first claim ascribes a disposition to the person: it says that the person has a tendency or propensity to smoke cigarettes. Clearly it does not say that the person is always or perpetually smoking a cigarette, or that they are smoking a cigarette now. The second claim does not ascribe a disposition to the person but mentions a certain occurrence – it says that an event is taking place. This is the sort of distinction which obtains, on the one hand, between saying someone knows or believes something and, on the other hand, that they have a pain or an itch. Ryle allows that in the case of certain dispositions (but not all) they could not exist unless certain occurrences took place. For example, if it is true that a person is a cigarette-smoker – has a disposition to smoke cigarettes – then that can be true only on condition there are certain occurrences – the person sometimes smokes a cigarette. Clearly, unless a person actually smoked cigarettes periodically, we could not properly call him or her a cigarette-smoker. But the fact that someone smokes just one cigarette does not make that person what we call 'a cigarette-smoker'. So there is both a difference and a dependence between occurrences and dispositions.

Introspection

Perhaps the seemingly most intractable concept for which a logical behaviourist analysis might be attempted is that of introspection. If it is true that among occurrences there exist special non-physical perceptions by which a mind detects its own operations, then it is hard to see how these could be explained in terms of a person's speech or bodily behaviour. Ryle's reply is, to put it bluntly, that introspection in this sense simply does not exist. This conclusion may seem less extraordinary once we have examined Ryle's reasons for subscribing to it.

Ryle points out that, if introspection exists, then that seems to commit us to the view that there is a kind of awareness of awareness, and that means we are performing two mental acts simultaneously. If you discover by introspection that you are deciding to get up early in the mornings, for example, then two things at once are true of you: you are deciding to get up early in the mornings and you are mentally paying attention to this resolution. Ryle doubts very much whether this sort of twin mental action ever takes place. He does not deny that it makes sense to speak of 'undivided attention' and so allows the contrasting possibility of divided attention – as when we are distracted or perform two tasks simultaneously. However, this phenomenon is best explained, he thinks, by our being able intermittently to switch attention from one task to the other. He appeals to our common sense in this matter to free us of the Cartesian picture:

Many people who begin by being confident that they do introspect, as introspection is officially described, become dubious that they do so, when they become satisfied that they would have to be attending twice at once in order to do it. They are more sure that they do not attend twice at once than that they do introspect. (*The Concept of Mind*, p. 165)

In addition, Ryle poses a severe problem for someone who believes in introspection: how do you know you introspect? If I know I introspect through introspection, then that would seem to require three simultaneous mental acts: the original act I introspect, my introspection of it and, finally, my introspection of that act of introspection. Not only is it commonsensically implausible that such mental triads exist, but the proposed solution generates an infinite regress – I introspect to know I introspect to know I introspect ... and so on. The alternative is to give up the idea that we know we introspect by introspection; but, once we have done that, we have allowed that we may know that we are in a mental state without introspecting it, and if introspection is not needed for knowledge of one of one's mental states, why should it be needed for any?

Naturally, if Ryle's demonstration that it is a mere myth that we introspect can resist criticism, then he had dealt a crippling blow to a number of non-behaviourist psychological methods; for example, to the extent that the theories of Jung and Freud rest upon the supposed findings of introspection, those theories are entirely vacuous if introspection does not exist. Nor can it be true, as Descartes thought, that knowledge derived from introspection is especially incorrigible, if there is no knowledge derived from introspection. Although Ryle does not overtly characterize his philosophy in this way, one clear result of it, if it is successful, is the clearing away of conceptual obstacles to the practice of behavioural psychology as an empirical science. Its upshot for how psychology should be practised is therefore fully congruent with the hopes of the early logical behaviourists like Hempel.

One World

It should further be noted that this repudiation of introspection is not just consistent with, but is a part of, Ryle's denial of mind–body dualism. It is part of his insistence that our everyday performances, including utterances, are not duplicated in a shadowy second world called 'the mind'. Indeed, it does not even make sense to talk about a mental world and a physical world:

To talk of a person's mind is not to talk of a repository which is permitted to house objects that something called 'the physical world' is forbidden to house; it is to talk of the person's abilities, liabilities and inclinations to do and undergo certain sorts of things, and of the doing and undergoing of these things in the ordinary world. Indeed, it makes no sense to speak as if there could be two or eleven worlds. (The Concept of Mind, p. 199)

There is then only one world, the one in which you are reading this book. Reading itself, on a Rylean analysis, does not divide into two processes, one physical and one mental. It is to abuse our ordinary concepts to claim such a bifurcation. It is only if we assume the truth of the dogma of the ghost in the machine that we are forced to believe that every process must be either mental or physical, or must contain separate mental and physical components. In fact, Ryle thinks most of what we say and do does not fall cleanly into either category, and if we do not take the dualism between mental and physical as our starting point it need not be our finishing point either.

It is an important tenet of logical positivism, logical behaviourism and of the sort of conceptual analysis which Ryle practises that philosophical problems arise through asking the wrong sorts of question. An example of such an inappropriate question is: is a person really mental or physical? It is not as though the answer is merely very difficult, or that it should be the role of the philosopher to devise ever more ingenious solutions. The correct tactic, according to this tradition, is, if a question has proved utterly intractable for literally thousands of years, to suggest that perhaps there is something mistaken about posing the question in the first place. Ryle takes this view, and he thinks this particular philosophical problem has arisen because philosophers abuse our ordinary language.

Whatever the force of Ryle's arguments against mind–body dualism and introspective psychology, there is still room to ask whether he can explain our emotions, sensations and mental images in terms similar to those used so far. Certainly one does not have to be a mind–body dualist to hold the common-sense view that each of us has experiences of pleasure and pain, goes through periods of depression and happiness, and can imagine things in the mind's eye and the mind's ear – where this imagining is not at all the same as perceiving the things in question. It also seems to be part of our everyday conception of these phenomena that they are in some sense private to us. They are subjective.

Ryle would certainly say that to call such mental states 'private' or 'subjective' is philosophically misleading, not only because it might lead us to Cartesian dualism but because, if it means that only the person having the emotion, sensation or image can know that, then our concepts of those events could not possibly take on the meaning they actually possess.

According to Ryle, the term 'emotion' is ambiguous in that it might denote a certain sort of occurrence or a certain sort of disposition. Feelings are emotions which are occurrences, and Ryle gives the homely examples of 'trills, twinges, pangs, throbs,

wrenches, itches, prickings, chills, glows, loads, qualms, hanker-
ings, curdlings, sinkings, tensions, gnawings and shocks (*The
Concept of Mind*, pp. 83–4). He notes that the language in which
we report our feelings is riddled with spatial metaphors. The
lesson of this, however, is not that feelings take place in some
private, subjective world with ghostly para-mechanical parts, but
that it does not make much sense to call them mental or physical.
Ryle is, I think, tempted to adopt the view of the American
philosopher and psychologist, William James, that feelings are
actually to be identified with sensations having specific spatio-
temporal locations in the body. He does not adopt this course
because it sounds to him too much like an answer to a question
he considers nonsensical. Instead he notes the fact that, for example, a glow of pride seems to pervade one's whole body to
show that strict mental/physical taxonomy is inappropriate and
that feelings, such as glows of pride, although they are occurrences, are not occurrences in a Cartesian mind.

Feelings should not be confused with moods. Moods are best
understood as dispositions, not as occurrences, so that a person
who is in a frivolous mood has a tendency or propensity, for
example, to laugh at jokes more readily than usual, and to go
about his or her daily tasks without much anxious concern. A
person in a depressed frame of mind has a tendency to adopt
certain bodily postures, perhaps to cry, and to make certain
avowals such as 'I feel depressed' (*The Concept of Mind*, p. 102).
An avowal of this sort is an expression of a mood and even is
part of what being in such a mood consists in, much as *avowing*
hatred or love for another person might be part of hating or
loving them. It would be a mistake, on Ryle's view, to think
avowals are primarily autobiographical reports on a person's
mental state; rather, they are parts of that state.

We are misled into thinking that moods are peculiarly private
or subjective occurrences because we ask a certain causal question in the wrong way: we ask, for example, whether someone did
something because they were depressed, as though depression
were a kind of hidden inner cause of their action. In fact, moods
are not causes in the sense of being events, they are dispositional
causes. To illustrate what he means by this, Ryle gives the example of a glass breaking because it was brittle. To say that the

glass is brittle is to say that it has a propensity to break when struck with a certain force; we do not mean by 'brittleness' an intrinsic property of the glass which could be explained in complete abstraction from its relations to other objects. Similarly, if we say that someone bursts into tears because she is depressed, we are mentioning her proneness or liability to do just that sort of thing, not mentioning an outer event which has the inner event as its cause.

Ryle says that moods are not experiences. But even if this is allowed, surely, it will be protested, sensations are experiences. In a way Ryle is prepared to concede this; but he urges us to recognize that the word 'sensation' is really a term of art used mainly by philosophers. It does not have much of a role in everyday life or in the writings of novelists. Normally we have recourse only to speaking of someone perceiving something, for example seeing a robin or smelling a cheese. Once we accept this, according to Ryle, then it does not help our understanding of what perception is to call it something purely mental. For example, if someone is watching a horse race, what does make sense is to ask whether he had a good or a bad view of it, whether he only glimpsed it or saw as much of it as possible. The idea that there are sensations in the 'other-worldly' sense arises from using words outside their everyday contexts. Once we relocate them – correct their logical geography – the artificial split between mental and physical occurrences is seen to be nonsensical.

Seemingly more intractable than sensations are mental images. My images of my childhood seem a paradigm case of entities which are purely mental and private just to me. To criticize this idea, Ryle draws a distinction between 'imaging' or 'imagining' and, on the other hand, non-optically peering at non-physical pictures. As he puts it: 'Roughly, imaging occurs, but images are not seen' (The Concept of Mind, p. 247). What he means is that if I imagine something then I am imagining that thing, not being inwardly conscious of a mental picture of that thing. I am not seeing that thing but it is as though I am. I seem to see it but do not. For example:

True, a person picturing his nursery is, in a certain way, like that person seeing his nursery, but the similarity does not consist in his really looking at a real likeness of his nursery, but in his really seeming to see his nursery itself, when he is not really seeing it. He is not being a spectator of a resemblance of his nursery, but he is resembling a spectator of his nursery. (*The Concept of Mind*, p. 248)

Indeed, this kind of imagining is dependent upon pretending, and much of what we call 'imagining' is to be explained as make-believe behaviour. For example, imagining being a bear might take the form of playing at being a bear. As with the other concepts he analyses, these take on their meanings through their use in the one publicly observable world of common sense and not by labelling private episodes in a Cartesian mind.

How should we appraise Ryle's thesis? To a mind–body dualist, Ryle will seem to be allowing the existence of everything except that which is most important –' that purely mental and perhaps spiritual centre of conscious awareness which each of us essentially is – and it is of course Ryle's central purpose to repudiate such an idea of the self. But even those of us who are not dualists may consider that Ryle at least tries to play down the importance of the lived experience of the individual, even though Ryle says it is no part of his project to deny the well-known facts of psychological life but merely to give us a clearer understanding of them. Materialists frequently find much that is conducive to their own position in Ryle's writing. But Ryle thinks materialism is almost as big a mistake as dualism. Perhaps the merit of his work lies, in the last resort, in his questioning the appropriateness of posing the mind–body problem at all with its clean mental–physical distinction. If the question is misguided, then his position is indeed a most radical one because we then have to rethink much of what passes for the philosophy of mind.

WITTGENSTEIN

Arguably, nobody has had a more direct or more thorough influence on English-speaking philosophy in the twentieth century than Ludwig Wittgenstein. Although Austrian born, he spent most of his productive life at the University of Cambridge. His philosophy is often thought to have passed through three phases: an early phase lasting into the 1920s, in which philosophical problems were to be solved by the devising of the logically perfect language; a middle phase in the early 1930s, during which the feasibility of such a project was called into question; and a late phase, lasting from the 1930s until his death in 1951, in which philosophical problems were thought to be muddles generated by the misuse of our ordinary everyday language. The masterpiece of the early phase is the *Tractatus Logico Philosophicus* (1921). Among several pieces from the middle period the most conspicuous are *The Blue and Brown Books* (1958) and *Philosophical Grammar* (1974), and the third phase is exemplified by another masterpiece, *Philosophical Investigations* (1953). (I give the publication date of the English translation in each case.) In what follows we shall be concerned only with the latter work, as it is this which has a direct bearing on the mind–body problem. For more on Wittgenstein I refer the reader to Anthony Kenny's *Wittgenstein* (see 'Further Reading').

The Private Language Argument and the Philosophy of Mind

Wittgenstein's private language argument is an argument against the possibility of a private language. Whether a private language is possible is a crucial issue for the philosophy of mind (and, indeed, for philosophy generally) for the following reason; it could be that several theories of the mind presuppose a private language. If they do, and if a private language is impossible, then those theories must be false. For example, both Plato and Descartes assume that we may have the concept of a mind or soul existing independently of any body. Descartes in particular thinks that one comes to acquire the concept of mind only from one's own case. For him, the mental is private in the sense that only the owner of that mind has direct cognitive access to its states, and it is a matter for doubt whether other people have minds. He also thinks that first-person psychological knowledge is peculiarly incorrigible; if I believe I am in a certain mental state, then that belief is true. In order to formulate this position, Descartes seems to be presupposing a language which could take on meaning just from referring to the contents of his own mind, a language which, perhaps, only he could understand.

Another example: solipsism is the doctrine that only one's own mind exists. Other people are just physical exteriors or appearances, but one's own mind *is*. If Wittgenstein's argument against private language works, it could be that solipsism may be formulated only on condition that it is false. The solipsist assumes – in formulating the sentence 'Only my mind exists', for example – that there may be a language which takes on meaning solely from referring to the contents of one's own mind. Clearly, for the solipsist, no one else could learn this language. There is no one else.

Solipsism is an extreme version of idealism which, as we shall see in the next chapter, is the theory that only minds and their contents exist. It is frequently assumed by idealists that all a mind is ever acquainted with is its own contents: thoughts and experiences. Any learned language, it would seem, is learned by the private labelling of such thoughts and experiences; they are the meanings of such a language. Again, if Wittgenstein can show that such a language is impossible, then this kind of idealism is false.

Phenomenology includes attempts to describe the contents of consciousness in a presuppositionless way, without prior commitment to the objective existence of those contents. Maybe, however, phenomenology cannot escape presupposing phenomenological language: a language which refers only to 'phenomena' or private appearances to a subject. If Wittgenstein has ruled out such a language, Wittgenstein rules out phenomenology.

A final example from the philosophy of mind: phenomenalism is the doctrine that sentences about physical objects may be correctly analysed by sentences about the contents of sense experience. The language we use to talk about physical objects is to be translated into a language just about sense contents, without loss of meaning. If sense contents are private – the content of your experience is not the same as the content of my experience – then it looks very much as though phenomenalism requires translation out of a public language into a private language. The question is: is such a private language possible?

The private language argument potentially has enormous eliminatory power in philosophy. If sound, it is a refutation not only of dualism, idealism (including solipsism), phenomenological philosophy and phenomenalism but also renders senseless the posing of certain sceptical questions; for example, the suggestion that we cannot know that or what other people think and the suggestion that your experience may be utterly different from mine both seem to presuppose a private language. Furthermore, according to more than one influential theory in the philosophy of language, the meaning of a word is an idea: something 'inner', private and psychological. Indeed, the whole philosophical tendency called 'empiricism' is essentially the view that all one's knowledge, including one's knowledge of language, is derived from experience. If experience is 'private', then so is language on the empiricist view. It follows that Wittgenstein, if successful, must inflict severe damage on the positions of philosophers as diverse as Descartes, Locke, Berkeley, Hume, Schopenhauer, Husserl, Russell and Ayer.

What exactly is a private language? Wittgenstein fully accepts that in some senses a private language is possible. For example, you may decide to write secrets in a diary and devise a code to translate these out of English. Sometimes one blames oneself or encourages oneself and frequently one talks to oneself in English or German. Clearly, too, young siblings or friends may devise a language just for their own use to conceal their communication from others. Wittgenstein is not concerned to argue against any of this.

Wittgenstein's target is the philosophically significant sense of 'private language':

a language in which a person could write down or give vocal expression to his inner experiences – his feeling, moods, and the rest – for his own private use ... The individual words of this language are to refer to what can only be known to the person speaking: to his immediate private sensations. So another person cannot understand the language. (*Philosophical Investigations*, p. 243)

The private language, then, has two putative characteristics: it refers only to the experiences of the speaker, and no one except the speaker can understand it. Those experiences too have certain alleged characteristics. They are 'inner', 'private' and 'immediate', and only the speaker knows what and that they are. Wittgenstein proceeds to launch an attack on the alleged privacy of both experience and meaning.

Is Experience Private?

Suppose someone said that his or her sensations were private in the sense that 'Only I can know I am really in pain' (*Philosophical Investigations*, p. 246). Wittgenstein thinks this is not true. According to him, on one reading it is just false, and on another reading it is nonsensical. It is false because other people frequently do know when I am in pain. In ordinary language the use of 'to know' allows this. It is nonsensical because 'I know I am in pain' adds nothing to 'I am in pain' except, perhaps, emphasis. It makes sense to talk of knowledge only when there is room for doubt or error. It does not make sense to talk about *doubting* whether one is in pain – in one's own case – so it does not make sense to talk of *knowing* that one is in pain either. Ironically, it is the possibility of doubt rather than the fact of absolute certainty that allows the use of 'to know'.

Wittgenstein does allow one use of 'sensations are private'. This is not to express some putative fact about sensations but to show how the word 'sensation' is used in English. It is an example of what he calls a 'grammatical proposition', one which shows the use of a word. It would be an error to think that 'sensations are private' expressed a fact in the philosophy of mind or some metaphysical insight. The sentence just shows us how a certain word is used in the English language.

Suppose someone claimed that his or her sensations were private in a different sense. This person says: 'Another person can't have my pains' (*Philosophical Investigations*, p. 253). Again, this claim makes sense only to the extent that there is room for error or doubt about whose pains are whose. Of course there could be error or doubt about which physical object is which – about whether the chair is the same one you saw yesterday or is one just like it – but there could be no mix-up about whether the pain you are feeling is really mine. That is a nonsensical supposition. Wittgenstein does allow certain cases to be imagined without nonsense. You could feel a pain in my body, or Siamese twins might feel a pain in the same body area. What does not make sense is the claim that another person can or cannot have my pains.

For Wittgenstein, the temptation to think that there are profound metaphysical problems is akin to an illness. In fact such problems are illusions, produced by misunderstandings of our ordinary language. He thinks it is the job of the philosopher to 'treat' a question, like an illness (*Philosophical Investigations*, p. 255).

Is Meaning Private?

Of course we may use everyday public language to refer to our sensations; Wittgenstein does not deny that. What he urges is that those sensations are in no philosophically interesting sense private and that our psychological vocabulary, although perfectly meaningful, does not derive its meaning from the labelling of those experiences. His attack on private meaning may be usefully divided into three components: a suggestion about how sensation words come to be learnt, an argument against the possibility of private ostensive definition, and, finally, a statement of the need for a background of rule-governed communication and public 'criteria' for the use of psychological concepts.

Sensation words like 'pain' do not take on their use in language from labelling something inner and private. Rather, Wittgenstein suggests, the word 'pain' comes to replace the primitive expressions of pain. Before the acquisition of language a child in pain simply cries, but adults teach the child new linguistic exclamations of pain, which are used instead of crying: 'They teach the child new pain-behaviour' (*Philosophical Investigations*, p. 244). On this account, 'pain' is an expression of pain, rather than a name for pain. Also, the child learns 'pain' by initiation into the uses of the public language, not by a process of secret inner labelling.

Wittgenstein is not saying that 'pain' means 'crying', nor, indeed, that 'pain' may be translated completely by reports of non-linguistic behaviour. However, he clearly thinks pain behaviour includes using 'pain'. On his suggestion, the first use of 'pain' is an acquired piece of pain behaviour: a verbal expression of pain. Notice, too, that if the use of 'pain' is part of what Wittgenstein calls 'natural expressions of sensation' (*Philosophical Investigations*, p. 256), then the language in which it features is not private but public. This is because such expressions are publicly observable pieces of behaviour.

The idea that 'pain' is a learnt public expression of pain is Wittgenstein's alternative to private ostensive definition. Ostensive definition needs to be distinguished from verbal definition.

In a verbal definition, the meaning of a word is explained only by other words. Dictionaries, for example, provide verbal definitions. In ostensive definition, in contrast, a word is defined by the showing of an example of what the word refers to. For example, to define 'square' verbally, one produces a sentence: '"Square" means equilateral, equiangular, right-angled closed plane'; but in defining 'square' ostensively, one points to a square and says 'Square'.

In *Philosophical Investigations* Wittgenstein systematically criticizes the view that words take on meaning from simple ostensive definition. Words have a wide variety of uses: to give orders, to ask questions, to insult, to implore, and so on. Words have uses or functions just as human artefacts such as tables or screwdrivers have uses. To take a word out of its behavioural and linguistic context – its 'language game' – and ask for its meaning is as misguided a procedure as taking a cog out of a machine and asking what it is. Replace the cog in the machine and its function is apparent. Replace the word in the living human context and its use is evident. Meaning is not inner, mysterious, private and psychological. Meaning is outer, evident, public and behavioural. Indeed, we should give up the quest for a theory of 'meaning' and direct our attention towards actual linguistic uses. Meaning is just those.

Ostensive definition is possible, but it presupposes the public language with what Wittgenstein calls its 'stage setting': its grammar, its rules, its common-sense world of human communicators. Ostensive definitions are useful in that they show the role or place of a word in that entire context. As philosophers, we should not forget the 'stage setting' which makes ostensive definition possible.

To show the impossibility of private ostensive definition, Wittgenstein invites us to consider the putative possibility of someone who decides to keep a diary about the recurrence of a sensation (*Philosophical Investigations*, p. 258). The idea is that the person writes a sign, 'S', each time the sensation occurs. Wittgenstein's point is that this would be impossible for someone who did not already have command of a public language within which 'S' could be allocated a role as the name of a sensation. There is nothing the putative private ostensive definition could consist in.

The person cannot point to his or her sensation. He or she could concentrate attention on the sensation and, so to speak, 'point inwardly', but it is an illusion to suppose that a referential connection between 'S' and the sensation could be established in that way. There is nothing that it consists in for 'S' to be the name of the sensation. There is nothing for it to consist in for the sensation to be named correctly or incorrectly by 'S'. There is no such thing in this case as being right or wrong in labelling the sensation 'S', so no such labelling takes place here. As Wittgenstein puts it: 'But in the present case I have no criterion for correctness. One would like to say: whatever is going to seem right to me is right. And that only means that here we can't talk about "right"' (*Philosophical Investigations*, p. 258).

Naming presupposes the possibility of naming correctly or incorrectly. This possibility exists only in a public language where there are criteria for being right or wrong. Private ostensive definition no more establishes the use of a word than consulting a railway timetable in the imagination is consulting an actual railway timetable. It is like buying several copies of the morning paper to make sure a news item is true.

Psychological concepts cannot be learnt only from one's own case. It is necessary that the learner be acquainted with third-person criteria for their use. If everybody only felt pain and never showed it then 'pain' could have no use in our public language. The same applies if no one ever knew when another was in pain. It is precisely because we may be sometimes right and sometimes wrong in our ascriptions of pain to others that the word may have a use. Behavioural criteria provide the conditions for the term's use.

If Wittgenstein's private language argument works, then he turns the tables on the Cartesian world-picture. Descartes thinks first-person-singular psychological knowledge the most certain and the most foundational. He thinks nothing is more certain than that he thinks, and he rests all his other knowledge claims on that, including the claim that he exists. If Wittgenstein's private language argument is successful, then Descartes' intelligibility of his own mind to himself rests on enormous assumptions: a public language and the common-sense world of human communicators. His doubts are possible only if groundless. Ironically, the meaningfulness of his own language in the *Meditations* is what Descartes most conspicuously fails to doubt.

3

IDEALISM

Idealism is the theory that only minds exist. It is clearly incompatible with dualism because that is the theory that both minds and physical objects exist. The implication of idealism, that physical objects do not exist, is potentially misleading and usually misunderstood. No idealist denies that there exist tables, bricks, pieces of wood and all other items we commonly take to be physical objects. Idealists merely deny two alleged facts about physical objects: they deny that they exist unperceived or unthought; and they deny that they are material, that is, made out of a substance called 'matter'. This is, perhaps, denying the existence of the physical objects in the sense of denying their essential properties, but it is clearly not the claim that there are voids or gaps in our visual or tactile field where most people take there to be physical objects. So far as I know, no philosopher has held that.

A central claim of the idealist is that physical objects do not exist independently of minds. Unless there were minds, so-called physical objects could not exist. What exists exists only within consciousness, so that what we commonsensically or prephilosophically take to be physical is in fact mental. The physical is mental.

Many people, when they hear about idealism for the first time, think it is a foolish theory: I mean so grossly and manifestly false and so hard to believe that only a philosopher divorced from the concerns of everyday life or one with dubious theological commitments could have formulated it. Sometimes, too, idealism is thought to be unscientific in the sense of incompatible with the findings of modern science.

None of these changes has any foundation. The theory that the physical is mental is consistent with any everyday, practical commitment, consistent with atheism, and consistent with modern science. Contrary to a widespread misconception, nothing at all in modern science rules out idealism. All the sentences of physics, biology and even neurology could be true, and all the sentences of idealism true too; their conjunction forms a self-consistent set. Obviously, idealism is incompatible with the old Newtonian idea of matter as a kind of material or stuff that the universe is made of, but physics gave up that idea long ago. Indeed, the idealist attack on matter anticipates in important respects the demonstration of the limitations of Newtonian physics by Mach and Einstein. Ironically, it might well turn out that, while idealism is compatible with science, materialism is incompatible with science.

In what follows I shall try to provide some intuitive plausibility for idealism, simply because it seems to so many people intuitively false. First, though I shall say something about the varieties of idealism. I have been talking as though idealism were a single homogeneous theory, but this is not really so. All idealists agree that in some sense reality is ultimately spiritual or mental, but there are, nevertheless, radically different kinds of idealism.

Idealism is essentially a British and German movement in modern philosophy. Idealism was not a doctrine in ancient Greek philosophy or in medieval Christian philosophy. An exception to this generalization is the dialectical and spiritualist metaphysics of the neo-platonist Greek-Egyptian philosopher, Plotinus, who lived and wrote in the third century AD. Plotinus argued that individual human consciousnesses are perspectives or points of view that the One unifying, cosmic consciousness has on the universe which, in a sense, it constitutes. In Plotinus's thought there are massive anticipations of the central tenets of German idealism. Indeed, in my view it is no exaggeration to say that German idealism is essentially neo-Platonism. Plato himself was not an idealist. Plato was a mind–body dualist. The Platonic theory of the Forms, for example, does not commit Plato to idealism because the Forms are not mental or spiritual, even though material particulars depend upon the Forms for their existence. Apart from Plotinus, then, there are no ancient idealists in the Western intellectual tradition.

The two idealists I have selected for study are the eighteenth-century Irish philosopher George Berkeley, and the nineteenth-century German philosopher G. W. F. Hegel. Berkeley thinks that physical objects do not exist over and above ideas, ideas either in the infinite mind of God or ideas in the finite minds of persons such as you and I. Hegel thinks that the physical world is ultimately to be understood as an expression of Spirit, a pantheistic cosmic mind for which human consciousnesses are agents or (rather as Plotinus thought) points of view.

Berkeley and Hegel are very different thinkers. Berkeley is an empiricist, that is, he thinks all knowledge depends ultimately upon experience. Hegel is a rationalist in that he thinks it is possible to obtain by intellectual means knowledge of the essential properties of reality as a whole. The differences between the two should not be overemphasized, however. Berkeley is a theist, and there can be no conclusive empirical proof of the existence of God; and, while Hegel's 'logical' writings exhibit his rationalism, an empirical or experiential side of his philosophy is found in his 'phenomenology'. Idealism is logically independent of both empiricism and rationalism.

I have excluded from consideration the critical philosophy of Immanuel Kant as he expounds it in his book *The Critique of Pure Reason*, even though that philosophy was called by him 'transcendental idealism'. Kant has been read as an idealist by almost every commentator since Hegel, but I think this view of his work is almost certainly false. Kant himself tried to dispel the misreading by including the chapter 'The refutation of idealism' in the second edition of *The Critique of Pure Reason* but the legend has persisted none the less. (I cannot argue the point in this book, but I think Kant was not an idealist but a materialist philosopher.)

The German idealists who have systems partially similar to Hegel's are J. G. Fichte and F. W. J. Schelling. It is in their hands that transcendental idealism becomes a kind of idealism. I shall say something briefly about their rather convoluted philosophical systems.

Fichte's book *The Science of Knowledge* is a synthesis of metaphysics and epistemology. Metaphysics is the study of what exists as it really or essentially is in itself. Epistemology is the study of philosophical problems about knowledge. By generating an idealist metaphysics, Fichte also hoped to define the limits of knowledge. What knows and what is most fully real is the individual, purely spiritual Ego or subjective consciousness. The Ego is irreducibly active and through its mental acts it is conscious of itself. The Ego's self-consciousness depends upon a self–not self distinction or upon an Ego-world distinction which is itself created by the Ego's 'positing' of the empirical world. The world of spatio-temporal enduring items which we confront in everyday life is, so to speak, constructed out of the experiences of the Ego, or, more precisely, out of appearances which the Ego is acquainted with. Because what passes for the objective world is an intellectual construct by oneself as Ego, Fichte's idealism is sometimes known as 'subjective idealism'. Hegel calls it that.

Fichte's partial contemporary, Schelling, thinks of his own 'absolute idealism' as a holistic unification or overcoming of a set of dualisms or separations which are in the last resort artificial or unreal. In reality there is no genuine bifurcation between object and perception, concept and image, person and external world. All these are created by conscious reflection, and are most appropriately viewed as aspects of a spiritual and unitary whole. Schelling considers persons as 'separated' from themselves by acts of reflection, and it is one ambition of his philosophy to reconcile persons with themselves. Reflection, because it produces psychologically damaging and metaphysically illusory dualisms, is regarded by Schelling as a kind of mental illness and he seeks to replace the oppositions of ordinary thinking by a 'philosophy of identity' which exhibits the mutual dependence between opposites. Philosophy itself, in so far as it is dualistic, is an evil, albeit a necessary one in the sense of necessary prerequisite for the formulation of his own philosophy. When we live and act without reflection, we are not conscious of dualisms between, say, objects and our mental representations of them. In this, and especially in the thesis that the overcoming of dualisms is in a universal spirit, Schelling anticipates many themes in Hegel's system.

Although Berkeley is the most celebrated British idealist, towards the end of the nineteenth century British philosophy was dominated by a group of thinkers deeply influenced by German idealism, especially by Hegel. This group comprised F. H.

Bradley, Bernard Bosanquet, Thomas Hill Green and John McTaggart Ellis McTaggart. These thinkers are little read nowadays, mainly because of the severity of criticism levelled at them, first by G. E. Moore and Bertrand Russell and later by the logical positivists. However, their writings display logical rigour and considerable metaphysical imagination. They are, in my view, just as worthy of study as their anti-metaphysical opponents.

In his *Appearance and Reality* (1893) Bradley argues that it is not possible to specify what something is, independently of specifying that thing's relations to other things. In particular, rather like Fichte, Bradley thinks it is not possible to make sense of the idea of self except in contrast with a not-self. The 'Absolute' is Bradley's name for the sum of all relations in their unity. It is a spiritual whole, which is more than the sum of those parts which are appearances to conscious selves, and it is more real than the physical world, which Bradley regards as an ideal construction or useful fiction postulated by the natural sciences.

Like Bradley, Bernard Bosanquet thinks that dualisms or oppositions are united in reality as a whole, which he too calls the Absolute. The most fundamental philosophical dualism to be overcome is that between individual and universal, or things and sorts of things. The unity of universal and particular is expressed in the political, religious and artistic progress of conscious beings. The Absolute, or reality as a whole, is best understood on the model of self-consciousness. We finite minds are parts or aspects of a single infinite mind which is identical with the Absolute, and the physical universe does not exist independently of its experience by finite minds. Bosanquet advocates this quasi-Hegelian metaphysics in his book *The Principle of Individuality and Value* (1912).

Thomas Hill Green acknowledges that mental events may have physical causes but argues that everything physical is nothing but a constituent of the world of experience: part of the content of experience. He concludes from this that what makes the whole of experience possible cannot be anything physical. Both experience and its contents depend, in fact, on certain spiritual principles which Green characterizes in his book *Prolegomena to Ethics* (1883).

In his two-volume work *The Nature of Existence* (1927) –

perhaps the master-work of this phase of British idealism – McTaggart argues that conscious spiritual selves are the fundamental constituents of the universe. Each of us is essentially one of these, and the empirical world logically depends upon its perception by us for its existence. According to McTaggart, there is no such substance as matter and, as spiritual selves, we are immortal. Interestingly, McTaggart rejects the claim that God exists, so combining a doctrine of personal immortality with atheism. This perhaps illustrates my point that theism and belief in one's survival of death are logically independent (see page 2, above).

Two contemporary British idealists with systems very different from one another are John Foster and Timothy Sprigge. Foster advocates an idealist phenomenalism in his *The Case for Idealism* (1982) and Sprigge a pan-psychic neo-Hegelianism in his *The Vindication of Absolute Idealism* (1983). Foster argues that the physical world is a logical construction out of sense contents and that ultimate contingent reality is at least not physical and plausibly mental. Sprigge argues that pan-psychism, the doctrine that everything that exists has at least one mental property, is the only metaphysics that adequately recognizes the existence of conscious subjects. Indeed, for Sprigge, consciousnesses are the ultimate constituents of the universe. If they did not exist, nor would anything else.

Why should anyone believe idealism? Two kinds of argument for idealism, one empirical and one metaphysical, can be discerned in this variety of thinkers. The empirical argument is that physical things are known to exist only through our perception of them. Further, physical things are not known with certainty to exist over and above our perception of them. Finally, it might even be incoherent – contradictory – to suppose that physical things exist independently of our perceptions at all. The metaphysical argument goes as follows. Science and much empirical thinking give us only a partial account of reality. This is because science and empirical thinking are essentially objective or third-person in their approach. They treat their subject matter as 'other'. Neither science nor empirical thinking can provide an account of subjectivity, in particular of consciousness, which is a subjective or first-person phenomenon. It follows too that purely objective modes of thought cannot explain the relationship between conscious subjects and the objects they experience. Science treats everything as physical. It cannot explain consciousness and it cannot explain the location of the conscious subject in the universe. Idealism explains just what science cannot explain.

BERKELEY

Berkeley's idealism is best understood against the background of his empiricism. Empiricism is the view that all knowledge is acquired through the use of the five senses. Sometimes it is held, in the weaker form: all knowledge is acquired through experience; but nearly all empiricists agree that no experience would be possible if sense experience were not possible. Berkeley shares his empiricism with the seventeenth-century English philosophers, Thomas Hobbes and John Locke, and the eighteenth-century Scottish philosopher, David Hume. Empiricism by no means necessarily leads to idealism: Hobbes, for example, was a materialist and Locke a dualist. But Berkeley thinks that strictly correct empiricist thinking should lead to idealism. He takes the view not only that knowledge is all acquired through experience but that only experience can be certainly known to exist. One's experiences are all one is ever directly acquainted with, so belief in anything else cannot be based on direct experience. Thus we can understand Berkeley's idealism as an extreme form of empiricism. He conceives of himself as pushing empiricism to its logical conclusions.

   Experience gives us absolutely no evidence for belief in two features of physical objects which we normally take to be essential to them. Experience does not teach us they exist unperceived; that they exist before and after not just during our perception of them. Experience does not teach us that they are material, that is, ultimately composed of a substance called 'matter'. Berkeley also thinks there is no sound philosophical justification for these two fundamental assumptions, and he argues they are both false.

Matter in Question

To understand why Berkeley denies the existence of material

substance we need to be familiar with a philosophical problem which had been addressed by Locke. A physical object – a chair or a book say – possesses certain properties or characteristics; for example, if something is a physical object, then it has a certain size and shape. It is solid and is either in motion or at rest. Physical objects may also appear coloured and have a smell and a taste to them. The philosophical issue is: what are these properties of? What is it that bears or supports all the properties of a physical object? Locke answered uncomfortably that there must be supposed to exist a substance or material or stuff which actually 'has' or bears these properties. Locke was reluctant to postulate such a substance because of his empiricism; clearly, matter in this sense could not be known to exist through any direct experience of it.

Viewed in this context, Berkeley's unequivocal denial of the existence of material substance does seem more strictly empiricist than Locke's postulation of it. His reasons for rejecting substance divide into arguments that substance could never be known to exist and arguments that the word 'substance' is really meaningless. He also has an interesting account of what it means to say that something exists.

To be clear about what it is that Berkeley is denying we need to know his definition of 'matter'. He says that matter is an 'unthinking substance' and that 'by matter ... we are to understand an inert, senseless substance, in which extension, figure and motion do actually subsist' (*Principles of Human Knowledge*, p. 69). To show that such a substance could never be known to exist, Berkeley poses this question: what means could we possibly use to detect it? The only two possibilities open to us are the use of the senses or reason. In other words, if we are to know that matter exists this can only be through observation, using one or more of the five senses, or by reasoning, the logical exercise of the intellect – or, perhaps, by a combination of the two. Berkeley's argument is that we cannot know that matter exists by either of these two means, these are the only means available to us, so we cannot possibly know that matter exists. Berkeley rules out the possibility of perceiving matter through the senses because 'by them we have the knowledge only of our sensations, ideas, or those things that are immediately perceived by sense' (*Principles of Human Knowledge*, p. 73). All the colours, shapes, sounds and other qualities we perceive fall into this category of ideas or of things immediately experienced through the senses. Berkeley's use of the word 'idea' is much broader than our twentieth-century use. It includes our sense of 'thought' or 'mental image' but also covers all experiences. It therefore may strike the modern reader of Berkeley as odd that he should speak of perceiving ideas. We should translate this as 'having sense experiences' or some such, unless the context makes it clear that he is speaking of thinking or imagining. So Berkeley's view is that through the senses we can know only our own experiences. Given this premiss Berkeley is entitled to conclude that the senses 'do not inform us that things exist without the mind, or unperceived' (*Principles of Human Knowledge*, p. 73). Material substances allegedly exist independently of minds, so material substance cannot be known to exist through the senses.

This leaves only the possibility that substance is known to exist by reasoning: by this, Berkeley means logically deducing the fact that substance exists from the fact that we have sense experiences. But, he argues, whatever the character of our experiences, it does not logically follow from the fact that we have them that they are perceptions of physical substances which exist when they are not perceived. To show the failure of any reasoning from subjective experiences to objective objects, Berkeley draws our attention to 'what happens in dreams, frenzies and the like' (*Principles of Human Knowledge*, p. 73). During dreams and hallucinations it seems to us that we are perceiving mind-independent physical objects, but none is really present to our senses: 'Hence, it is evident the supposition of external bodies is not necessary for the producing [of] our ideas' (*Principles of Human Knowledge*, p. 73). So we are not entitled to reason, from the fact that we have experience, to the conclusion that there are physical objects which exist unperceived.

If Berkeley is correct in concluding that we cannot know of substance through the senses or by reason, and if these are our only means of knowing, then he is right that we cannot know that matter exists. Berkeley's argument is in fact a strong one. He insists, for example, that it is contradictory to suppose that there could be perception of an unperceived object, and he is right in that because perceiving an unperceived object means both perceiving it and not perceiving it at the same time. Also, it seems plausible to argue that what I perceive now does not necessarily exist before my perception or after my perception, and would not necessarily exist without my perception existing. In considering these arguments, we should bear in mind that Berkeley maintains he is being more strictly an empiricist than the other empiricists, especially Locke.

Even if we may not perceive unperceived objects, or reason to their existence, may we still not imagine them? It certainly seems to us that we may imagine the trees in a park when we are not there, or think of the books in a cupboard when it is closed. Berkeley considers this fact because it could be argued that the most likely explanation for our being able to imagine objects unperceived is that they do indeed exist unperceived. To refute this conclusion, Berkeley invites us to consider carefully what such imagining consists in, and asks 'but what is all this, I beseech you, more than framing in your mind certain ideas?' (*Principles of Human Knowledge*, p. 75). The mere imagining of the books or the trees only proves that we have a power of thinking in certain mental images, and it certainly does not follow from that that there exist physical objects independent of our minds. To establish that would require our imagining objects unimagined, or conceiving objects unconceived, which – like perceiving objects unperceived – is contradictory or, as Berkeley puts it, 'a manifest repugnancy' (*Principles of Human Knowledge*, p. 76).

There remains the possibility that the existence of material substance is the probable, even if not the certain, cause of our experiences. Berkeley wonders whether the fact that we have our experiences might not be best explained on the supposition that they are the effects of such a material substance, 'and so it might be at least probable that there are such things as bodies that excite their ideas in our minds' (*Principles of Human Knowledge*, p. 73). He comes to reject this hypothesis because it suffers from one of the central defects of mind–body dualism: the problem of how it is possible for mental and physical to interact causally if they belong to radically distinct ontological categories, that is, if they are utterly different sorts of entity. Berkeley thinks that his maintaining that only minds and their ideas exist enables him to bypass the question of how psycho-physical interaction is possible. If he is right, then his idealism is immune to an objection which is possibly fatal to dualism, and he has also refuted the conjecture that physical objects exist as the causes of our experiences, if it is true that only things of fundamentally the same type may interact causally.

If we know only our own experiences, then it does follow from that that we do not know that material substances exist independently of those experiences. But Berkeley wants a stronger conclusion than that. He has already indicated that there is something contradictory about the supposition that objects exist unperceived or unthought. He takes up this theme to try to show that concepts like 'matter' and 'material substance' are in fact devoid of meaning. This is important because, from the fact that we do not know that something exists, it does not follow that it does not exist. But from the fact that the concept which putatively denotes that thing is meaningless, it does follow that that thing does not exist. Indeed, if the definition of the concept contains a contradiction, it is logically impossible for that thing to exist. So Berkeley seeks to prove 'that the absolute existence of unthinking things are words without a meaning, or which include a contradiction' (*Principles of Human Knowledge*, p. 76).

Qualities

He begins with an attack on Locke's distinction between primary and secondary qualities of physical objects. Locke thought that a physical object possesses certain characteristics irrespective of whether it is being perceived. For example, an object is a certain size, has a shape, is either in motion or at rest, is solid and occupies a specific part of space and time whether a person perceives it or not. Nor is the number of physical objects which exist altered by the perception of them. Locke called these objective characteristics 'primary qualities'. On the other hand, Locke also maintained that objects possess properties which are only powers or dispositions in the objects to produce experience in us. These so-called 'secondary qualities' are colour, taste, sound and smell. They do not exist in the objects as we experience them, but only as capacities to excite subjective sensations of taste, sound, etc. in conscious beings. So Locke's theory is that our ideas of primary qualities resemble characteristics actually possessed by the object, but our ideas of secondary qualities resemble nothing at all in the object.

Berkeley's attack is two-pronged. He tries to show that primary qualities are just as mind-dependent as secondary qualities, and then denies that ideas of qualities can resemble anything which is not yet another idea. One argument for the mind-dependence of secondary qualities is that they seem to be relative. What colour an object is, what it tastes like and whether it smells, all depend on the nature and position of the observer, as well as environmental conditions like lighting. Berkeley says that exactly the same is true for primary qualities. What shape something is, what size it is and how fast it is moving are all also relative to some observer, and these qualities may vary with context, and indeed appear different to different observers. Berkeley concludes that if the fact that secondary qualities are relative proves they are subjective, then, if primary qualities are relative, they too must be subjective. In addition, Berkeley argues that primary qualities depend upon secondary qualities for their existence so that, for example, size and movement cannot be imagined to exist without being coloured according to his view. If it is true that primary qualities depend upon secondary qualities, and if it is true that secondary qualities depend upon the mind, then it is true that primary qualities also depend upon the mind.

The other prong of the attack is 'an idea can be like nothing but an idea' (*Principles of Human Knowledge*, p. 68), so ideas of primary qualities cannot be like the alleged primary qualities, because they are not ideas but objective characteristics of physical objects. But ideas of primary qualities exist, so there cannot be qualities like them really in the object, otherwise an idea could be like something that was not another idea.

Berkeley uses these criticisms of the primary–secondary distinction as premises for the conclusion that 'matter' is an incoherent concept. We need to bear in mind the definition of 'matter' (see page 70, above) as a mind-independent substance which objectively possesses size, shape and motion. This definition is contradictory if Berkeley's premises are true because it contains the assertion that primary qualities are mind-independent; that is, it contains the thesis that characteristics which do not exist independently of minds exist independently of minds – which is blatantly self-contradictory. So postulating matter on Berkeley's view is not some kind of empirical or factual mistake, it is a deep conceptual muddle. It involves the claim that what only exists perceived exists unperceived, or what only exists in thought exists unthought. For this reason he feels able to claim 'the very notion of what is called matter or corporeal substance involves a contradiction in it' (*Principles of Human Knowledge*, p. 69). Berkeley assumes – quite rightly – that if the definition of a word contains a contradiction, then the word is meaningless. So if his argument is sound, he has shown that 'matter' is meaningless and hence that matter cannot possibly exist.

Another component of the concept of material substance is that it is the substratum or support of the properties of a physical object. Berkeley points out that the word 'support' is either being used as a spatial metaphor here or else is being used with no meaning at all. He asks: 'It is evident "support" cannot here be taken in its usual or literal sense – as when we may say that pillars support a building; in what sense therefore must it be taken?' (*Principles of Human Knowledge*, p. 72). No coherent answer can be provided, so another part of the definition of 'matter' is shown to be meaningless.

Esse Est Percipi (To be is to be Perceived)

Berkeley brings together his two sorts of argument against the existence of matter by an account of what it means to say that something exists. According to Berkeley, to say that something exists means nothing more than that it is or may be perceived. If we do not take this view, he thinks the word 'exists' becomes unintelligible. His theory of existence therefore includes that theory of perception called phenomenalism – the thesis that statements about physical objects ultimately mean the same as statements about actual or possible experiences, and so may be translated by them without loss of meaning. Berkeley does not use the term 'phenomenalism', but his answer to the question 'What is meant by the term exist when applied to sensible things [?]' is that those things are or may be perceived. For example: 'The table I write on I say exists, that is, I see and feel it; and if I were out of my study I should say it existed – meaning thereby that if I was in my study I might perceive it, or that some other spirit actually does perceive it' (*Principles of Human Knowledge*, p. 66). This doctrine is summed up by Berkeley in his famous slogan '*esse est percipi*': to be is to be perceived.

Now, it is clear that material substance does not meet the '*esse est percipi*' requirement. Matter is never directly perceived, nor could it be, because we perceive only our own ideas. But 'to be perceived' is the only sense there is to 'to exist', so matter does not exist. If we reject Berkeley's theory of existence because we find its conclusion unpalatable, then the onus is on us to say what existence is. For his part, Berkeley admits 'The general idea of being appeareth to me the most abstract and incomprehensible of all other' (*Principles of Human Knowledge*, p. 72). There is a final twist to Berkeley's argument here. He says that, once we dismiss the idea of substance being a support of properties as incoherent, all we are left with is substance as being in general. But that is an idea he finds senseless. He has then adduced yet a further ground for maintaining that 'matter' is a meaningless concept. 'Support' and 'being' are only empirical concepts according to Berkeley, so he feels that he can state with justification 'When I consider the two parts or branches which make the signification of the words material substance, I am convinced there is no distinct meaning annexed to them' (*Principles of Human Knowledge*, p. 72).

Minds

Whatever the merits of Berkeley's arguments against matter, two fundamental questions remain: what are minds? and do they exist? Berkeley's answers are that minds do exist and they are of two sorts, finite and infinite. There is only one infinite mind and that is God, who possesses all the traditional divine attributes of omniscience, omnipotence and omnibenevolence. The finite minds are human souls. We should examine next Berkeley's reasons for believing these entities exist. For them, to be is *to perceive*.

Berkeley's argument that minds exist is that ideas exist, and the existence of ideas consists in their being perceived. But they could not be perceived and so could not exist unless perceivers also exist. Therefore perceivers – or minds – exist. Berkeley is quite clear that a mind, or a self is not just another idea. It is that which has ideas, and so cannot be found among the ideas themselves. For the same reason, at least in the case of human minds, minds are irreducibly active and subjective. They do not perceive themselves directly, they perceive only their own ideas. Berkeley presents his argument in this way:

This perceiving, active being is what I call mind, spirit, soul, or myself. By which words I do not denote any one of my ideas, but a thing entirely distinct from them, wherein they exist, or which is the same thing, whereby they are perceived – for the existence of an idea consists in its being perceived. (*Principles of Human Knowledge*, pp. 65–6)

Far from it being the case that physical substances exist, the only substances according to Berkeley are mental or spiritual, and we know these exist only because ideas are perceived. As he puts it, 'it is evident there is not any other substance than spirit or that which perceives' (*Principles of Human Knowledge*, p. 68).

In addition to finite human minds or souls, according to Berkeley, there must also exist an infinite, divine, mind, otherwise we could not explain how our ideas are caused. Berkeley notes that in perception – if not in imagination – we are not free to control the content of our experiences. If we open our eyes, for example, we cannot just choose what visual experiences will then occur. Berkeley concludes from this that we are not the cause of our own ideas. Nor are they, he thinks, the cause of each other. It follows that there must exist a cause of our ideas which is not an idea or one's own mind. Berkeley dismisses one seemingly plausible candidate for this role, which is, of course, matter. Matter is held by those who believe in it to be inert or inactive, and also unthinking. But something inert and unthinking cannot be the cause of ideas, argues Berkeley, so matter is not the cause of our ideas. He concludes that the order and beauty and complexity of his ideas are such that their cause can be nothing less than God, so God must exist, and he is 'one, eternal, infinitely wise, good, and perfect' (*Principles of Human Knowledge*, p. 140).

In these ways, then, Berkeley attempts to convince us that material substance does not exist, and that only minds and their ideas are real. His philosophy of mind is a powerful one and is largely internally consistent. But a defender of Berkeleyan idealism needs to find answers to the following objections. What does 'exists' mean when applied to God and human minds? Does it really make sense to talk of perceiving ideas, even when these are understood to be experiences? Is the concept of a spiritual substance really any clearer than that of a material substance? Does not Berkeley's God have much of the same role as Locke's material substance anyway? How does Berkeley know that other people have minds? In other words, how does Berkeley know solipsism is false? (Solipsism is an extreme form of idealism: idealism is the theory that only minds exist; solipsism is the view that only one's own mind exists.)

Despite these problems, Berkeley's books are philosophical classics and his contribution to the philosophy of mind is valuable because it does not seek to diminish the reality of conscious experience.

HEGEL

The philosophical works of G. W. F. Hegel form a systematically interrelated whole and it is fair to say that no one aspect of his thought may be fully appreciated in complete abstraction from the rest. Extracting Hegel's solution to the mind–body problem therefore requires doing some violence to his holistic conception of philosophy. I shall try to keep this to a minimum by first stating his solution and then outlining its role in his philosophy as a whole.

I should warn the reader in advance that Hegel's idealism is very different from Berkeley's, and many find his prose style tortuous in the extreme. Hegel uses several ordinary words with extra, philosophical senses, and I shall try to make these reasonably clear as we encounter them. In addition, Hegel's thinking is frequently of a complexity many would call 'convoluted', but which others find subtle and original. Many great philosophers are at least as lucid as the commentators who try to make them intelligible; but in the case of Hegel it is certainly wise to read secondary literature to obtain an overview his aims and methods before tackling the primary texts. His contribution to the philosophy of mind is concentrated in two books, *The Phenomenology of Spirit* of 1807 and volume three of the *Encyc-*

lopaedia of the Philosophical Sciences (1830), which is called
The Philosophy of Mind. It is better to read the latter work first
as it is clearer and shorter and was regarded by Hegel as a more
definitive statement on the nature of mind than the 1807 Phenomenology. I advise this despite the fact that Hegel conceived of the
Phenomenology as an introduction to the philosophy of the En-
cyclopaedia, and it is the order I shall adopt here.

A useful way to read the first section of Hegel's Philosophy of
Mind is as an attempt to avoid the philosophical shortcomings of
mind–body dualism, and to replace that theory with a kind of
idealism. As we have seen, idealism and dualism are mutually
inconsistent – they cannot both be true simultaneously – because
dualism is the view that there are two substances, one mental
and one physical, but idealism is the view that there is ultimately
only one substance: mental substance or mind. Indeed, idealism
is a monism and materialism is a monism, because according to
each of those only one sort of substance exists and, as the names
suggest, monism and dualism are incompatible. We should now
inspect Hegel's rejection of dualism and his reasons for adopting
that monism called idealism rather than the one called materialism.

The Critique of Dualism

Hegel has an interesting account of how mind–body dualism
comes to be a theory of the mind at all. It is his view that as
children we are not mind–body dualists; on the contrary, we
have an intuitive or taken-for-granted feeling of unity between
ourselves and nature. He suggests that because we are alive, and
so parts of the single life-process which is nature, we have a
sympathy which extends so far as feeling ourselves to be a part
of nature. Naturally, as children we do not rationally represent
these thoughts to ourselves in language, but nevertheless this is
the intuitive and pre-philosophical character of our experience.
However, according to Hegel, as we grow older we lose this
feeling of being at one with nature and reflect rationally on our
experience instead. It is precisely this act of reflection which
gives rise to an apparent split or bifurcation between oneself, as
a subjective mental substance, and the rest of the world, as an
objective physical substance. In the act of reflective awareness

there appear to exist two separate and independent entities: the observer and the observed, or the subject and the object.

It is worth pausing at this point to ask why rational reflection should produce the appearance of a mind–body dualism. It will be Hegel's sophisticated answer that this is one of the structures of self-consciousness; but some immediate plausibility in his view may be adduced in the following way. If you consider for a moment the states of mind you are in typically during the course of the day, it seems likely that many of them are not what we would call 'self-conscious' states. I mean by this that you are conscious of whatever you are thinking about or perceiving; so, for example, you think about posting a letter, and then your attention is absorbed in the actual posting and so on. Arguably it is only intermittently that you are conscious of being conscious of the letter or of anything else. This would seem to require a new and special act of awareness – a kind of awareness of being aware. If this is correct, it supports Hegel's case in that there is no self or subject or observer present to consciousness most of the time; one appears only during those acts called acts of self-consciousness. As we shall see in *The Phenomenology of Spirit*, Hegel describes many different aspects of self-consciousness, but I note this everyday fact about our mental lives to give one reason for making dualism rely on self-awareness.

Hegel makes two important points about mind–body dualism as generated by reflection: it gives rise to insuperable philosophical problems, and it is illusory. I shall take each of these in turn.

The philosophical problems cluster around the relationship between the mental and the physical substance. There is notably the time-worn problem for dualism of how causal interaction between mental and physical is possible if each is so different in kind from the other. Hegel also notes that the empirical sciences of physiology and psychology are powerless to state what the nature of the psycho-physical relation is. This importance is due to the seeming utter heterogeneity of mental and physical. I appear to myself as a single unified subjective self, faced by a multifarious composite objective world. I have a mental life of thoughts and perceptions which is in some sense internal to me, but I am confronted by an 'external world' of physical objects.

Within the Cartesian picture produced by reflection, my thoughts seem merely temporal, but the world of nature about me appears both temporal and spatial. It seems to fly in the face of common sense to deny the reality of either side of this polar opposition between mental and physical.

Mistaken metaphysical philosophies have been built on the findings of reflection, according to Hegel. Not only Descartes but also his rationalist contemporaries, Leibniz and Spinoza, tried to account for psycho-physical interaction. Hegel has some sympathy for Spinoza but thinks that in the last resort it is a mistake to try to state how mental and physical interact at all, because the question of how they interact is inappropriate. If we ask 'How do mental and physical interact?' then Hegel's answer is 'The question thus posed [i]s unanswerable' (*The Philosophy of Mind*, p. 33). Once we concede that mental and physical are really two different substances, it is impossible to explain their interaction, so the solution is to deny that they are really two substances: 'If soul and body are absolutely opposed to one another as is maintained by the abstractive intellectual consciousness, then there is no possibility of any community between them' (*The Philosophy of Mind*, p. 33).

Part of dualism's mistake is to think of the mind as a kind of thing, not as a physical thing but as a peculiar kind of individual, a non-physical thing. Reflection gives rise to this idea of the mind because it belongs to that kind of thinking which Hegel calls '*Verstand*' or 'understanding'. The primary role of the understanding is to make intelligible to us the empirical world, the world of spatio-temporal objects we observe around us. When we try to use the concepts appropriate for that purpose for a quite different role – to think about thinking – we lose ourselves in incoherences. Concepts like 'thing' and 'indivisibility' or 'unity' mislead us into Cartesianism if we try to use them to make our mental lives intelligible to us. The argument Hegel deploys here is to be found in the writings of his German anti-metaphysical predecessor, Immanuel Kant.

Dialectic
Hegel also follows Kant in distinguishing *Verstand* from '*Vernunft*' or 'reason'. Where he parts company with Kant is in

claiming that the use of reason can provide us with knowledge of the world as it really is in itself, not just as it appears to us through observation or reflection. If reason has this power, then it follows that we may use it to discover the truth about the mental and the physical; so it is appropriate at this point to explain part of Hegel's conception of it. According to Hegel, reason divides into two parts, dialectic and speculation. Dialectic is the sort of thinking which exhibits philosophical problems as contradictions or apparent contradictions. For example, it is apparently contradictory to state that persons are completely free yet also wholly causally determined in what they do; it is also apparently contradictory to say that the world is both wholly mental and wholly physical. Yet philosophy contains many such opposed positions. For example, libertarians hold that we perform our actions by free will, but determinists say that our actions are caused and perhaps therefore inevitable and so not performed freely. Idealists hold that reality is really mental, materialists that it is really physical. Dialectic takes these oppositions seriously and tries to show that the oppositions in fact depend upon one another for their formulation – they define themselves in opposition to one another. In his book *The Science of Logic* Hegel describes the mutual dependences between the most general and fundamental concepts that he thinks we use to make sense of the world. The other part of reason, speculation, is used to transcend or overcome the oppositions by exhibiting the truth in both of the old positions in a new 'synthesis' or reconciliation.

Whether we think dialectic is a genuine or a spurious mode of problem solving, it is worth noting that the two concepts 'mental' and 'physical' often do seem to contain equally semantically opposed sub-concepts, at least within the Western intellectual tradition: private–public, subjective–objective, internal–external, temporal–spatial one–many, free–determined, active–passive, I–other, sacred–profane, indivisible–divisible, and so on. It is also arguable that adopting a position in the philosophy of mind often partly consists in emphasizing one side of each pair or some of these opposites while playing down the importance of the other. In what follows, then, we should bear in mind that Hegel thinks he is employing a kind of reasoning which is peculiarly appropriate to philosophy. We should also perhaps bear in mind the question, whether his own version of idealism is itself 'one-sided' or succeeds as a genuine speculative synthesis.

A key statement in Hegel's criticism of dualism and his transition to idealism is this: 'The separation of the material and the immaterial can be explained only on the basis of the original unity of both' (The Philosophy of Mind, p. 33). This counts as a piece of dialectic, because it is the claim that two seemingly opposed elements have this status because they are in fact two aspects of one reality. This underlying reality will turn out to be spiritual for Hegel, but he does not conceive of himself as an idealist in the Berkeleyan sense because that would require his making merely one opposite depend on the other – the physical on the mental. Nor does he accept materialism, because that would be just to make the mental depend on the physical. His own 'absolute idealism' is the view that mental and physical exist in a new synthesis called Spirit, which is the synthesis of all oppositions. This is what he means by the 'original unity' just quoted.

How does Hegel arrive at this conlusion? It will take the remainder of this chapter to explain that process, but first we should examine Hegel on conventional idealism and materialism.

Hegel has two main criticisms of these theories. First, they are undialectical or one-sided. This means that idealism is the attempt to minimize the significance of physical reality and reduce it to mind, and that materialism is the attempt to minimize the significance of mental reality and reduce it to matter. They are in fact mutually dependent philosophies because idealism is partially defined as the negation of materialism and vice versa. The second objection is that each is an answer to an inappropriate question. If we ask whether reality is really mental or physical Hegel says: 'It is just this form of the question which must be recognized as inadmissible' (The Philosophy of Mind, p. 33). So Hegel's answer to the mind–body problem as traditionally conceived is, roughly, 'Do not pose the question'. Why does he feel entitled to this answer?

Universal and Particular

Within the Cartesian framework we tend to think of the relation between mental and physical as that of particular to particular, and this misleads us into thinking we are dealing with the relationship between two substances. In fact the relation is universal to particular. To make sense of this, we need to understand what Hegel means by 'universal' and 'particular'. The problem of universals in philosophy may be formulated in several different ways, but some of them are as follows. What are examples, or instances, instances of? What do we mean by meaning when we speak of the meaning of some general term – a term which may be used to refer to more than one thing? What do all the things we call by the same name have in common? What entitles us to speak of kinds or sorts of things? So the problem of universals is a problem about what generality consists in, especially what the relationship is between the specific and the general or, as it is usually put, between the particular and the universal.

This bears on the mind–body problem because Hegel thinks the psycho-physical relation is universal to particular. In some sense the physical world is an exemplification of mind. He uses picturesque language to describe this relationship, sometimes he talks of nature as an expression of mind, or of mind pervading nature, or as embracing it. For example:

In truth the immaterial is not related to the material as particular to a particular but as the true universal which overarches and embraces particularity is related to the particular; the particular material thing in its isolation has no truth, no independence in face of the immaterial. (The Philosophy of Mind, p. 33)

Despite this, it is not as though the mental could exist without the physical. It is an important part of Hegel's views on politics, history, art and religion that mind cannot exist independently of its expression in these fields. Mentality is not distinct from its growing expression in human activities, and this is revealed in different kinds of political organization from the ancient Greek polis to the European societies which post-date the French Revolution of 1789. Again, religious practices, from those of the ancient Egyptians and Greeks to modern Christianity, and works of art from the first sculptures to modern music and painting are all stages in the historical manifestation of mind.

It follows that the psycho-physical relation is very close according to Hegel. Neither mind nor matter is an independent substance, because each depends on the other. Matter is the expression of mind. Here is his description of this relationship as it holds for a human being.

Under the head of human expression are included, for example, the upright figure in general, and the formation of the limbs, especially the hand, as the absolute instrument, of the mouth – laughter, weeping, etc., and the note of mentality diffused over the whole, which at once announces the body as the externality of a higher nature. (*The Philosophy of Mind*, p. 147)

It is clear then that Hegel is not an idealist in Berkeley's sense. But still less is Hegel a materialist, despite the fact that the existence of mentality depends on its expression. His verdict on materialism is: 'The explanations given in materialistic writings of the various relationships and combinations which are supposed to produce a result such as thought, are unsatisfactory in the extreme' (*The Philosophy of Mind*, p. 34). Materialism does have the merit of being a monism. It is an attempt to repudiate Cartesian dualism but ironically it still operates within a fundamentally Cartesian framework. Materialists either simply deny the existence of one of Descartes' two substances – the mental one – or else they speak incoherently of causal relations between mental and physical by making mind causally dependent on matter.

If this is Hegel's philosophy of mind, why should we call him an idealist at all? Would it not be better to include him under the heading of neutral monism, as holding that mental and physical are two aspects of some underlying reality? The description provided so far is consistent with Hegel being a neutral monist, but the rest of his system is not. Furthermore, Hegel himself says that he is an idealist, albeit a special sort of idealist, an 'absolute idealist'. We should take him at his word in this and try to decide next what exactly absolute idealism is. In this we shall take up the theme that mental and physical are united in an ultimate reality called 'Spirit', where Spirit is the unity of all dialectical oppositions, including universal and particular. To examine the grounds for this claim, we should turn to Hegel's other book concerned with the philosophy of mind, *The Phenomenology of Spirit*.

The Phenomenology of Spirit is a work of considerable

intricacy, complexity and originality and, although it was the first sizeable book that Hegel wrote, it is regarded by many as his greatest philosophical achievement. A good way to approach its central theme is to try to make sense of its title. The word translated as 'Spirit' is 'Geist', which in ordinary German may have the sense of 'mind', 'intellect', 'intelligence', 'wit', 'imagination', 'genius', 'soul', 'morale', 'essence', 'ghost' and 'spectre', as well as 'spirit', and most of these translations seem appropriate at different points in the Phenomenology. Of these, 'Spirit' is to be preferred because it captures the implication of a divine character, which Hegel certainly intends Geist to possess; but this choice must be taken to preclude Geist's mental and intelligent character which is also essential to it. It would not do much harm to translate 'Geist' as 'consciousness', meaning 'consciousness in general', so long as we do not forget the connotation of divine intelligence.

The other problematic term in the title is 'phenomenology'. Phenomenology is the sort of philosophy which attempts to describe what is given to consciousness just as it presents itself. The aim is to make no prior commitment about the objective causes or nature of what appears to consciousness and in this way to provide our knowledge with foundations in experience, and thus not to rely on dubious preconceptions. In this the project of phenomenology is rather like that of Descartes' search for certainty in his first Meditation, examined in our first chapter. If phenomenology describes what appears to consciousnesses, and if Geist is consciousness, then a 'Phenomenology of Spirit' is a description of how consciousness appears to consciousness, or a description of how Spirit appears to Spirit. This is in fact exactly what Hegel attempts in the book.

In keeping with his practising phenomenology, Hegel does not offer us any explanations, only descriptions. The Phenomenology is in fact a description of all the various stages or states of consciousness which Hegel thinks are possible. These range from the poorest and most rudimentary naïve awareness through the senses, called 'Sense-Certainty', to reality's complete knowledge of itself in so-called 'Absolute Knowing'. Geist is in fact the whole, or the totality of what exists as it really is, and Hegel's aim is to describe the various stages in Geist's growing self-realization. It is clear that Hegel is a metaphysical philosopher, because he thinks it is possible to obtain knowledge of reality as a whole and of reality as it really is in itself, and these are two of the concerns traditionally held to be essential to metaphysics as a branch of philosophy. Hegel does not expect us to accept these rather grandiose claims at the start of his book, but he thinks we should be led to them as our concept of what consciousness is becomes progressively enriched. Before we examine the various stages of consciousness, an ambiguity needs to be dispelled. It is sometimes thought unclear whether Hegel is describing a chronological process or a kind of conceptual or logical structure. On the first view, one kind of consciousness is superseded in time by a new, more sophisticated version which retains its merits, and so on in a chronological progression. This reading gains support from Hegel's writings on history. In *The Philosophy of History* Hegel argues that different historical epochs are characterized by different mentalities, so that it makes sense to talk of an 'Oriental World', a 'Greek World', a 'Roman World' and 'German World', where 'world' means something like *Weltanschauung* or 'world view'. These epochs are manifestations of the 'World Spirit' (*Weltgeist*). On the other reading however, Hegel is describing conceptual or dialectical relationships between different sorts of consciousness irrespective of their expressions or temporal inter-relations. Thus some kinds of consciousness are necessarily individualistic, others social, others religious, and so on, and these are arranged in a hierarchy in which some make others possible and some can be discerned as included within others. Although commentators read Hegel with different priorities in mind, I think it is best to regard the two interpretations as complementary. We can read the *Phenomenology* as describing the structures of consciousness in general, or in the abstract, and think of *The Philosophy of History* as what consciousness has amounted to in actuality. Clearly, that consciousness has a certain dialectical structure does not preclude its having a certain historical realization.

We may read the chapters of *The Phenomenology of Spirit* as a sustained and increasingly satisfactory answer to the question: what is consciousness? A glance at the book's contents gives an outline of the broad sorts of consciousness Hegel thinks possible. These are: Consciousness, Self-Consciousness, Reason, Spirit, Religion, and Absolute Knowing. Clearly it is impractical, in this short compass, to comment on all the subdivisions which have been philosophically influential.

The part of the book called 'Consciousness' divides into three, called 'Sense-Certainty', 'Perception' and 'Understanding' respectively. The first two are dialectically opposed or antithetical, and the third is the synthesis or reconciliation of the first two. Sense-Certainty is the bare sense experience of particular objects. Pre-philosophically it seems to us the richest and most certain kind of consciousness, but, according to Hegel, it is in fact the poorest and least sophisticated. Its limitations are revealed as soon as we ask: what are the objects of consciousness in sense-certainty? or who is conscious in sense-certainty? Then it is apparent that immediate sense experience cannot be all that our consciousness consists in. It also involves the use of general concepts but, as soon as we admit this, sense-certainty has given way to the second state of consciousness: perception. Within the confines of sense-certainty each of us is merely presented with a bare this and a bare now. Although sense-certainty presupposes a distinction between an experiencer and an experienced or between subject and object, it cannot even make this distinction intelligible because it has no conceptual resources.

'Perception' allows the experience of the objects of perception, including oneself, as different sorts of things. This kind of consciousness includes the ability to make discriminations and generalization which require the use of language. Language is inherently universal or general in what it can express so 'Perception takes what is present to it as a universal' (The Phenomenology of Spirit, p. 67). This applies equally to subject and object, so I can perceive myself to be a certain kind of being. As he puts it: '"I" is a universal and the object is a universal' (The Phenomenology of Spirit, p. 67). Within perception we use the universal or general concepts of language to make sense of the objects of perception, and so we are not confined to sensing them in their bare, given particularity. Perception involves both sensing and thinking.

But understanding the nature of the objects we perceive does not just consist in perceiving them according to different classifications. We try to explain them. The sort of consciousness called 'understanding' subsumes phenomena under natural laws and postulates forces and chemical elements in a 'supersensible realm'. Hegel means that we use the natural sciences to explain the perceptible partially by reference to the unperceptible. This scientific understanding is a synthesis of sense certainty and perception because it does justice to both particular and universal. Natural laws are absolutely universal because they are exceptionless and because they use general concepts yet subsume particulars under them. So he can say 'the absolute universal which has been purged of the antithesis between the universal and the individual ... has become the object of the understanding' (The Phenomenology of Spirit, p. 87).

Hegel's view of the natural sciences is that they are extremely useful in their proper role, making the empirical world intelligible – explaining the natural phenomena we perceive – but they are powerless to explain what consciousness is. Nor can they yield a metaphysical picture of reality as a whole which includes ourselves as perceiving subjects. Because science is empirical, 'the understanding in truth comes to know nothing else but appearance' (The Phenomenology of Spirit, p. 102). But because appearance is always appearance to someone or other, the question arises: who? or what am I? In this way understanding gives way to different sorts of self-consciousness. There is another, typically Hegelian aspect to the transition from understanding to self-consciousness. It is his idealist view that the natural laws and postulates of natural sciences are ultimately best understood as intellectual constructs. They pertain to our understanding of the world not to reality as it really is in itself. For this reason he feels entitled to say 'the understanding experiences only itself' (The Phenomenology of Spirit, p. 103). The conscious realization of this clearly requires an act of self-consciousness, so the next stage of the Phenomenology is to describe 'what consciousness knows in knowing itself' (The Phenomenology of Spirit, p. 103).

Self-Consciousness

At first glance some of Hegel's characterizations of self-consciousness are rather paradoxical, but I think it is possible to make sense of them. For example, he says 'consciousness makes a distinction, but which at the same time is for consciousness not a distinction' (The Phenomenology of Spirit, p. 104). What he means is that self-consciousness is consciousness' consciousness of consciousness – consciousness' consciousness of itself. It follows that in one sense consciousness is divided – between that which is conscious and what that consciousness is of. But in another sense that division must be artificial or not the whole truth, because in self-consciousness that which is conscious is what consciousness is of. This is what he means when he says of self-consciousness 'what it distinguishes from itself is only itself' (*The Phenomenology of Spirit*, p. 105). Understood in this way, there is nothing illogical or contradictory about such a claim.

The first kind of consciousness Hegel describes under 'Self-Consciousness' is 'Self-Certainty', and this is not a fully fledged kind of self-consciousness. In self-certainty, consciousness is indeed conscious of consciousness, but it is not aware that that which is conscious is the same as what consciousness is of. There is a subject–object split in self-certainty but there is no realization of the identity of subject and object. That is one of the further steps required before we can properly speak of self-consciousness. It is Hegel's view that this transition to self-consciousness proper can be facilitated only by the encounter or meeting of two would-be self-consciousnesses. In other words, 'self-consciousness achieves its satisfaction only in another self-consciousness' (*The Phenomenology of Spirit*, p. 110).

The social conditions for self-consciousness are described in the famous 'Master and Slave' chapter of the *Phenomenology* but before we examine that, one other concept needs to be mentioned; this is desire. Hegel attaches particular importance to desire in giving rise to self-consciousness. It is as though only a being capable of feeling desires can be capable of self-consciousness. I think the reason for this is that, in desiring some object in the world about us, we make a distinction between ourselves and the object we desire. A kind of mismatch or asymmetry is set up between oneself as desiring but unfulfilled and the object which could fulfil that desire. In so far as desire is correctly described in this way, it seems reasonable to hold that it is an emotion which produces self-consciousness. It creates a self–not self distinction.

Master and Slave
However, it is only through social interaction that we become

entitled to speak of self-consciousness proper. The 'Master and the Slave' chapter opens with the claim that self-consciousness can exist only if it is acknowledged as a self-consciousness. Being one partially consists in being recognized as one. Hegel says that many and varied meanings are contained in this claim, and I shall try to separate some of them out. First, we may ask, why should there not be a completely private self-consciousness? Why could there not be a self-conscious being who had had absolutely no contact with similar beings? An answer to this question may be found if we reflect on what our ordinary commonsensical self-consciousness consists in. Each of us is aware of ourselves as a human being, as a person, as a woman or as a man. But how are such thoughts about ourselves possible? Part of the answer seems to be because we have encountered other human beings, people, men or women. The concept of oneself is modelled on others. Our self-consciousness requires that I think of myself as a person, and this means one person among others, or as a human being and this means one human being among others. Hegel does not illustrate his rather abstract descriptions with these specific examples, but I think they illustrate part of his point. We can also read Hegel at a deeper level. Self-certainty established a self–not self distinction, but self-consciousness requires a self–other distinction. It must be possible to think of oneself as the same sort of being as another but also to think of oneself as a different one from the other. Additionally, modelling oneself on another further facilities making a distinction between oneself and one's environment – I can think of myself as an autonomous individual like the others. I can think of myself as another.

To see why recognition is important, consider the converse possibility. Other self-consciousnesses do not recognize you as a self-consciousness. Or, to use my examples, other people do not recognize you as a person, other humans do not recognize you as human. It is not just that you would perhaps not count yourself as such, but that you would not be one. The concepts 'self-conscious', 'person' or 'human' would not apply to you, and that would amount to your not being those things. It is not as though you could invent such concepts for your own private use, you would simply not belong to the community of persons, human beings or self-consciousnesses where those concepts have their meaning.

Self-consciousnesses need each other to count as such: 'they recognize as mutually recognizing each other' (*The Phenomenology of Spirit*, p. 112). Thus, as self-consciousnesses we are inextricably bound up with one another for what we are. So although self-consciousness seems the most private and individual sort of consciousness, it is in fact necessarily public and social. As Hegel puts it: 'Action by one side only would be useless because what is to happen can only be brought about by both' (*The Phenomenology of Spirit*, p. 112) and 'each is for the other what the other is for it' (ibid., p. 113).

Our mutual recognition as self-consciousnesses takes the form of an antagonistic struggle, in which each tries to obtain recognition from the other. This is the 'Master and Slave' dialectic proper. On one level, each seeks the death of the other – as though that would prove its independence of the other for its own existence. Indeed, it is Hegel's view that full self-consciousness is possible only for a being which has risked its own life. What I think he means is that one fully appreciates one's own existence – one is brought up sharply, so to speak, with the very fact that one exists – only if that very existence has been threatened. He is not talking here about our habitual day-to-day self-consciousness but of a stark and immediate existential self-consciousness. But clearly, if one kills the other, the sought-for recognition is ironically frustrated. A lull in the conflict is established by the temporary victory of one self-consciousness – the master – in acquiring recognition from the other – the slave. But this provisional solution contains the seeds of its own destruction. The slave exists for the sake of the master and manufactures commodities for the master's enjoyment. But, ironically, the slave gains independence from the master by perceiving his own handiwork in the commodities. He perceives his own consciousness embodied or realized in the objects he has worked, and this gives him a new self-consciousness which the master lacks. Finally, the master realizes that a slave self-consciousness does not recognize him properly because it does not recognize him freely. To see what Hegel means here, compare the case in which a person may enter into a sexual relationship either freely or under duress. One partner (A) wants the other (B) to want him or her sexually but freely, that is, with the possibility (but not the actuality) of B not wanting A. In these two themes – labour and freedom – lie the slave's escape from servitude to the master.

Hegel is at pains to point out that each self-consciousness is both master and slave; it would be one-sided or undialectical to think otherwise. One question worth raising at this point is whether Hegel is really describing necessary structures of any self-consciousness or just engaging in some acute observations on social relations. We could no doubt substitute 'man' and 'woman', 'employer' and 'employee', 'teacher' and 'pupil' for 'master' and 'slave' in Hegel's text and thereby obtain many insights into power and knowledge relations. But Hegel intends the chapter to be part of a necessary exposition of what consciousness is, a contribution to the phenomenology of mind. Perhaps the fundamental question in the philosophy of mind here is: is a self-conscious mind necessarily social? If so, must it exhibit the social properties Hegel ascribes to it?

Absolute Idealism

The stage of the *Phenomenology* which follows Self-Consciousness is Reason, and this is a dialectical synthesis of consciousness and self-consciousness. It is facilitated by the 'Unhappy Consciousness', which is a kind of self-conscious mind which is divided against itself. The master and slave struggle is here enacted within one mind rather than two, and this mind is unhappy because it is divided between what it is and what it would like to be. This sort of consciousness is prevalent in any community which conceives of God as a transcendent being, rather than one omnipresent in the world humans know. Reason is the realization that the dualisms between the ideal and the actual self and between a transcendent God and the empirical world are in fact illusory, and that consciousness is itself what is most fully real. As Hegel puts it: 'Reason is the certainty of consciousness that it is all reality' (*The Phenomenology of Spirit*, p. 140). Clearly this is a kind of idealism, but a kind of pantheistic, metaphysical idealism where, in the last resort, the individual finite minds of human persons will be seen to be points of view or perspectives of one universal divine mind called 'spirit':

'Spirit is – this absolute substance which is the unity of the different independent self-consciousnesses' (The Phenomenology of Spirit, p. 110).

The truth is expressed imperfectly in the forms of consciousness called 'Spirit' and 'religion'. Under 'Spirit', Hegel charts the expression of spirit in the different ethical and legal institutions which have existed historically. In religion, people come close to a true understanding of the nature of reality – so spirit comes to a close understanding of itself – but this understanding is still metaphorical and not wholly rational. This is because the great world religions rely upon images and analogies in their language. It is the role of philosophy – Hegelian philosophy – to express the real truth of religion in apposite, rational language. For example, Hegel has a dialectical interpretation of the Christian doctrine of the Trinity. The father is the transcendent God of traditional Christianity. The son is nature, the material world which is God's creation. But the Holy Ghost is the synthesis of the two: God as both immanent and transcendent; God as the whole or Geist.

The culmination of the Phenomenology is Absolute Knowing. Here 'Spirit ... knows itself as spirit' (The Phenomenology of Spirit, p. 493). Spirit is reality as a whole as it really is in itself, and in Absolute Knowing there is a 'unity of thought and being' (The Phenomenology of Spirit, p. 488). Hegel means by this that there is ultimately no difference between reality's knowing what it is and its being what it is; and it is in this that his idealism consists. Reality is self-consciousness, so, in so far as it comes to know what it is, it becomes what it really is. Consciousness and what exists are, when fully understood, understood to be absolutely identical.

What are we to make of this absolute idealism? Many thinkers regard it as the most abominable nonsense, others as a work of outstanding genius. Some have seen in it the merit of an intellectual framework within which to make sense of many puzzling problems. Others see this as no merit at all: by appearing to explain everything, Hegel explains nothing. That Hegel provokes such sharp disagreements is perhaps a sign that his work does contain genuine philosophical contention and that he should be taken seriously as a thinker, even if one would not wish to endorse his system. His importance for the philosophy of mind is that he takes our thinking outside the narrow confines of the psychology of the solitary individual and explores the social, religious and universal aspects of consciousness. He is also a philosopher who tries to provide a sustained if sometimes obscure answer to the question: what is consciousness? and this cannot safely be ignored by any serious theorist in the philosophy of mind.

4

MATERIALISM

Materialism is the theory that if something exists then it is physical. For example, the theses that only physical objects exist and only physical events exist are both materialist theses. Sometimes the doctrine is held in a weaker form which allows that physical objects or events may possess non-physical properties — for example, mental or abstract properties — but even then it is maintained that any such putatively non-physical properties logically depend upon the existence of physical things. No non-controversial definition of 'physical' has ever been given, but it is thought that if something is physical then it is spatio-temporal. In addition, physical objects are those objects which possess essentially the properties of shape, size and solidity and are capable of motion. More controversially, materialists usually maintain that physical things are composed of a substance called 'matter'. Indeed, the term 'materialism' is sometimes used to denote the theory that matter exists, as well as the theory that everything that exists is physical. 'Matter' has proved even more recalcitrant to definition than 'physical'.

Several versions of materialism have been advocated in the history of philosophy. In what follows I shall concentrate on a particularly sophisticated and influential, twentieth-century version: the so-called mind–brain identity theory. This is the view that any mental event is literally identical with some event or state in the brain. It has been developed by two contemporary Australian philosophers, J. J. C. Smart and David Armstrong, but finds an early and succinct expression in a 1956 paper by the English philosopher and psychologist U. T. Place. The paper is called 'Is consciousness a brain process?'. After examining the version of materialism defended by Place there, I shall turn to an important adaptation of the mind–brain identity theory by the North American philosopher Donald Davidson. Finally, I shall examine the philosophy of mind of a materialist who finds short-comings with the mind–brain identity theory and who advocates instead a materialistic or physicalist non-identity theory: Professor Ted Honderich of the University of London.

Before discussing these three contemporary views, however, I shall distinguish some varieties of materialism through their exponents in the history of philosophy.

Democritus, the Greek atomist philosopher who wrote in the fourth century BC, maintained that everything that exists is composed of physical objects which are so minute as to be imperceptible. These he called 'atoms'. The word 'atom', in its etymology, means 'indivisible' and it is indeed Democritus's view that the atoms are indivisible and impenetrable. They are physical because they have the properties (size and shape) essential to any physical object. Not only do atoms exist, according to Democritus, but only atoms exist. Everything that exists is either an atom or a collection of atoms, so it is clear that Democritus is a thoroughgoing materialist. The atoms are located in what Democritus calls 'the void' – pure nothingness – absence of being. All the atoms are in motion and there exist an infinite number of them, but if we ask what the atoms move in or what they move through, the only true answer on the Democritian view is 'the void' or 'nothing at all'.

The atomism of Democritus was used as a set of premisses for a humanistic ethical philosophy by Epicurus, also a Greek, who lived later in the same century. Epicurus thought that all the atoms move downwards but not every atom moves parallel to all the others, so collisions sometimes occur. The material universe which we inhabit is the result of one such original collision. The fact that collisions occur between atoms introduces a certain indeterminacy into the universe which makes it impossible to predict human actions with certainty, and Epicurus thinks that this leaves room in the universe for human freedom. It follows that Epicurus combines materialism and libertarianism – the view that humans have free will – in his philosophy. It is clear too that, although Epicurus thought that the gods have no influence over human affairs, and although the human soul is not immortal because it is just a collection of atoms that will disperse, he is nevertheless not an atheist. The gods do exist but they too are composed of material atoms, albeit atoms of an especially minute or rarefied kind. It follows that Epicurus not only combines libertarianism with materialism but also theism with materialism.

Theism and materialism are also combined by the seventeenth-century English philosopher and political theorist, Thomas Hobbes. According to Hobbes, everything that exists has the physical dimensions of size, that is, everything that exists has length, depth and breadth. Also, everything that exists is composed of matter. He not only maintains that all our thoughts and sensations are caused by physical objects, he also maintains that those very thoughts and sensations are themselves physical. Hobbes does not deny that God and the soul exist, he merely denies that they are immaterial. God and the soul are physical entities, but the particles of matter which compose them are so minute as to be undetectable by the human senses. For this reason it is impossible for us to perceive God or the soul. Hobbes notes that the soul allegedly travels to heaven or to hell, where it may burn, and that souls in the form of ghosts allegedly haunt people on earth. His thought about these phenomena is that their intelligibility depends upon their being conceived in physical terms. To talk of travelling, or burning, or being present in a churchyard is necessarily to talk in physical terms. To think of something non-physical doing these things is patently absurd, in Hobbes's view. This is a powerful materialist thought: when we think we have succeeded in thinking of something non-physical, we have in fact only succeeded in imagining something physical, for example an invisible or perhaps transparent physical object.

Hobbes is both a materialist and an empiricist. He thinks that everything is physical, and everything known depends upon observation through the five senses. These two positions, the first ontological and the second epistemological, are logically independent of each other. Nevertheless, not only Hobbes but also the French Enlightenment thinker, de la Mettrie, subscribed to both philosophies. De la Mettrie tried to present a purely mechanistic account of human thought and action in his *L'Homme Machine* (1748). His project was adequately to describe a person as a highly complicated physical object with moving parts and hence to dispense with the Cartesian notion of the person as essentially an immaterial soul. Thought and sensation, according to de la Mettrie, are nothing over and above the complicated motion of matter. The most complete expression of the materialist strain in the French Enlightenment is Baron d'Holbach's *System of Nature* (1770). D'Holbach argues that the universe is one enormous deterministic system of physical objects, and that nothing else exists.

The most famous materialist of the Western intellectual tradition was not a materialist at all. I am thinking of the nineteenth-century revolutionary thinker, Karl Marx. True, the topic of Marx's doctoral dissertation was the materialism of Democritus, mentioned above. True, Marx did try to reverse the order of priorities in the philosophy of his idealist predecessor, Hegel, by 'turning Hegel on his head'. It is important to note, however, that Marx, when called a materialist, is called a special sort of materialist. He is sometimes called a 'dialectical materialist' and sometimes a 'historical materialist'. What both of these views entail is that it is the material, especially the economic, facts about a society which determine that society's other features. What laws, religion and other patterns of thinking obtain in a society is closely dependent upon the way in which that society is organized economically: the way in which it can reproduce itself. Now, the view that the physical determines the mental is not the same as materialism. Materialism is the view that the mental is the physical. Materialism is the theory that all the mental facts are nothing over and above all the physical facts, and there is nothing in Marx's writings to suggest that Marx was a materialist in that sense. The view that the mental is determined by the physical is consistent with most of the ontologies of the mind described in this book. To show that determinism implies materialism requires special argument, in fact argument of the sort deployed by Honderich and to be examined later in this chapter.

Ironically, Marx's determinism may be inconsistent with materialism. Arguably, if A determines B then B is 'something over and above' A. If Marx did adopt an ontology, then this was the 'naturalism' he describes in the *Economic and Philosophical Manuscripts* of 1844. His naturalism, he claims, will dissolve the contradiction between idealism and materialism. Marx, I think, was not much interested in the mind–body problem. His concern was the overthrow of capitalist society and its replacement by communism. His materialism is a doctrine of material determinism and not an ontological materialism. It is fine to call Marx a materialist so long as we use the term in this special sense.

Could materialism be true? Could it be true that you and I are just highly complicated physical objects? One common misunderstanding needs to be dispelled straight away. When people hear about materialism for the first time, they often say: no, I am not just a complicated physical object because I think, I perceive, I have emotions, and so on. Now, it is not a very good objection to materialism to mention the fact that people think. No materialist, or hardly any materialist, would deny this. Materialists accept – just as you or I or anyone else would – that we all have thoughts, perceptions, emotions, mental images. The materialist is not denying that we think. The materialist is saying that our thoughts are physical. That fully fledged mental life each of us has is a series of physical events – a set of electro-chemical processes in the brain, according to the most modern version of materialism. Matter can think. You and I and everyone else are thinking matter.

We may turn now to the materialism of Place, Davidson and Honderich.

PLACE

When Place suggests that consciousness is a brain process, he does not mean that our thoughts and experiences are merely caused by events in the brain; he means that those mental events are exactly the same events as events in the brain. A causal correlation between mental and physical is not of itself sufficient for the truth of materialism, because a dualist might plausibly maintain that mental events are caused by physical events yet cling to the view that those mental events nevertheless occur in a non-material mind. So Place wants a stronger theory than causal correlation.

A Scientific Hypothesis
He says that he advocates that consciousness is a brain process

as a scientific hypothesis and goes on to argue that this claim cannot be dismissed on logical grounds alone. What does Place mean by calling 'consciousness is a brain process' a scientific hypothesis? A hypothesis is a statement which is designed to be a solution to a problem and which is open to test for its truth or falsity. If a statement has the status of a hypothesis, then we do not yet know whether it is true or false, but it is true or false. We are putting it forward for confirmation or refutation. By calling the hypothesis 'scientific', Place means that it is the procedures of the natural sciences – especially perhaps neuro-psychology – which will demonstrate its truth or falsity. So we need to be clear that Place does not take himself to have proved the mind–brain identity theory. He conceives of himself as removing logical obstacles to its plausibility so that it may be handed over for use by scientists in explaining what consciousness is.

Place's first clarification of his thesis is a denial that sentences about consciousness mean the same as sentences about processes in the brain. He takes it that his thesis would be manifestly false if it was that our terms for sensations and mental images were semantically equivalent to our terms for describing the central nervous system. This is clearly right to the degree that what a person intends to convey by saying, for example, that they are in pain is not that they are in a certain neurological state but that they are undergoing a certain sensation. The two sorts of meaning seem to be quite distinct, whether or not the mind–brain identity theory is true. So even if pain is exactly the same thing as C-fibre stimulation, 'pain' does not mean 'C-fibre stimulation'. It is worth pointing out here Place's relationship to logical behaviourism. Place thinks a logical behaviourist programme for translating our dispositional mental concepts – like 'knowing', 'believing' and 'intending' – into sentences about our actual and possible behaviour is fundamentally sound. Nothing essential to their meaning would be lost. But he thinks our occurrent mental concepts like 'is having an after image' or 'is in pain' contain an irreducible experiential dimension which resists the analytical translation attempt. He allows that in principle there may come a time when the behaviourist thesis may be extended to cover concepts of occurrent states also, but Place is pessimistic about the current prospects for this. So we may read Place as in a sense supplementing logical behaviourism by a new sort of theory which will cope with the seemingly private, internal and experiential dimension to the mental; and we can read his denial, that our occurrent mental state concepts may be translated into sentences about brain processes, as part of his pessimism about an extension of logical behaviourism into that area. Place does not simply assert baldly that mental and physical concepts have different meanings – even though to many it will no doubt appear self-evident. He has three arguments in support, and it is to these we should now turn.

It is possible for a person to know the meanings of words like 'image', 'pain' and 'sensation' without knowing anything about neurology – indeed, perhaps, without even knowing that they have a brain. It follows that it cannot be any part of the meaning of such words to be about synapses, ganglions, or any other part of the central nervous system. Otherwise a person unacquainted with facts about his or her central nervous system could not know the meanings of the words for his or her thoughts and experiences.

Further, there are two qualitatively distinct modes of verification for statements about consciousness and statements about brain processes. This means the way in which we find out whether it is true that a certain conscious thought or experience is happening, and the way we find out whether a certain brain process is happening, are radically different. We verify that we are thinking or experiencing by introspection – or perhaps we do not even have to introspect. Perhaps if we are thinking or experiencing, we already know that. But no amount of introspection or thinking will reveal to me what is going on in my brain. That can be discovered only by empirical observation. So there is a severe asymmetry between the verification procedures for the two sorts of sentence. On several influential accounts of what meaning is, how the truth or falsity of a sentence is decided is largely constitutive of that sentence's meaning. If that is right, then if two sentences require different sorts of verification procedure they cannot possibly mean the same.

Place also maintains there is nothing self-contradictory about a person's claiming that he or she is in pain but – at the same time – claiming there is nothing going on in his or her central nervous system. It would no doubt be false to conjoin these two claims, but not self-contradictory. A man would have contradicted himself if he said he was in pain but could not feel it, or that his C-fibres were stimulated but nothing was happening in his nervous system, because part of what it means to have a pain is to feel it, and part of what it means for C-fibres to fire is for something to happen in the central nervous system. The fact that we do not produce contradictions when we say we are in a mental state but deny any nervous activity proves that mental concepts do not mean the same as neurological concepts.

Two provisos need to be made about Place's arguments here. He has said we are not talking about brain processes when we talk about consciousness, and his reasons are convincing. However, we should note that if the mind–brain identity theory turns out to be true then we will be – and presumably will have been – talking about brain processes when we talk about consciousness. Compare 'the person in the blue suit' does not mean the same as 'the philosophy lecturer'; but if it turns out to be true that the person in the blue suit is the philosophy lecturer, then when you were talking about the person in the blue suit you were talking about the philosophy lecturer – even if you did not know that the person in the blue suit was the philosophy lecturer.

Also, if the mind–brain identity theory is proved – shown to be true – and if it becomes widely accepted, then it is not impossible that the meanings of our mental words would change. Then it would be part of the meaning of words like 'pain' to be about the central nervous system. If that happened, it would also become contradictory to claim to be in a mental state but deny any nervous activity, because speaking of nervous activity would be part of defining a mental concept. I do not know, whether Place would accept these two observations, but it does not seem damaging to his theory for him to do so.

Contingent Identities

We are now in a position to approach Place's claim that '"Consciousness is a process in the brain", although not necessarily true, is not necessarily false' (Borst, p. 44). If a statement is necessarily true then not only is it true but it could not not be true. If a statement is necessarily false, then not only is it false but it could not not be false. So Place is saying that if his thesis is true it is contingently true: even if it is true it could conceivably have been false. This view is consistent with two claims he has made already. Someone who denied the mind–brain identity theory would not have contradicted himself, and if the denial of a statement produces a contradiction, then that statement is a necessary truth. Also, the thesis is a scientific hypothesis. If it is a hypothesis it might be true or false, so it is not necessarily true. Place hopes that formulating his position in this way makes it immune to purely logical objections and open to empirical or scientific test. This is the force of his saying that the thesis is not necessarily false – it is not an incoherent or self-contradictory or meaningless thesis, so it is genuinely open to be treated as a scientific hypothesis.

To understand Place's theoretical position more clearly, we need to examine closely exactly what is being claimed by saying that consciousness 'is' a brain process. Place argues that his hypothesis is 'a contingent identity statement' (Borst, pp. 43–5). We have seen what he means by 'contingent'. What exactly are identity statements? These are sentences capable of truth or falsity which have the form 'the such and such is a such and such', where 'is' means 'is identical with' or 'is the same thing as'. But it is important for Place's thesis that a distinction be drawn between two different senses of the word 'is'. We use the word in one of these senses when we assert that 'red is a colour' or 'a square is an equilateral rectangle' (Borst, p. 44). This is the so-called '"is" of definition'. It takes this description because it features in sentences which are definitions. It is, for example, true by definition that red is a colour just because if someone claimed that something was red but denied that it was coloured the person would have contradicted him or herself. This in turn is because saying that something is coloured is part of what is said about something when it is claimed that it is red. 'Coloured' is part of the meaning of 'red'.

In clear contrast with this sense of 'is' is the so-called '"is" of composition'. In this use of 'is', what something is is said, without any definition being produced thereby. Place provides these examples: 'Her hat is a bundle of straw tied together with string', 'His table is an old packing case', 'A cloud is a mass of water

droplets or other particles in suspension' (Borst, p. 44). Perhaps
the first two examples are clearer illustrations of this use of 'is'
than the third, because it might plausibly be argued that part of
what we mean by a cloud is a mass of liquid particles, and, if
that is right, then 'is' is being used in the first, 'definitional'
sense, as well as in the second sense. However, it is clearly not
any part of the meaning of the word 'hat' to be 'straw', nor could
one correctly use 'packing case' as part of the definition of 'table'.
These two illustrations show, I think, that Place's distinction is
made out correctly.

The point of these examples is that Place intends 'is' in 'consciousness is a brain process' to be taken in the second of these
two senses, not in the first. This reinforces his earlier claims that
the thesis is not a necessary truth and that mental state words do
not have the same meanings as words for parts of the central
nervous system. Identity statements using the 'is' of composition
are contingent because they are not self-contradictory to deny,
and the fact that they are not definitions illustrates the fact that
the words connected by 'is' are not synonyms. The relevance of
allocating the thesis to this logical category is that it makes it
more impervious to objections of a purely logical or semantic
nature. It would be wrong, for example, to say that the thesis
'consciousness is a brain process' contains a contradiction or
does not make sense.

Two remarks are worth making about the theory as it has been
depicted so far. Place's desire is to show the plausibility of a
certain kind of materialism, and this requires him to show that
consciousness is nothing 'over and above' a brain process. It
might in principle be possible for someone to develop a view of
the psycho-physical relation in which it was conceded that some
consciousness is a brain process but not all consciousness, or in
which there were some physical things, some things which are
both mental and physical, but still others which are purely mental.
Perhaps on such speculation there are both minds and physical
objects, but our experiences are a kind of interface between the
two and so may be described as either mental or physical. Place
can have none of this. To be a materialist he needs to show that
consciousness is just or only a brain process: a brain process and
nothing else.

Place hopes that if the mind–brain identity theory can be proved then it will indeed be proved that consciousness is a brain process and nothing else. This is provided for precisely by his making 'is' the 'is of identity', as opposed to what he calls the 'is' of predication. The 'is' of predication is used to ascribe some property to something, as when, for example, one says that 'Her hat is red'. This is not an identity statement even though the word 'is' features in it, because it is not the claim that a certain hat is exactly the same thing as a certain colour. In contrast, the truth of the mind–brain identity theory would not establish that consciousness is some kind of property or characteristic of a brain process but that a brain process is what consciousness is. It makes no sense to say that 'Her hat is red and nothing else' (Borst, p. 44), but it does make sense to say that a table is a packing case and nothing else or that consciousness is a brain process and nothing else. Notice that these 'nothing else' claims would still make sense if Place had chosen the other sort of 'is' of identity – the 'is' of definition; for example, it would make sense to say 'red is a colour and nothing else'. He does not, however, pursue that line.

The other remark worth making is that Place recognizes an important asymmetry between the claim that consciousness is a brain process and the examples of identity statements using the 'is' of composition he has given. They are assertions of particular or specific identities. One hat or one packing case in particular was being specified. But the claim that consciousness is a brain process is a general one: the claim that all consciousness is a brain process. Now, if all packing cases were tables, claims Place, then the two concepts 'table' and 'packing case' would not be logically independent. This comes very close to answering 'yes' to the question I raised earlier (on page 105) about whether our mental words could take on new meanings if the mind–brain identity theory should turn out to be true.

Place takes great care over the formulation of his theory because he wants it to have the best possible chance of being true. Part of the force of his claim that there can be identity statements which are contingent is that, from the fact that two words do not have the same meaning, it does not at all follow that they do not refer to the same thing. To use my example, from the fact that 'person wearing the blue suit' and 'philosophy lecturer' do not have the same meaning, it does not follow at all that they cannot refer to the very same person. 'The person wearing the blue suit is the philosophy lecturer' is, then, a contingent identity statement, and it is the sort of claim which may be tested empirically for its truth or falsity. Similarly, Place thinks it is quite open for 'consciousness' to refer to the very same thing as 'brain process'.

The next important step in the argument is to try to decide under what sorts of condition two words which differ in meaning may have a single reference; in other words, what the truth conditions are for contingent identity statements, that is to say, what the conditions are which would make them true. We can state these quite straightforwardly: 'consciousness is a brain process' is true if and only if consciousness is a brain process. But to advance the theory further, we need to be able to say under what circumstances we are entitled to claim that two sets of observations are observations of the same thing or event. In some cases this is not difficult. We are entitled to say that the observation of a cloud is the observation of a collection of water particles because we could observe the cloud from a distance and (if we were on a hill, say) walk into it and, perhaps using instruments, inspect its microscopic constituents. There is a direct continuity between the two observations and they are observations of a roughly similar sort.

But in the case of consciousness and brain processes the situation is not nearly so straightforward. Not only is the introspection of consciousness a very different sort of observation from the perceiving of physical processes in the brain, but also there is no continuity between the two. In fact, there is a radical discontinuity because, as was noted above (page 104), no amount of introspective scrutiny will reveal to me the functioning of my brain, and no amount of observation by scientists of the electrical activity inside my skull will reveal to them my thoughts and emotions as I have them.

Place does not think these problems are insuperable. In fact he thinks there already exist true contingent identity statements within science, which have been established, despite the fact that two radically different sorts of observation were needed and despite the fact that these observations were discontinuous. He offers as an example 'Lightning is a motion of electric charges' (Borst, p. 47). It is not possible to observe a bolt of lightning from a distance, then gradually move closer and on that nearer scrutiny notice the electric charges. What has happened is that scientists have discovered that there are electric charges through the atmosphere and, when this happens, we may have observations of those events we call 'lightning'. Place wishes to argue that, in a similar way, what we commonsensically and pre-scientifically call 'consciousness' may be discovered by the scientist to be identical with electrical activity in the brain.

Although the lightning analogy is more satisfactory than the cloud one, there remains here a severe problem for the mind–brain identity theorist. How do we know that lightning is – is identical with – an electrical discharge? How do we know that consciousness is identical with a brain process and not merely causally correlated with a brain process? As we have seen (on page 102 above), casual correlation between mental and physical events is consistent with dualism, a philosophy Place emphatically wishes to repudiate. Perhaps as serious, suppose it is true that consciousness exists always and only when brain processes exist. This may be empirically false, but, if it is not, then it leaves open the possibility that it is consciousness which causes brain processes and not vice versa. This is just as unacceptable to a materialist as dualism because it sounds like a kind of idealism – a kind in which the physical is causally dependent on the mental.

There are no doubt cases in which we confidently speak of identities instead of causal relations as when (to use an example Place does not) we say that water is H_2O. The 'is' here would seem to be the 'is' of composition. Or is it? Perhaps a liquid could not be water unless it were H_2O. In the case of consciousness and brain processes, the relation still seems open. It could be constant correlation, it could be causal correlation (in one or both directions), it could be identity. We should remember, however, that Place does not claim to have proved the mind–brain identity theory – that is up to the scientists. So, the philosophical question remains about what is to count as identity as opposed to (causal) correlation. This problem certainly needs to be solved by the mind–brain identity theorists because, arguably, if A causes B then it follows that A is not B, and 'A is B' is what the theory demands. 'A is not B' is dualism.

We may note that Place's own position on the correlation/identity distinction is:

We treat the two sets of observations as observations of the same event in those cases where the technical scientific observations set in the context of the appropriate body of scientific theory provide an immediate explanation of the observations made by the man in the street. (Borst, p. 48)

Whether, this entitles us to talk about identity in the case of consciousness and brain processes depends heavily on what meaning can be attached to 'immediate explanation'.

Verifying Materialism

So how satisfactory is Place's version of the mind–brain identity theory? If it is true, then dualism is certainly false. Its relation to idealism is rather more ambivalent. Materialism is the view that what we commonsensically take to be mental is in fact physical. Idealism is the view that what we commonsensically take to be physical is in fact mental. So the materialist thinks the mental is physical and the idealist thinks the physical is mental. These positions seem at first sight to be diametrically opposed. But are they? If the mental is physical, does that not imply that the physical is mental? And if the physical is mental, does that not imply that the mental is physical? These possibilities – horrendous to materialist and idealist alike – mean that the theories need careful formulation if they are not to collapse into each other. Ironically, materialism and idealism might turn out to be essentially the same philosophy.

Another problem is as follows. The mind–brain identity theory is supposed to be a scientific hypothesis. This means that some observation within the sciences will confirm or refute it empirically. But could it? If we have another thousand years of science, or another twenty thousand, what sort of empirical observation would exhibit the identity of consciousness with a brain process? It could be that consciousness is just not the sort of thing that – logically – could be observed. If that is so, then it might not be possible even in principle to verify or falsify the mind–brain identity theory. This means, not just that it is very difficult to decide whether the theory is true, but that the theory might even be meaningless – nonsensical. As we have already seen (on page 37–8, above), according to the logical positivists, if there is no way of verifying or falsifying what is expressed by a certain sentence, then that sentence is in fact meaningless. On that account of meaning there are two and only two classes of meaningful statement: on the one hand there are empirical hypotheses and, on the other hand, tautologies or statements true by definition. Place wants the mind–brain identity theory to fall into the first category – he says explicitly that it is not intended as a definition. But suppose, as I am suggesting, it is not an empirical hypothesis because nothing empirical could ever confirm or refute it. Then it could only fall into the disastrous middle category of nonsensical metaphysical sentences.

I am not saying that these difficulties are necessarily insuperable. It could be, for example, that some test for the theory can be devised. Nor is it clear that the logical positivists have the correct theory of meaning. But I think the objections do show that further work needs to be done if the theory is to receive a fully satisfactory formulation.

The Phenomenological Problem

An objection which Place seeks to refute is an anxiety some neuro-scientists have, that it is not possible to explain mental events by describing processes in the central nervous system. The problem is that, no matter how complete the physical description of the person, or no matter how complete an explanation is in terms of a person's physical constituents, all mention of the mental is still omitted. The mental is not 'captured' by any physical theory. For example, it is possible to describe in physiological detail light waves contacting a retina and the transmission of an electrical impulse to the brain-cortex, where these are links in a causal chain. But the result of this causal chain is something qualitatively different: a visual perception, an experience. There seems to be an abrupt discontinuity between the nature of the physical events and the mental event: the chain of physical events seems to come to an abrupt but unintelligible halt when the mental event occurs. This leads one to suppose that there are in fact two distinct series of events, mental events and physical events, or, to put it another way, dualism seems to be true.

Place's reply to this objection is that it rests on a kind of logical error which he calls 'the phenomenological fallacy'. As we have seen (on page 88, above), phenomenology is the description of what appears to consciousness as it appears. The error Place detects here is that of taking phenomenological appearances to be entities or events. The mistake is to think that in describing how something appears – sounds, feels, tastes and so on – a person is actually describing mental items – sounds, feels or tastes. To use Place's example, if a person is having a green after image, then it would be to commit the phenomenological fallacy to suppose that person was mentally perceiving something green. There is no green mental object or event called the 'after image'. Rather, Place favours an account similar to that which Ryle gave of the functioning of the imagination (see page 55, above). The person is in a mental state which is like the perceptual state he would be in, were he perceiving a publicly observable green physical object.

If Place is entitled to this quasi-Rylean manoeuvre, then it seems he has succeeded in redescribing the findings of introspection in a way that does not preclude the truth of the mind–brain identity theory. Clearly, it would be inconsistent with that theory only if it could be maintained that when we introspect we introspect mental events or entities which could exist independently of physical processes. Place perhaps needs an argument that the thinking he calls the phenomenological 'fallacy' is in fact fallacious, particularly as he allows that psychological and physical terms are semantically independent of one another, and this leaves open the fact that nothing mental logically follows from any physical description of the world.

Type–Type or Token–Token?

What, then, is the status of Place's theory? It is clear from the findings of neurologists that it is simply empirically false that the same sort of mental event has to be correlated always with the same sort of brain event. So, if you and I are having the same type of thought – suppose, for example, you and I are both thinking this sentence – then it does not follow that our brains are in the same sort of physical state. This means that, if the mind–brain identity theory is true, the identities cannot always hold between the same types of mental event and the same types of physical event. It must be the case that qualitatively similar mental events are each identical with a physical event – but sometimes those physical events are qualitatively dissimilar. For this reason it is generally recognized that a thoroughgoing type–type version of the mind–brain identity theory is untenable – even though room seems to remain for many cases of broad types of mental events to be identified with broad types of brain event in the case of human beings.

It is suggested instead that the mind–brain identity theory should be construed as a token–token theory. This means that any mental event is in fact identical with some physical event, so that each particular mental event is the same as a particular physical event. This allows the possibility that the mind–brain identity theory is true, despite the fact that it is not always true that similar types of mental events are correlated with similar types of physical event. This perhaps makes the proof of the theory a more complex matter than before, and seems to rule out the possibility that mental events are related to physical events in a law-like way.

Whichever form of the mind–brain identity theory is adopted, it might be objected that as a form of materialism it is highly reductionist. It reduces the mental to the physical in that the mental is held to be ontologically 'nothing over and above' or 'nothing but' the physical. Even if it is true that the mental is the physical, it would seem to require further argument to show that the mental does not exist over and above the physical. After all, the mental must exist in some sense to be identified with the physical. Arguably, a person has irreducibly mental properties – thoughts, moods and emotions – even if these are not properties of an immaterial substance. The construing of the mind–brain identity theory as a kind of materialism requires playing down the mental, subjective, private and experiential aspects of the person, just as idealism depends upon underestimating the physical, objective, public and observable aspects. If this is correct, then the debate between idealism and materialism has by no means been concluded.

DAVIDSON

The contemporary North American philosopher Donald Davidson is a materialist because he holds the view that any mental event may in principle be given a true physical description. Davidson nevertheless thinks human freedom of action is to be taken seriously, so a kind of materialism has to be found which does justice to the reality of the control we have over our own action. His philosophy of mind is concentrated in three influential papers: 'Mental events' (1970), 'Psychology as philosophy' (1974), and 'The material mind' (1973) – all in his *Essays on Actions and Events*. In what follows I shall draw most heavily on the first of these.

Three Principles

A materialism which will leave room for freedom is possible, according to Davidson, if the appearance of contradiction between three principles may be relieved. The principles are the principle of Causal Interaction, the principle of the Nomological Character of Causality, and the principle of the Anomalism of the Mental. By 'causal interaction' Davidson means the bringing about of a physical event by a mental event or the bringing about of a mental event by a physical event. His view is in fact that both sorts of causality occur; for example, beliefs, intentions, judgements and decisions may be among the causes of the sinking of a battleship in a naval engagement. Conversely, the perception of a ship – a physical object – may alter a person's belief and other mental states. So he thinks it is true that 'at least some mental events interact causally with physical events' (*Essays on Actions and Events*, p. 208). By 'nomological' Davidson means 'law-like', in the sense of falling under the generalizations expressing natural scientific laws. A scientific law is deterministic if the events mentioned in the law are also predicted by it. Now we can understand the second principle: Davidson thinks that if two events are causally related – one is the cause of the other – then they always fall under some strict deterministic law. 'Anomalous' is the opposite of 'nomological', so, if some event is anomalous, then there could exist no natural scientific law on the basis of which that event could be predicted. Davidson's third principle is that mental events are anomalous.

Davidson claims that these principles appear to be mutually inconsistent but that they are all in fact true. Some sentences are mutually inconsistent if the truth of at least one of them precludes the truth of at least one of the others, so Davidson has to show that the appearance of inconsistency is illusory if all three are to be true. Before examining how Davidson does this, it is worth inspecting the appearance of contradiction. On the face of it, if mental events cause physical events, they may be subsumed under deterministic natural laws; but the third principle is precisely that this is not the case. Conversely, it seems at first sight that if mental events could never be subsumed under natural laws, then either they do not cause physical events or else, if they do, then not all events related as cause and effect fall under strict deterministic laws. To reconcile the three principles, Davidson advocates a version of the mind–brain identity theory, or at least a physical event/mental event identity theory. As he puts it: 'mental events are identical with physical events' (*Essays on Actions and Events*, p. 209).

Anomalous Monism

Davidson's theory is that every mental event is identical with some physical event, but not every physical event is identical with a mental event. What does Davidson mean by 'mental' and 'physical'? An event is physical if it can be described using only physical terms, and an event is mental if it is describable in mental terms. Davidson is content to say that a physical term is one that features in the vocabulary of physicists, but he offers a single criterion for something's counting as mental: 'The distinguishing feature of the mental is not that it is private, subjective, or immaterial, but that it exhibits what Brentano called intentionality' (*Essays on Actions and Events*, p. 211). The nineteenth-century German philosopher Brentano suggested that all and only mental events exhibit the feature of being directed towards an object, so all thinking is thinking about something, all perceiving is perceiving something – even if the object of thought or perception is purely imaginary. Davidson actually thinks it is false that only mental events are intentional and he counts certain human actions as intentional, but this does not matter for his thesis, because he just needs to locate a feature all mental events do possess.

To make clearer his own version of the identity theory, Davidson contrasts it with three competitors. There is the kind of materialism which not only includes the view that every mental event is a physical event, but also the view that there are psychophysical laws, so that the occurrence of any given mental event could in principle be predicted, given enough knowledge of the physical events with which they are correctly identified. Davidson accepts the first of these theses but not the second. Their conjunction he calls 'nomological monism'. Then there exists the opposite of this theory, according to which no mental event is identical with any physical event, and no mental event may be predicted, however complete our knowledge of physical events. Davidson accepts the second of these theses but not the first. Davidson calls their conjunction 'anomalous dualism' (or 'Cartesianism'). 'Nomological dualism' is the name of the theory that mental events and physical events are correlated in some way, such that sufficient knowledge of physical events would make possible the prediction of mental events, even though no mental event is identical with any physical event. With all of these is to be contrasted Davidson's own theory, according to which every mental event is identical with some physical event, but no mental event may be predicted, no matter how complete our knowledge of physical events. Davidson's name for his own thesis is 'anomalous monism'.

The two central tenets of Davidson's anomalous monism are the materialist view that every mental event is identical with some physical event, and the view (usually denied by materialists) that there are no psycho-physical laws. It remains an open possibility on Davidson's theory that every event is mental under some description, but he holds it as certain that, if some event is mental, then it is also physical. The fact that there exist no psycho-physical laws – that no mental events may be subsumed under deterministic scientific generalizations – entails that mental events cannot be explained in purely physical terms. For example, no law about physical events enables any prediction about a mental event.

Despite the fact that Davidson denies there are any psycho-physical laws, he holds that by the truth of the identity theory the mental is in a sense dependent upon the physical. He calls this the 'supervenience' of the mental on the physical. This means that if two events are similar in all physical respects, then they cannot differ in any mental respect, and that nothing may change in any mental respect without thereby changing in some physical respect. Davidson denies that this commits him to the thesis that there are psycho-physical laws or that mental terms may be defined in physical terms. So, clearly, anomalous monism is inconsistent not only with the usual materialist view, that the mental may be explained by scientific investigation of the physical, but also with the logical behaviourist claim, that mental terms can be translated into physical terms without loss of meaning.

This theory reconciles the principles of Causal Interaction, the Nomological Character of Causality, and the Anomalism of the Mental in the following way. There is not just the relation of causal interaction but the relation of identity between mental and physical events. Those events which are in fact mental may be subsumed under natural scientific laws only by virtue of the physical descriptions which are true of them, but the mental *qua* mental – mental events as described using only mental terms – may not be subsumed under any natural scientific law. This preserves the three theses: that mental and physical interact causally, that where there is causality there is some law, and that the mental is not law-like. Mental events possess their causal efficacy by virtue of physical descriptions being true of them. Davidson is prepared to allow that there may be true scientific generalizations about the relationships between mental and physical events; for example, which mental events there are may be reported using only physical terms. If we discovered specific identities between individual mental and physical events, then lists of such identities would be such generalizations. But even if they looked grammatically like laws, they would not be, because a scientific law enables us to predict future events and to know what would happen in hypothetical cases, by induction. It is precisely Davidson's thesis that reports of particular identities are not sufficient for such explanations.

It is worth noting the relationship between anomalous monism and the other theories of the mind discussed so far in this book. Davidson's theory is incompatible with dualism because that is the theory that no mental event has any physical description and no physical event has any mental description. Its relation to idealism is more ambivalent, because that includes the theory that every physical event has a mental description. Davidson would certainly reject the thesis that an event may exist only if a mental description is true of it, but he leaves it open as a possibility that any physical event may tenuously fall under some mental description. Anomalous monism is also incompatible with any version of materialism on which there exist psycho-physical laws. The theory with which Davidson most explicitly contrasts his own is logical behaviourism. This is perhaps because the logical behaviourists were his most influential immediate predecessors in the philosophy of mind. We should examine that contrast now.

Davidson's repudiation of logical behaviourism is part of his more general opposition to a certain kind of reductionism in philosophy. This reductionism is found, for example, in naturalism in moral philosophy (the attempt to explain the meanings of moral concepts entirely in non-evaluative terms) or in phenomenalism in the philosophy of perception (the attempt to explain what a physical object is by the claim that any sentence or set of sentences about physical objects may be translated into a sentence or set of sentences about actual or possible sense-contents without loss of meaning). Such projects are doomed to failure, according to Davidson; and analytical behaviourism is one of them, because it is the theory that sentences about mental states may be similarly 'reduced' to sentences about physical behaviour. For example, if someone says something, this cannot be entirely understood as the production of sounds: such an action is intentional, it presupposes the understanding of some language, say English, and it may be a reply to something also said in English. No matter how detailed or complicated the purely physical description of such actions, some mental terms will always be needed for their adequate characterization.

The Holism of the Mental
Because in Davidson's view the entire programme of logical behaviourism is a failure, he substitutes for it a proposal of his own about how we should explain human thought and action. This is

his theory of the holism of the mental. It was a drastic mistake of the logical behaviourists to assume that it was possible to explain what someone thought or did on a particular occasion in abstraction from the whole network of that person's beliefs, desires, intentions, hopes, fears and other mental states. We have to devise instead some theory which makes sense of, say, a single action or belief in terms of what else the person does or believes. In particular, Davidson thinks that understanding what a person believes and what a person desires are mutually dependent parts of understanding what a person does. The logical behaviourists were wrong to think that a person's beliefs and desires could be specified independently of one another, and decided solely by the inspection of individual tokens of behaviour.

This is a holistic theory of the mental because it contains the assumption that a person's mental states largely cohere with one another. According to Davidson's view, what we mean when we treat someone as a person is that their beliefs, desires and other attitudes form a rational pattern. Indeed, it would not make sense to attribute universal inconsistency or irrationality to people in their thought and actions because the ideas of mistake and confusion are thinkable only against a background of rationality and truth. If everyone were mistaken, there would be nothing to be mistaken about. It follows from this that there is a close correspondence between what a person believes and what a person means when he or she uses language. In particular, what people mean cannot be different from what they believe, hope, fear, intend, etc., because these mental attitudes have a linguistic content. To believe is to believe that such and such is the case, to hope is to hope that such and such is the case, and so on. In each case the word 'that' is followed by some proposition, 'P', so that a person may believe that P, wish that P, regret that P, and so on, where P is what is expressed by a sentence. Mental states described this way are called 'propositional attitudes' because they are psychological attitudes to propositions, or what is expressed by some indicative sentence. Clearly, the content of various attitudes, what is believed, hoped, wished for, etc., may be the same across several of an individual's attitudes. Davidson's holistic programme for studying the mental allows for this and includes the thesis that we cannot discover what a person believes and desires without finding out what he or she means by using his or her language. Conversely, it is not possible to find out what a person means by his or her use of words without discovering the content of some of his or her propositional attitudes.

This holistic approach to the mental is closely linked to Davidson's work in the philosophy of language. Davidson proposes the following requirement on any adequate theory of meaning: a theory of meaning for some language, L, will enable us to determine the meanings of the sentences of L. But such a theory will help explain human thought and action too, on Davidson's assumption that what a person means by some sentence cannot be different from what a person believes when he believes that sentence, and on the assumption that making sense of a person's beliefs helps make sense of his desires and actions.

Davidson's holistic approach to the mental owes something to his twentieth-century predecessors in Anglo-American philosophy; for example, the concept of a propositional attitude is employed by the British philosopher Bertrand Russell, and the idea of a holistic dependence between sets of sentences, and the connection between understanding meanings and understanding propositional attitudes, may be found in the writings of the American philosopher W. V. O. Quine, with whom Davidson studied.

Materialism and Freedom

It follows from the holistic theory of the mental that any purely physicalist programme for the explanation of mental events cannot possibly succeed. This is because explanations of mental events make a reference to other mental events and linguistic phenomena, but physicalist explanations make reference only to physical events. As Davidson puts it:

It is a feature of physical reality that physical change can be explained by laws that connect it with other changes and conditions physically described. It is a feature of the mental that the attribution of mental phenomena must be responsible to a background of reasons, beliefs, and intentions of the individual. (*Essays on Actions and Events*, p. 222)

Despite this, Davidson insists that his denial of psycho-physical laws is no threat to a materialist, mental–physical identity theory. On the contrary, Davidson thinks his anomalous monism proves a version of the identity theory. His proof goes as follows. If we suppose some mental event caused some physical event, then it follows, by the Nomological Character of Causality, that there is some way of describing those two events such that they fall under a natural scientific law. But if those two events fall under a natural scientific law then they must both have a physical description. It follows that 'every mental event that is causally related to a physical event is a physical event' (*Essays on Actions and Events*, p. 224), that is, has a physical description. So, on Davidson's theory, it is at least true of every mental event which is causally related to some physical event that it is a physical event. Clearly this conclusion is a version of the psycho-physical identity theory.

It should be clear now how Davidson's anomalous monism leaves room for human freedom. Although the scientist may discover that some mental event is identical with some physical event, and even though he or she may discover which mental events are identical with which physical events, if there are no psycho-physical laws then it is impossible for the scientist to predict mental events, and so impossible for the scientist to predict human thought and action. As Davidson puts it:

Even if someone knew the entire physical history of the world, and every mental event were identical with a physical, it would not follow that he could predict or explain a single mental event. (*Essays on Actions and Events*, p. 224)

Yet the freedom of mental events from natural law is conjoined by Davidson with the thesis of their causal efficacy. Mental events may be the causes of physical events because they are physical events, so a person's thoughts and actions may have effects in the material world. That one's thoughts and actions be causally efficacious, and that they be inexplicable *qua* thoughts and actions by any deterministic natural science, is arguably a large part of what we mean by saying they are performed freely.

HONDERICH

Ted Honderich is a philosopher of Canadian origin who is currently a professor of philosophy in the University of London.

Until recently, Honderich was best known for his controversial
work in political philosophy and for a number of papers on the
question as to whether people have free will or whether their
actions are causally determined in a way that necessitates them.
In his political philosophy Honderich is a socialist who has
produced penetrating critiques of would-be justifications of
punishment, and radical reflections on the role of political violence in the removal of unfair inequalities. In his papers on freedom
and determinism, Honderich remains implacably a determinist.

The work of Honderich to be examined in this section is the
massive and influential 1988 work, *A Theory of Determinism*. In
it Honderich provides a materialist model for the explanation of
human thought and action.

A Theory of Determinism is divided into three parts. In Part 1
Honderich presents a sophisticated determinist theory of causation and specifies, as closely as he thinks possible, what the
psycho-physical relation is. As well as this, he presents a view of
how human actions have neurological events among their causes.
The whole of Part 1 is concerned with the explanation of theory
and includes no attempt to prove it. Part 2 in contrast is concerned
with the truth of the theory. Here Honderich argues that the
theory of determinism is very likely true. It is as likely to be true,
for example, as is the theory of evolution in biology. In particular
Honderich argues that the findings of two sophisticated branches
of science are no threat to his theory. These are quantum theory
and neuroscience. Indeed, Honderich maintains that evidence
from both tends to confirm rather than refute the theory of determinism. Finally, in Part 3 of the book Honderich examines the
consequences of determinism. Suppose determinism is true, then
what follows for morality, for politics, for our conceptions of
human societies and for our individual hopes about what we may
achieve in life, what Honderich calls our 'life hopes'? Part 3 ends
with a discussion of the relation between determinism and political freedom.

Examining each of the three parts of Honderich's book in
turn, in Part 1 I shall concentrate on three claims Honderich
makes: a claim about what the psycho-physical relation is, a
claim about what causation is, and a claim about how actions are
caused; in Part 2 I shall briefly examine the claim that quantum

mechanics and neuroscience confirm rather than refute the theory of determinism; and finally, in Part 3 I shall try to decide whether the theory has some of the consequences Honderich thinks.

Honderich's theory is rich and complex and I can only introduce it briefly here. Like Hegel, Honderich refuses to abstract the philosophy of mind from the study of both the natural world and the world of all things human. Like Russell, Honderich is concerned that philosophy should be consistent with the findings of modern science.

Honderich's theory of determinism is essentially the conjunction of three hypotheses. These hypotheses are called, respectively, the Hypothesis of Psychoneural Nomic Correlation, the Hypothesis on the Causation of Psychoneural Pairs, and the Hypothesis on the Causation of Actions. The formulation of these takes up Part 1 of Honderich's book and I shall now say something about each of them, explaining the technical terms in which they are couched.

Psychoneural Nomic Correlation

A hypothesis is a sentence or set of sentences capable of truth or falsity and designed to explain something. It is also thought to be part of the idea of a hypothesis, in that it be capable, at least in principle, of being confirmed or refuted. This means there must be some possible procedure to demonstrate its truth or falsity if it is to count as a genuine hypothesis.

If we say that something is 'neural', this means it is some part of, or some event in, a central nervous system. If we say something is mental or psychological, this means it is or pertains to some mental event commonsensically so conceived. For example, thoughts and emotions are mental events, so are sensations. If two things stand in 'correlation' with one another, this means that they exist in a one–one mapping to each other according to some criterion. For example, two events are correlated if they exist at all and only the same time. (Also, if two things are correlated with one thing, then they stand in a two–one mapping to that thing, and so on.) Finally, if we say that two things are in 'nomic' connection, this means that there is some scientific law which connects the two things.

We can now understand something of the name of Honderich's

first hypothesis. He is advocating a claim, which may at this stage be true or false, that there is a relationship between mental events, like thoughts and perceptions, on the one hand and physical events, like synaptic firings in the brain, on the other hand, which is of a scientific law-like nature. Here is a formulation of the hypothesis by Honderich, one of several in the book:

For each mental event of a given type there exists some simultaneous neural event of one of a certain set of types. The existence of the neural event necessitates the existence of the mental event, the mental event thus being necessary to the neural event. Any other neural event of the mentioned set of types will stand in the same relations to another mental event of the given type. (A Theory of Determinism, p. 107)

What does this mean? It means that, if a mental event occurs, then a neural event occurs at the same time, and, if a neural event occurs, then a mental event occurs at the same time. Mental and neural events occur at all and only the same time, so they are 'correlated' in the sense explained above. Additionally, mental events may be divided into types and neural events may be divided into types. If a specific type of mental event occurs, then one of a set of specific types of neural event occurs and, if a specific type of neural event occurs, then a specific type of mental event occurs. It follows that types of mental events are correlated with types of neural events. Mental events of one type happen at all and only the same time as neural events of certain types.

Next, Honderich says that the neural event 'necessitates' the mental event. This means that, if the neural event happens, then the mental event cannot fail to happen. To put it another way, the occurrence of the neural event is a sufficient condition for the occurrence of the mental event; it is enough to make it happen. For any neural event 'N' of a given type and any mental event 'M' of a given type 'If N then M' is true. This is the central claim of Honderich's determinism. Determinism is the doctrine that causes necessitate their effects: if the cause happens, then the effect cannot not happen, and Honderich is claiming exactly that the neural determines the mental in a way that necessitates it. It is true, as Honderich points out, that, on most determinisms, causes pre-date their effects in time, but on his determinism neural events do not ante-date the mental events they necessitate. However, the fact that the neural necessitates the mental is sufficient to warrant the title 'determinism' for the theory.

Honderich also claims that the mental event is necessary for the existence of the neural event. As he is aware, he is logically committed to this thesis by the theory as expounded so far. To say that a mental event is necessary for the neural event is to say that, unless the mental event happens, the neural event does not happen. 'Necessary' here means 'necessary for' or 'needed for' or 'prerequisite for'. Now, if it is true that a neural event is a sufficient condition for a mental event, then it logically follows that that mental event is a necessary condition for that neural event. We can see this intuitively because, if N is sufficient for M, then M happens always and everywhere N happens, but, if that is right, N could not happen unless M happens. According to Honderich's account, it follows that, although the neural necessitates the mental, the mental is a necessary condition for the neural. Although the neural makes the mental happen, if the mental did not happen, neither would the neural.

Finally, we should note that at the end of this formulation of the Hypothesis of Psychoneural Nomic Correlation Honderich makes a claim about types. He says that any neural events of more than one type stand in the same relation to any mental event of a given type. This means that, although a neural event necessitates a mental event which is its necessary condition, this is a relation which holds between sets of neural events and sets of mental events. A consequence of this is that the psychoneural relation is not a one–one mapping or a many–many mapping but a one–many mapping. I take it that this is an empirical consequence which follows from criteria for individuating neural events and criteria for individuating mental events.

The Causation of Psychoneural Pairs

This second hypothesis is designed to do two things. It tells us more about the precise nature of the psycho-physical relation and it provides an account of how mental events and neural events can be causes and effects. Honderich says that our theoretical position as inquirers into the mind–brain relation is akin to that of people inquiring into a cell or an organism or a machine to which they have no direct access. The point is, I think, that we have no direct perceptual acquaintance with the mind–brain relation but we know that it exists to be characterized. We know *that* it is but not *what* it is. As Honderich points out, early research into the gene was once at this stage.

Our situation is not, however, impossible. We have what Honderich calls 'constraining' knowledge of the psychoneural relation. There exists of course the overriding constraint on any rational inquiry – that it be free from contradiction. This is because, if some theory is or contains a contradiction, that is a sufficient condition for that theory's being false. Similarly, if a theory is free from contradiction, although that is no guarantee of its truth it is a necessary condition for its truth.

Honderich specifies seven constraints on his theory in particular. We should think of these in the following way: whatever the explanation of mental events is like, it must be at least like this. The constraints are: (1) Mental Realism. Mental states exist and cannot be reduced in some abstract or formal way. Each of us has a fully fledged mental life with its distinctive phenomenology. (2) Psychoneural Intimacy. Each mental event necessarily occurs simultaneously with some neural event. (3) Mental Indispensability. Mental events, neural events and bodily actions have mental causes, not only neural causes. (4) Personal Indispensability. A person must be among the causes of their own actions. (5) Over-determination. The explanation of mental events should be simple and not suggest more than one set of conditions sufficient for their occurrence. (6) Neural Causation. Neural events have neural causes. (7) Causation. Any adequate theory of the mind must rely on an adequate theory of causal connection.

The explanation of mental events produced by the observation of the seven constraints is the Hypothesis on the Causation of Psychoneural Pairs. Here is Honderich's formulation of the hypothesis:

Each psychoneural pair, which is to say a mental event and a neural event which are a single effect and in a lesser sense a single cause – each such pair is in fact the effect of the initial elements of a certain causal sequence. The initial elements are (i) neural and other bodily elements just prior to the first mental event in the existence of the person in question, and (ii) direct environmental elements then and thereafter. (*A Theory of Determinism*, pp. 247–8)

What is a psychoneural pair? Understanding this furthers our understanding of Honderich's view of the psycho-physical relation. Honderich says a psychoneural pair is a mental event and a neural event standing in the mutual relations specified by the Hypothesis of Psychoneural Nomic Correlation. We are to think of 'pair' here in the sense of 'pair of scissors' or 'pair of trousers'. The two components of the pair must 'function together as a unit' (A Theory of Determinism, p. 165). A neural event and the simultaneous mental event it necessitates form a pair in this sense. Even though the formulation is still partly metaphorical, we have here an exciting and novel way of thinking of the mind–body relation.

The next part of the hypothesis is as follows. The pair that is the neural event and the mental event constitutes just a single effect (not two effects) and the pair that is the neural event and the mental event constitutes just a single cause (not two causes). The mental event considered singly does not constitute either a cause or an effect and the neural event considered singly does not constitute either a cause or an effect.

Finally, any psychoneural pair is a result of two kinds of antecedent cause: neural and other bodily events inside the organism and physical events in the environment of the organism.

Honderich's name for the psychoneural relation is the 'Theory of Psychoneural Union' or the 'Union Theory'. The Union Theory is the name given to the conjunction of the two hypotheses discussed so far: the Hypothesis of Psychoneural Nomic Correlation and the Hypothesis on the Causation of Psychoneural Pairs. The Union Theory is therefore both the claim that neural events necessitate their simultaneous mental necessary conditions and the claim that such neural and mental events form psychoneural pairs and, as such, are single causes and single effects. Honderich thinks we may never come to specify the psychoneural relation more precisely than by the Union Theory.

The Causation of Actions

This, the third central hypothesis of the Theory of Determinism, is an explanation of how actions are caused. It is logically consistent with the two hypotheses described so far:

Each action is a sequence of bodily events which is the effect of a causal sequence one of whose initial elements and some of whose subsequent elements are psychoneural pairs which incorporate the active intention which represents the sequence of bodily events. The other initial elements of the causal sequence, at or after the beginning of the active intention, are neural events, non-neural bodily events, and direct environmental events. (*A Theory of Determinism,* p. 248)

This hypothesis includes a definition of 'action' which depends partly upon the account of how actions are caused. The first clause is uncontroversial. Clearly, smoking a cigar and typing both are or involve sequences of bodily movements. It is also uncontroversial that actions are caused and that those causes are at least partially mental. Actions are events and on any determinist view every event has a cause, so actions have causes. The causes of actions include mental events, because nothing would count as an action unless some motive, wish or intention counted among its causes and those are mental events. Finally, actions are arguably intentional, not accidental or arbitrary.

Honderich is claiming that among the causes of actions are psychoneural pairs, and those pairs include the intention to do the action. So, the intention to do the action features among the causes of the action. Honderich also says that the intention represents the action. I take it that this is because, in order for an intention to be an intention to do a particular action, it must be or include a representation of that action. If I intend to do x, then as part of that intention I think of doing x.

Finally, earlier components of the causal chain leading to the action are neural events, other bodily events and events in the organism's environment.

What Honderich has presented in the first part of his book is a unified deterministic account of the psychoneural relation and the causation of actions. I turn now to the question of the truth of the theory.

Neuroscience and Quantum Mechanics

Possible objections to the Theory of Determinism come from two sources: neuroscience and quantum mechanics. I shall take each in turn.

Honderich claims that 'the theory of determinism of this book, consisting in the three hypotheses, is at least given very strong and clear support by standard neuroscience' (A Theory of Determinism, p. 304). Why does he feel entitled to claim this? He argues, in fact, that neuroscientific evidence tends to confirm each of the hypotheses separately. For example, the first hypothesis, the Correlation Hypothesis, is made more likely by the confirmation of psychoneural intimacy by findings in the study of 'sensation, perception, learning, memory, pleasure and pain' (A Theory of Determinism, p. 283). The second hypothesis receives some confirmation from the absence of an 'originator' or uncaused cause of actions, because it is part of Honderich's view that the psychoneural pair that causes an action is itself an effect. Finally, the third hypothesis is not only consistent with the control of bodily movements through the central nervous system but does not depart severely from our pre-scientific concept of an action. The plausibility of Honderich's claim that his theory tends to be confirmed by these empirical findings depends in part upon his being able to refute all possible alternative ontologies of the mind consistent with those empirical findings. I leave it to the reader to decide whether Honderich succeeds in this.

Quantum theory is the branch of physics which postulates 'quanta' – emissions of energy in discrete packets. The famous problem to which quantum theory gives rise is that it does not seem possible to specify precisely both the momentum and the position of a sub-atomic particle at the same time. In so far as the position of the quantum may be specified, it appears particle-like; in so far as the momentum of the quantum may be specified, it appears wave-like. This problem is known as Heisenberg's Uncertainty Principle because of our inability to be simultaneously certain of both properties of the quantum. It is sometimes thought that quantum mechanics proves indeterminism in so far as some of the events postulated within it possess unpredictable properties. The thought is that in a deterministic universe every event is in principle predictable – given enough knowledge of causes, we may predict their effects. It has even been thought, on the basis of quantum theory, that there exist uncaused events.

Quantum theory may be thought to threaten the Honderich theory in the following way. Suppose quantum theory does (as is debatable) imply that there is indeterminism in the universe –

some of its properties may not be predicted. Suppose too it
requires us to postulate uncaused events. If this may be maintained, then Honderich's second and third hypotheses may be
in doubt. If there are uncaused events, then perhaps a mental
event may be a cause but not an effect. This violates the Honderich tenet that psychoneural pairs are both causes and effects.
Further, a mental event might be the uncaused cause of an action;
this would violate the third hypothesis, because that includes the
view that there are causes of the intentions that cause actions.
Quantum mechanics might provide the conceptual tools for an
indeterminist theory of the mind and, indeed, has been thought to
do so by Sir Karl Popper and John Eccles.

Honderich's reply is, in part, that quantum theory is a problem
rather than a support for indeterminist theories of the mind.
Suppose quantum theory allows uncaused events. If that is right,
then there are chance events, but this is not really what the
libertarian about the mental needs. It is no argument in favour of
our having free will in our actions to say that those actions have
no causes. That would make them random occurrences over which
we have no control. Rather, Honderich maintains, determinism is
essential to a correct account of agency, because being an agent
partially consists in being among the causes of one's own actions.
'Chance events', Honderich concludes, 'are inconsistent both with
determinism and with freedom and responsibility' (A Theory of
Determinism, p. 333). Also, Honderich independently doubts that
quantum theory gives good grounds for indeterminism in any
case.

Honderich, it is clear, thinks the Theory of Determinism is true.
He is aware that it has not been proved beyond any conceivable
doubt and is prepared to concede that any scientific theory is in
principle open to revision. He therefore says that the theory is
'very strongly supported' (A Theory of Determinism, p. 374). Its
strengths are that it provides a theory of the mind that is
consistent with modern science and it receives some confirmation,
and no refutation, from neuroscience.

Life Hopes
In the third and final part of A Theory of Determinism, Honderich
considers the theory's consequences for seven issues, some of

which are personal, some moral and some political. They are: (1) What may we each realistically hope for in the remainder of our life? (2) How should we feel about others who affect us for good or ill? (3) Is it possible for us to know the truth? (4) Should we hold ourselves and others morally responsible for actions? (5) What is the moral worth of people? (6) Should particular actions be judged right or wrong? (7) What should politics be like? Each of these is an enormous and complex philosophical question, and to explore them would unfortunately take us beyond the scope of this book. I should say, however, that Honderich distinguishes two families of response to these questions: one based on the idea of an originator – a self as an uncaused cause of actions – and one which rejects such an originator. It is the second of these which is compatible with his own theory of determinism. For example, with regard to question (7), political conservatism must be ruled out in so far as it presupposes an originator – an individual self who is not caused to be what he or she is. The theory of determinism is no threat to the hopes we have about the future that are worth having. We may have 'life hopes' even if determined where 'to have a life hope ... is either to hope that one will achieve a certain thing, or else that some state of affairs will come to obtain' (A Theory of Determinism, p. 508). The idea of punishment as simple retribution should be given up because people are caused to do what they do, they do not act as uncaused causes. Honderich ends his book by distinguishing two fundamental attitudes to life: dismay and affirmation. He urges affirmation.

5

FUNCTIONALISM

Functionalism is the theory that being in a mental state is being in a functional state. A functional state is a state which may be individuated or picked out in virtue of its causal relations; so a mental state is one with a particular kind of cause, say a sensory input, and a particular kind of effect, say a behavioural output. Mental states are also causally related to one another, and the totality of the causal relations which a given mental state enters into is known as that state's 'causal role' or, sometimes, 'functional role'. Being a particular sort of mental state is having a particular sort of functional role. Being a particular mental state, a particular one, is having a particular functional role, just that functional role.

Functionalism is, in a sense, an attempt to bypass the mind–body problem. It provides a philosophical framework within which to devise a scientific psychology without any need to address the ontology of the person. It is notable, however, that many functionalists are also materialists. Many people who think that the answer to the question, what is the mind?, is the answer to the question, what is the mind for?, also think that mental states are physical states, and that a person is just a highly complicated physical object. It is necessary, therefore, first to say something about the relation between functionalism and materialism.

Functionalism and materialism are not the same theory. Functionalism is the theory that a mental state is essentially an effect of some perceptual input and a cause of some behavioural output. Mental states are also among the causes and effects of one another. Materialism is the theory that every mental state is identical with some physical state, say a state of the brain or the rest of the central nervous system. Now, clearly, somebody who is functionalist may be tempted by a materialist view of the person, because brain states seem good candidates for the effects of sensory inputs and the causes of behavioural outputs. Clearly also, brain states stand in causal relations to one another. It is important to note, however, that functionalism *per se* does not logically entail materialism. From the fact that there exist mental states, states with a particular kind of causal role, it does not logically follow that those mental states are physical states. That they are physical states, for example brain states, is a scientific hypothesis not a necessary consequence of functionalism.

Functionalism does entail materialism with the addition of just one extra premiss. This is: all causes and effects are physical causes and effects. Clearly, if only physical items – physical states, events, objects and so on – may enter into causal relations, then, if functionalism is true, materialism is true. Functionalism entails that every mental state is both a cause and an effect. The new premiss is that only physical states may be causes or effects or both. It follows that, if functionalism is true, then every mental state is a physical state: materialism.

The premiss that, if something is a cause or an effect, it is physical needs argument; but two considerations may be adduced here in its favour. We saw in the chapter on dualism that there is a metaphysical problem as to how qualitatively distinct substances may interact causally. If mental causes and effects are physical causes and effects, that problem need not be addressed. Also, a non-physical cause of a physical effect or a non-physical effect of a physical cause could not be incorporated into the system of scientific laws as we know them. Such relations would be outrageously at variance with any natural scientific view of the universe. They would be 'something new under the sun'. Despite this, I see no sound and so decisive argument in favour of the thesis that causal relations hold only between physical entities.

Functionalists therefore divide between those who are materialists and those who feel committed to no particular ontology of the mind. All functionalists hold that a particular kind of mental state may be realized in a number of different ways; for example, on a functionalist view, being in pain is being in a functional state. Being in pain is being in a state which results from certain sensory inputs and causes pain-behaviour. This account holds true for any beings capable of being in pain: humans, cats, dogs, Martians. However, the way in which the state of being in pain is realized may differ radically according to the make-up of these beings. Pain may be realized by the firing of C-fibres in a human central nervous system, but the way they fire in dogs may be physiologically different. Perhaps Martians do not have C-fibres — or, indeed, central nervous systems. A mental state of one kind may have several different sorts of realization, and in principle this realization need not be physical. Suppose you and I are essentially souls or essentially consciousnesses. In that case, being in pain could be realized as an intrinsically spiritual event or an intrinsically mental event, so long as it resulted from a specifiable kind of perceptual input and behavioural output and stood in the requisite causal relations to the rest of our mental states. This is what I meant when I said that functionalism in a sense bypasses the mind–body problem. Being in a mental state is being in a functional state. It logically follows that any kind of being capable of being in that functional state is capable of being in that mental state. It does not matter what that being is made of, so long as he, she or it is capable of realizing that state.

If the thesis that all causes and effects are physical is false, then functionalism is logically consistent with any of the theories of the mind in this book, with the exception of logical behaviourism. Being a functionalist is quite compatible with being a mind–body dualist, an idealist, a materialist, a neutral monist or a phenomenologist. (Notice that all mental states might be physical states, even if not all causes and effects are physical, so functionalism is still compatible with materialism about the person even if the materialist premiss about causes and effects is false.)

The reason why functionalism is logically inconsistent with logical behaviourism is that, as we saw in Chapter 2, according to the logical behaviourist, being in a mental state is being in a behavioural state. Having a mind is either behaving or having a propensity to behave in certain ways. This is quite incompatible with functionalism. Functionalists define the mental not as behaviour but as the cause of behaviour. Logically, if A is the cause of B and B is the effect of A, then A and B are not identical. Only distinct entities may stand in causal relations.

Functionalism has come to be a theory of the mind by two fairly independent routes. We saw in Chapter 4 that one of the motivations of the mind–brain identity theorists was to overcome one of the deficiencies of logical behaviourism. They thought a logical behaviourist analysis could plausibly be given for one important sub-class of our mental states: the dispositional ones, that is, beliefs, intentions, motives and desires. However, they thought there was not much intuitive plausibility in maintaining that our occurrent mental states are only behavioural. Thoughts and emotions, for example, were treated not as behavioural states but as brain states. Now, one mind–brain identity theorist in particular, the Australian philosopher David Armstrong, argued forcefully that the mind is not behaviour but the inner cause of behaviour: the inner physical cause of behaviour. Armstrong is, of course, a materialist, but he argues for a functionalist materialism in his important 1970 paper 'The nature of mind'. Armstrong agrees with the behaviourists that the concept of mind is logically tied to the concept of behaviour but not by way of identity. The mind is defined as that which brings about behaviour. In Armstrong's paper, the central moves of functionalism are made: the individuation of mental states through their causal relations and the identification of mental states with functional states.

The other avenue in recent intellectual history issuing in functionalism is thought about artificial intelligence. In particular, the English mathematician and computer scientist Alan Turing wrote an influential paper in the philosophy journal *Mind* in 1950. This was called 'Computing machinery and intelligence'. Turing is there concerned to defend the logical possibility of machine intelligence, and part of his strategy in doing so is the devising of a test that has subsequently become known as the 'Turing Test'. It provides us with a criterion for deciding whether computers are intelligent. The idea is that, first, a man and a woman in one room should provide answers to questions posed by an interrogator in a separate room. The questions are typewritten or sent via a teleprinter to the interrogator, who is to decide in each case whether the question has been answered by the man or the woman. Then, secondly, the woman is replaced by a computer. In this second case the interrogator has to decide whether each question has been answered by the man or the computer. To the extent that the interrogator succeeds in judging correctly more often in the computer case than in the woman case, we should say the computer is intelligent.

Now, whatever the merits or demerits of the Turing Test as a criterion of artificial intelligence, the connection with functionalism is as follows. The states of a computer which is running a program are defined by input and output relations and by their relations to each other. The software description of the operations of a computer is a functionalist description where, if a certain input is received, a certain state results, or where, if the machine is in one state but no input is received, then it moves to a new state, and so on. Importantly, a system may be described functionally in this way without any ontological commitment to what would realize the running of such a program. Software descriptions are functionalist descriptions, and this is the second large impetus to functionalism as a theory of the mind.

In what follows I shall consider the work of two philosophers, each of whom came to functionalism by a different route. They are the contemporary North American philosophers, Hilary Putnam and David Lewis.

PUTNAM

Brain States and Pain States

Putnam begins 'The nature of mental states' by arguing that the mind–brain identity theory cannot be dismissed on a priori grounds. He addresses the particular issue as to whether pain is a brain state. (Putnam uses the term 'brain' broadly to denote the central nervous system as a whole. He is not here concerned with the partially empirical question: which part of the central nervous system is pain to be identified with? but with the philosophical question, whether it may be significantly identified with any part of it.) His conclusion is that, from the fact that 'pain' and 'brain state' have different meanings in English, it does not follow that pain is not a brain state. From the fact that the concepts are semantically distinct, it does not follow that they do not refer to one and the same state. In this respect, Putnam's position is so far fully consistent with that of Place, examined in Chapter 4. To convince us that the mind–brain identity theory may not be refuted a priori on semantic grounds, Putnam provides us with an analogy. It is, for example, true (a truth of physics) that temperature is mean kinetic energy; but, clearly, 'temperature' and 'mean kinetic energy' do not mean the same. The fact that the concepts are distinct does not falsify the truth of physics because the concepts denote in fact one and the same thing. A person might know that something has a certain temperature but not know that temperature is identical with mean kinetic energy; but that does not prevent mean kinetic energy being exactly what temperature is. Similarly, a person might know that he or she is in pain but not know that he or she is in a certain brain state, but this is no grounds whatsoever (according to Putnam) for maintaining that his or her pain is not identical with that brain state. That might be exactly what his or her pain is. Nothing follows from distinctions between concepts about distinctions between things. Ontological conclusions may not be soundly derived from purely semantic premisses. Which things are identical with which others is to be decided empirically or scientifically, according to Putnam, and not a priori.

Thus far Putnam has defended the mind–brain identity theory, but only against a priori objections. In fact Putnam thinks the mind–brain identity theory is not the best theory of the mind; his view is that functionalism is superior. After we have decided what functionalism is, we may decide whether it is consistent with the mind–brain identity theory.

Putnam formulates his own theory succinctly thus:

My strategy will be to argue that pain is not a brain state, not on a priori grounds but on the grounds that another hypothesis is more plausible ... I propose the hypothesis that pain, or the state of being in pain is a functional state of the whole organism. (*Mind, Language and Reality*, p. 433)

Notice that Putnam calls his view that pain is a functional state of the whole organism a hypothesis. This is fully consistent with his thesis that what is to be identified with what is an empirical matter. A hypothesis is a claim or set of claims which may or may not turn out to be true. An empirical or scientific hypothesis is one which could be verified or falsified by scientific observation. It is the role of philosophy not to advocate scientifically refined hypotheses but 'hypotheses schemata' (*Mind, Language and Reality*, p. 433), that is, hypotheses which may be made more precise and testable by the natural sciences. That pain is a functional state is one such hypothesis schema. What does it mean, to say a mental state is a functional state?

Turing Machines

To understand Putnam's theory, we have to appreciate the concept of a Turing Machine and, more generally, the concept of probabilistic automata. Broadly, a Turing Machine is a simple computer comprising facilities for the input and output of information and an internal mechanism for the internal processing of that information. At any one moment a Turing Machine is in a particular state of processing information, which it does by mechanically scanning a tape divided into squares. It manipulates symbols on the squares by erasing some and replacing them by others, and it outputs the result by a printing mechanism. The set of possible states a Turing Machine may be in during the processing of some defined piece of information is represented in a machine table. In a Turing Machine it follows with certainty that, if it is in one state of a certain type, then it will next adopt another of a certain type; in other words, a Turing Machine is a deterministic system. The probability of its moving into a certain state from a previous one is one, and the probability of its not doing so is zero. In the case of any probabilistic automaton which is not a Turing Machine, the probability of its moving from one state to another specified state is somewhere between one and zero, so all those systems are not deterministic. We could put the point this way: all Turing Machines are probabilistic automata, but not all probabilistic automata are Turing Machines. As Putnam puts it: 'A Turing Machine is simply a special kind of Probabilistic Automaton, one with transition probabilities 0,1' (*Mind, Language and Reality*, p. 433).

Putnam thinks that probabilistic automata provide good models for the understanding of organisms, so his particular brand of functionalism in the philosophy of mind is sometimes known as Turing Machine Functionalism. He has some special adaptations of the idea of a probabilistic automaton for the purposes of his theory. In particular, the inputs are assumed to be sensory and the outputs motor. In psychology, sensory inputs are those received via the five senses, and motor outputs are bodily movements, including, for example, breathing. He also adds the notion of an 'instruction' which tells us the probability of the probabilistic automaton moving from one state to another.

It is important to understand that a probabilistic automaton is a theoretical entity which may be realized in physically different ways. One and the same physical system may be the realization of several distinct probabilistic automata, and one theoretical automaton may be realized in several distinct physical systems. The description of a probabilistic automaton could, for example, be the description of a cat, a robot or a human being. The probabilistic automaton could be realized or made real (rather than remaining purely theoretical) in any of those ways. Putnam, for present purposes, assumes that we know what the physical realization of the input and output mechanisms is but do not know what the internal realization of the state of the automaton is. This corresponds to our knowing, for example, roughly what inputs and outputs to the person are associated with pain but our not knowing what pain is. We know only the state the probabilistic automaton is in as described on its 'machine table'.

Finally, before we can be in a position to appreciate Putnam's functionalism we need to acquire one further concept. This is the concept of a 'description' of a system. Putnam defines 'description' in this way:

A Description of S, where S is a system, is any true statement to the effect that S possesses distinct states S_1, S_2 ... S_n which are related to one another and to the motor outputs and sensory inputs by the transition probabilities given in such and such a Machine Table. (*Mind, Language and Reality*, p. 434)

So a description is a statement, about a physical system Putnam labels 'S', which is the realization of at least one probabilistic automaton. The description, to count as such, must be a true statement and report the different states of the system S, where these states are labelled by Putnam S_1, S_2 ... S_n. The machine table for the probabilistic automaton lists the probabilities of the machine adopting one (particular) state if it is in another. Such a machine table, based on the truth of a particular description, is called by Putnam the Functional Organization of the system S. Clearly, at any given time, the description will report the total number of states, S_1, S_2' ... S_n, that the machine is in. Putnam's name for this is the 'total state' of the system. We are now in a position to understand Putnam's functionalism.

Functional States

The claim that being in pain is being in a functional state, a state of the whole organism, may be broken down into four separate sub-claims. I shall consider each of these in turn. The first, for Putnam, is trivially true:

1. 'All organisms capable of feeling pain are Probabilistic Automata' (*Mind, Language and Reality*, p. 434). This claim is trivially true because, in Putnam's view, anything may be described in such a way that it is true that it is a probabilistic automaton. He does not justify this rather sweeping claim, but I think he has in mind the fact that anything is located within a nexus of causes and effects, and its existence as an intermediary between such causes and effects will make a difference to the nature of causal sequences. In short, anything can be thought of as either a system or a part of a system and modelled using the distinctions between input, processing and output. However, it is clearly true in any case that any organism feeling pain is a probabilistic automaton in Putnam's sense if, as seems plausible, all organisms which feel pain causally interact with their environment: if their states are the results of certain inputs and their states help to effect certain outputs. If this is right, then the first component of the claim, that pains are functional states, is reasonably uncontroversial.

Second, Putnam claims that:

2. 'Every organism capable of feeling pain possesses at least one description of a certain kind (i.e. being capable of feeling pain is possessing an appropriate kind of Functional Organisation)' (*Mind, Language and Reality*, p. 434). There are two claims here, each of which may be made clear in terms of Putnam's

characterization of probabilistic automata. It follows that there exists a description of the states of an organism capable of feeling pain from the fact that such organisms are probabilistic automata, because all probabilistic automata have descriptions of their states. It follows that being capable of pain is possessing a certain kind of functional organization just so long as being is pain is a state of the organism. This, I think, may be conceded to Putnam, because again it is relatively uncontroversial that being in pain is a state of some kind. The functional organization is the set of states the system is capable of, as specified in the system's machine table, so Putnam is claiming that pain is one such specifiable state. Notice that being capable of being in pain is identified with the functional organization. This is because the functional organization of the system is what the system is capable of: the set of possible states it can be in, given a certain description. Having a certain functional organization is not identified with being in pain. Being in pain is being in a functional state.

The third part of the hypothesis is as follows:

3. 'No organism capable of feeling pain possesses a decomposition into parts which separately possess descriptions of the kind referred to in (2)' (Mind, Language and Reality, p. 434). This sentence is added to preclude a certain possibility: this is that the subject of pain – the system that is in pain – might not be a unified system. Putnam is concerned to model the behaviour of only a single organism, so he needs to rule out his model applying to, say, swarms of bees (Mind, Language and Reality, p. 435). Claim (3) ensures that no sub-component of an organism is an organism, or, for the purposes of the model, no sub-system of the system is of the type captured by the description of the system.

The final and crucial claim is this:

4. 'For every description of the kind referred to in (2) there exists a subset of the sensory inputs such that an organism with that description is in pain when and only when some of its sensory inputs are in that subset' (Mind, Language and Reality, p. 434). It will be recalled that in the description of a probabilistic automaton the states of the system are specified not only in relation to one another but in relation to inputs and outputs. Thus it is possible to discriminate one state from another not only by their mutual relations – state B is the state between state A and state

C, and so on – but also through their input–output relations – state A results from input I and causes output O. It is possible to say what a particular state is in terms of the inputs (which are preconditions for it) and the outputs (for which it is a precondition). If that is right, then it follows that there will be certain states such that the system will be in one of those states when it receives certain inputs and when it produces certain outputs and will be in that state only when the system receives those inputs and produces those outputs. Putnam is maintaining that pain is precisely such a state or, more precisely, being in pain is being in such a state.

This is in fact a most radical position in the philosophy of mind. If pain is a functional state of the whole organism, then pain cannot be a state only of the brain or only of the central nervous system. Indeed, according to Putnam, it does not even have to be that. For functionalist purposes, we may bracket or leave on one side the various ways in which pain is realized in the organism. We may specify pain in relation to certain inputs and outputs and other functional states of the system. Indeed, Putnam asserts that 'the functional-state hypothesis is not incompatible with dualism' (Mind, Language and Reality, p. 436). It should now be clear why this is so. So long as the probabilistic automaton has the relevant inputs and outputs and so long as its functional states are specifiable in a description, it does not much matter if those functional states are states of a mind, brain, soul or, indeed, anything else constitutive of the organism. I should emphasize, however, that functionalism is by no means incompatible with materialism and that many functionalists are materialists. It will be recalled that Davidson thinks that only physical states (or events) may enter into causal relations. Anyone who thinks this will think that functionalism can be true only if materialism is true because, if a state results from an input or produces an output, it is caused by that input and causes that output. If only physical states can be causes and effects, and functional states are causes and effects, then functional states are physical states. The assumption that all causes and effects are physical is, however, by no means uncontroversial.

It is also worth pointing out the bearing of Putnam's

functionalism on logical behaviourism. Putnam thinks it is a mistake to identify pain with pain behaviour, and he rejects the view, outlined in Chapter 3, that sentences about mental states may be translated without loss of meaning into sentences about actual and possible behaviour. Like the materialists, he thinks pain is the cause of pain behaviour, but maintains that that cause is a functional state of the whole organism. 'It would be more plausible to identify being in pain with some state whose presence explains this behaviour disposition' (*Mind, Language and Reality*, p. 439).

Because Putnam thinks that pain 'is the state of receiving sensory inputs which play a certain role in the Functional Organisation of the organism' (*Mind, Language and Reality*, p. 438), we need to know more about what functional organization is. This naturally will vary from system to system, but Putnam has some interesting suggestions about the functional organization necessary for an organism to feel pain. Such an organism must possess a 'preference function' (*Mind, Language and Reality*, p. 435), that is, be able to discriminate what it favours from what it seeks to reject. This capacity is, so to speak, 'built into' the function of pain. It must be able to learn from experience, as this too is part of the function of pain. Also, its input facilities must include 'pain sensors', or, clearly, the organism could never be in the functional state called 'pain'. Such sensors would, for example, provide information about damage to the organism, as it is a part of the function of pain to do.

Putnam thinks his functional theory of mental states provides a much more fruitful model of the mental than the mind–brain identity theory for the future progress of psychology. It seems to me there is some merit in this; for example, suppose we wish to study pain from a psychological point of view but do not wish to restrict ourselves to human psychology. It might turn out that various organisms feel pain defined functionally but that, between species, pain is not at all to be identified with a specific sort of brain state. It might be that there is not much in common between the state of the nervous system of a frog, of a chicken and of a human being when we say correctly that they are in pain; but, using the functionalist model, we have criteria to decide whether it is pain that they do all have. Functionalism is also consistent with a psychology which considers the organism in relation to its environment and does not simply consider the brain in abstraction from all else. In this sense, functionalism perhaps has more of a chance of correlating its findings with those of the biological and social sciences than a psychology based only on the mind–brain identity theory.

Perhaps the reader is left feeling, as with logical behaviourism and materialism, that the essential point has been omitted – what it feels like to be in pain. Pain is after all a sensation. In reply, the functionalist is likely to say: yes, of course pain is felt, but that is not an important consideration in understanding its functional role. It is to be defined in terms of its inputs, outputs and functional relations to other states. Perhaps it is worth pausing to ask whether pain could have that functional role if it did not hurt.

LEWIS

David Lewis argues for a materialist version of functionalism in two important papers, 'Psychophysical and theoretical identifications' (1972) and 'Mad pain and Martian pain' (1978). I shall discuss the later paper here.

Lewis thinks that any adequate theory of the mind must be both materialist and functionalist. It must be part of the theory that any mental state is a physical state and any mental state is a functional state. This conclusion is forced upon us to solve a philosophical problem.

The philosophical problem is as follows. It seems a logical possibility that a person should be in a mental state of a specific kind, say pain, where that state possesses none of the causal relations we typically associate with states of that sort. Also, it seems a logical possibility that a being should be in a mental state which exhibits all or most of the causal relations we typically associate with being in that state, where that state is realized by or correlated with nothing like the state of the central nervous system a human being is in when in that sort of state. In the first case, the person is in pain but shows none of the causes or effects of pain. In the second case, the person is in pain, shows the causes and effects of pain, but is not in the neurological state of pain. Lewis thinks both of these are genuine possibilities.

The Madman and the Martian

To make them clearer, Lewis invites us to conduct a thought experiment for each case. Imagine a person whose pain is not caused by damage to his body but by physical exercise, which has the effect not of making him groan but to snap his fingers. The person is not distracted by his pain and makes no efforts to avoid it. Lewis calls this 'mad pain'. Although the person in mad pain is not in pain in exactly the same sense as you or I when we are in pain, he is nevertheless in pain. There is a sense of 'pain' in which we and he are both in pain. His pain feels to him as our pain feels to us.

Imagine next a Martian, a physical being who writhes and groans when in pain just as we humans do. The Martian's pain is caused by the sorts of things that cause our pain, for example pinching. When we pinch the Martian, he tries to stop us. However, the Martian has no central nervous system. Instead pain is realized in him by a quasi-Newtonian hydraulic system of fluid-filled cavities. Although the Martian is not in pain in exactly the same sense as you or I when we are in pain, he is nevertheless in pain. There is a sense of 'pain' in which we and he are both in pain. His pain feels to him as our pain feels to us.

If the reader has little patience with strange thought experiments in philosophy, then I should say that we may take them as mere heuristic devices. Lewis's conceptual points could be made without them. In philosophy, one of the things we try to do is decide a priori what mental states are, and this requires considering logical possibilities, not just empirical actualities. We can make sense of the idea of pain in abstraction from its typical causal relations or from its typical physical realization without being committed thereby to the view that such pain exists.

Lewis's materialist and functionalist theory of mind is designed to capture the fact that our pain and mad pain and Martian pain are all cases of pain. The lesson of mad pain is that it is only a contingent fact about pain that it has the causal relations it in fact has. The lesson of Martian pain is that it is only a contingent fact that pain has the physical realization it in fact has. It follows that pain does not necessarily have a particular kind of causal role and pain does not necessarily have a particular kind of physical realization. Lewis's theory has to do justice to both these facts.

The mind–brain identity theory presents a solution to the problem of mad pain but fails to solve the problem of Martian pain. Functionalism or logical behaviourism presents a solution to the problem of Martian pain but fails to solve the problem of mad pain. On the mind–brain identity theory, we can say that mad pain is identical with a state of the central nervous system, just as my pain or your pain is identical with a state of a nervous system. On a functionalist theory, we can define Martian pain and our pain in terms of its causal role; and on a logical behaviourist theory, we can define Martian pain and our pain in terms of pain behaviour. However, on the mind–brain identity theory, we cannot identify Martian pain with a state of the Martian's nervous system as we may identify our pain with states of our nervous systems, because the Martian has no nervous system. On the functionalist theory, we cannot define mad pain in terms of its typical causes and effects as we may with our pain, because those causes and effects differ so greatly between the two cases. Similarly, on a logical behaviourist theory, we cannot identify mad pain with pain behaviour as we may in our case, because the behaviour associated with pain differs so greatly between the two cases. The madman and the Martian each seem to exhibit some of the features of pain, but they do not share those features. The madman's pain has the correct physical realization but the wrong causal relations; the Martian's pain has the correct causal relations but the wrong physical realization.

Causal Roles

The theory of the mind that correctly characterizes pain in all three cases is one which was also developed by David Armstrong, but independently of Lewis. It is the theory that the concept of a mental state is the concept of

a state apt for being caused in certain ways by stimuli plus other mental states and apt for combining with certain other mental states to jointly cause certain behaviour. (Block, p. 218)

The most conspicuous feature of this definition is that it is a functionalist definition. The concept of a mental state is the concept of a functional state, so the concept of pain for example is essentially the concept of that which occupies a particular kind of causal role. It is important to note in addition Lewis's use of the word 'apt'. A mental state is one that is apt or appropriate for being the effect of certain causes and being the cause of certain effects. This is an important part of his functionalism because it leaves open what sorts of state are the appropriate ones to stand in those causal relations.

Now, suppose the firing of C-fibres in a central nervous system is the state that does stand in the causal relations, the description of which defines 'pain', then pain is the firing of C-fibres. This is because 'If the concept of pain is the concept of a state that occupies a certain causal role, then whatever state does occupy that role is pain' (Block, p. 218). In this way Lewis offers us a theory of mind in which materialism and functionalism are mutually consistent.

Materialist Functionalism

To understand the theory further, an important distinction needs to be made. Although pain is a state of the central nervous system, the concept of pain is not the concept of part of the central nervous system. The concept of pain is the concept of that with a certain causal role. It is that, whatever it is. Pain happens to be a state of the central nervous system because that is what turns out to have the appropriate causal role. To put it another way, pain is necessarily that which has a particular causal role, but pain is contingently a state of the central nervous system because it is as a matter of fact that which has the causal role. 'Pain' is defined functionally but pain is realized physically.

For these reasons Lewis feels able to maintain that 'Pain might not have been pain' (Block, p. 218). Pain necessarily is the occupant of the causal role, but the occupant of the causal role might not have been C-fibres firing. Pain could not have failed to be the occupant of the causal role, but the occupant of the causal role might have been other than the actual occupant.

It is clear how this materialist functionalism should work for humans. Pain, in our case, is essentially the occupant of a certain causal role: the result of stimuli plus other mental states and the cause of pain behaviour. Pain, in our case, is realized by, and so is contingently identical with, a state of the central nervous system, that is, C-fibres firing. How does the theory of work for Martians?

Because pain is necessarily or essentially the occupant of a certain causal role, this must hold true in all possible worlds and so also on Mars. Martian pain, like pain everywhere else, is a state apt or appropriate for being a certain type of effect and cause. However, in the case of Martians the occupant of the causal role is different. While for humans the occupant of the causal role is C-fibres firing, in Martians the occupant of the role is hydraulic pressure changes. Pain is still essentially the occupant of the causal role in the Martian case, but pain is contingently changes in hydraulic pressure. Thus Lewis's theory captures both the human and the Martian cases. What of mad pain?

It may seem to be a fairly obvious difficulty for Lewis that he has defined 'pain' in causal terms, but in the case of mad pain the requisite causal relations are absent. It seems either that, by definition, mad pain is not pain after all, which is counter-intuitive because it feels like pain, or else that the madman is both in pain and not in pain, which is contradictory. In fact this is not a difficulty for Lewis. It will be remembered that Lewis, like Armstrong, says that pain is a state apt to produce certain effects, not that it always and everywhere does cause those effects. Now, in the thought experiment, the madman feels pain, and this sensation is realized physically by a state of his central nervous system. But that – C-fibres firing – is precisely the state apt for producing the effects constitutive of pain's causal role in humans. The madman is in the state apt to produce the effects of pain and to be produced by the causes of pain, so he is in pain. In order for that sentence to be true of him, those causal relations do not have to obtain in his particular case. Certainly, his case is atypical, but his is a case of pain nevertheless.

In these ways Lewis devises a materialist functionalism which does justice to both the causal role and the physical realization of pain. It should not be objected to his account (as it could to some) that he ignores the phenomenological properties of pain. Mad pain is a felt sensation as are Martian pain and, of course, our pain. As Lewis says: 'Pain is a feeling. Surely that is uncontroversial. To have pain and to feel pain are one and the same' (Block, p. 222).

6

DOUBLE ASPECT THEORY

The double aspect theory is the theory that mental and physical are two properties of some underlying reality which is intrinsically neither mental nor physical. It follows that it is incompatible with dualism, idealism and materialism because it includes the denial of mental substance and the denial of physical substance. It has it in common with idealism and materialism, however, to be a monism rather than a dualism because it includes the thesis that only one substance, or only one kind of entity, fundamentally exists.

It would be misleading in the extreme to suggest that there is just one kind of theory which could correctly be called 'double aspect theory'. Nevertheless, the three philosophers I have chosen to examine under this heading do share something essential in common. The English twentieth-century philosophers, Bertrand Russell and Peter Strawson, as well as the seventeenth-century Dutch philosopher, Benedictus de Spinoza, all reject dualism, idealism and materialism. Further, each of them in his different way thinks that the mental/physical distinction is not ontologically fundamental, and that our making the mental/physical distinction depends upon either the existence of, or our prior acquaintance with, some substance or entity which is in itself either (a) neither mental nor physical or (b) both mental and physical.

Spinoza thinks there exists only one substance and that this is identical with the totality of what exists. It has two and only two attributes: consciousness and size. In this way Spinoza devises a dualism of properties or characteristics with which to replace the Cartesian dualism of substances. Spinoza is a monist about substance. Russell maintains that our talk about mental and physical events depends logically upon our talk about the contents of sense perceptions he calls 'sense data'. Sense data, according to Russell, are intrinsically neither mental nor physical but count as such only according to the kinds of knowledge that are possible of them. Not only does Russell reject Cartesian dualism, he argues against the existence of any kind of substance: mental or physical. Strawson argues that, unless we were already possessed of the concept of the whole person, we could not have the concept of a consciousness as something distinct from a body. Our making the mental/physical distinction in our thought and language depends logically upon our prior acquaintance with the whole person, the concept of which cuts across any clean mental/physical distinction.

One version of the double aspect theory is sometimes called 'neutral monism'. Russell, for example, calls his theory this. As the term 'monism' implies, this is partly the view that only one kind of entity exists. These entities are purportedly 'neutral' between mental and physical descriptions of them. Russell's sense data, for example, fall into this category. I shall now discuss some varieties of double aspect theories presented in the history of Western philosophy, including 'neutral monism'.

David Hume, the eighteenth-century Scottish philosopher, does not use the expressions 'double aspect theory' or 'neutral monism' to refer to his philosophy of mind. However, he thought that we are directly acquainted through sense perception with a class of entities which are intrinsically neither mental nor physical, and our having knowledge of these is a condition of our having the concepts of mind and matter. Indeed, on Hume's empiricist epistemology, it is impossible to have an idea of anything without having been aware of certain impressions. If we ask what mind and matter are on Hume's account, then a mind is nothing over and above a collection of perceptions. Matter is a mere fiction, postulated to explain the identity of physical objects; and to speak of those physical objects themselves is to speak of the possibility of certain impressions. Minds and physical objects exist for Hume, but they are not Cartesian entities. Hume rejects the view that they are substances and refuses to separate out the questions of what they are and how we can know that they exist. Any talk about them is to be explained in terms of the possibility of ideas and impressions. Minds and physical objects do possess an identity over time but this is not the identity of substances. The identities of minds and physical objects over time is constituted by relations between the contents of perceptions which give those minds and physical objects their unity and coherence. These relations are thought by the imagination, a faculty which makes empirical knowledge possible.

'Neutral monism' is usually used in connection with the philosophy of William James, the North American philosopher and psychologist who lived and wrote at the turn of the twentieth century. It is true that James's 'pure experience' cannot be straightforwardly classified as either mental or physical, and it is also true that pure experience is what makes possible the classification of things as mental or physical. However, James's ontology of the mind is less clear than the label 'neutral monism' might lead us to suppose. For example, in his celebrated The Principles of Psychology he argues that the self has a fourfold structure: the material self, the social self, the spiritual self and the pure ego. The material self is essentially the body but may include physical objects we call our own, our clothes and home for example. The social self is the recognition a person obtains from others. Indeed, a person has as many social selves as there are persons who recognize him or her, according to James. Most interesting for our ontological purposes is James's account of the spiritual self. He says that various views of this are possible. Intuitively or pre-philosophically, it is perhaps best regarded as the awareness or consciousness that a person has of the contents of their perceptions. We obtain the concept of the spiritual self by thinking of ourselves as thinkers. It is a product of reflection. James conjectures that the spiritual self may be nothing over and above the stream of our consciousness, or perhaps some essential or conspicuous component of that stream. There seems to exist a distinction between the active and the passive ingredients of perception. Although I passively receive a sensory input, I seem to be actively aware of such input. Perhaps the spiritual self is this mental activity.

James's speculations about the spiritual self are derived from introspection; the paying attention to one's own mental processes by a kind of direct inner awareness or mental 'watching'. Now, interestingly, James maintains that, if we introspect carefully enough, we will notice that in introspection we never manage to catch an act of spontaneous awareness. All we are really aware of is some bodily sensation, especially in the head and throat. It follows that what normally passes for spiritual activity is in fact physical. What people take to be their innermost self is in fact some bodily movements between the head and the throat. The pure ego is a pure fiction. Philosophers have postulated this because of the shortcomings of previous empiricist theories of mind.

We should not conclude from this account that James is a materialist philosopher. He is not a materialist, a dualist or an idealist. For him, sensations are intrinsically neither mental nor physical, and there exists no mental substance and no physical substance. It is part of his 'radical empiricism' that there is no empirical justification for the postulation of such substances.

Neutral monist or double aspect theories of the mind have one singular advantage and one singular drawback. The advantage is that they avoid the shortcomings of materialism, dualism and idealism. The materialist tends to underestimate the reality of the mental and the idealist tends to underestimate the reality of the physical. Double aspect theorists try to do justice to both, without facing the metaphysical difficulty the mind–body dualist faces of accounting for causal interaction between two qualitatively dissimilar substances. The drawback is that it is typically unclear what the 'neutral' entities postulated by the neutral monist are. It is equally unclear what mental and physical properties are properties *of* on the double aspect theory. These unclarities are at least as serious as the unclarities about what mind and matter are on all these theories. Perhaps Hume, however, would reply that there is nothing we could know more directly than our own impressions and, if we cannot know what they are, then we are unlikely to know what minds and physical objects are. The neutral monist reverses our normal order of priorities. We normally think we are directly acquainted with our own minds and external physical objects; and there then arise the questions: whether both of these are real; if so, what the relations are between them; whether one may be reduced to the other, and so on. The neutral monist typically postulates the content of our experience – our impressions of sound, shape and colour for example – as that with which we are most directly acquainted. Minds and physical objects are then described as intellectual or logical constructs out of those contents of experience. The contents themselves are neither mental nor physical.

Whether or not any of these strategies work as a solution to the mind–body problem, some intuitive plausibility may be adduced for neutral monism. It might be that most of the things we come across in everyday life are not clearly either mental or physical, and it might be that some are both mental and physical. Perhaps the classification of things into mental and physical is neither mutually exclusive nor collectively exhaustive. In that case, the mind–body problem could be a product of the philosophical assumption that everything is either mental or physical but not both. Now we may examine the arguments of three philosophers who call this fundamental assumption into question: Spinoza, Russell and Strawson.

SPINOZA

One Substance

Spinoza's central metaphysical idea is that only one substance exists and that this substance may be thought of in two important ways. It is conscious and it has size. He means that the one world which exists – the one we are acquainted with, are a part of, and may think about – has two essential properties or attributes: thought and extension. What exists has these two attributes objectively, that is, whether we believe it or not; and reality may be named in two ways, depending upon whether we are considering it under the attribute of thought or the attribute of extension. If we think of the world as extended, then we should call it 'Nature'. If we think of it as conscious, then we should call it 'God'. 'God' and 'Nature' are two alternative terms denoting one and the same single substance which possesses both mental and physical characteristics.

To appreciate Spinoza's metaphysical theory, we need to make sense of some of the vocabulary he uses. His concept of substance is rather similar to the one Descartes inherited from Aristotle via the medieval scholastics:

I understand 'substance' [substantia] to be that which is in itself and is conceived through itself; I mean that the conception of which does not depend on the conception of another thing from which it must be formed. (Ethics, p. 1)

If something is in itself, then it exists but does not depend upon the existence of anything else for its own existence. If it can be conceived through itself, then, as Spinoza explains, it is possible to obtain the concept of it without thereby needing to think the concept of anything else upon which it might be thought to depend. So a substance depends upon nothing except itself for its own existence and nature. No other thing can cause a substance to be or to be what it is.

Spinoza thinks the only plausible candidate for a substance in this sense is reality as a whole — the totality of what exists. We can suggest, perhaps, why the whole of what is might meet this specification. First, it exists — what is, is. Secondly, what is, is all that there is, so there cannot possibly be anything upon which the totality of existence depends for its own existence. It follows that all that there is depends only upon itself for its own existence, or 'is in itself' as Spinoza puts it.

It follows that the only substance, if it has a cause, is the cause of itself. Given that it exists, and that it is all that there is, there cannot be any cause of its being, nor any cause of its being what it is, except itself. Spinoza explains something's being the cause of itself as follows: 'I understand that to be "cause of itself" [causa sui] whose essence involves existence, and whose nature cannot be conceived except existing' (Ethics, p. 1). Something's essence is what that thing is, so Spinoza is saying that, if something is the cause of itself, then in order to specify adequately what that thing is it has to be mentioned that that thing exists. Its existing is part of what it is. It is reasonable to suppose that the individual existing things we come across depend upon one another for their existence. For example, one event is caused by an earlier event and so on, and this seems equally true of mental and physical events. The Spinozistic thought is that this sort of regress of explanations cannot go on ad infinitum; explanations have to stop at some point. His solution is that the world system as a whole — the one substance — includes its own explanation. Its existence is part of its essence. It is its own reason for being.

Individuals

Spinoza's solution to the mind–body problem consists in locating human beings within the metaphysical picture described so far. We are parts or aspects of the one substance. Just as the one substance may be conceived either under the attribute of thought and so be known as 'God', and just as the one substance may be conceived under the attribute of extension and so be known as 'Nature', so the individual human being may be conceived as mental or physical, and so may be thought of as a mind or as a body: 'The mind and body are one and the same individual, which is conceived now under the attribute of thought, and now under the attribute of extension' (*Ethics*, p. 58). This is Spinoza's central statement on the mind–body problem and needs to be borne closely in mind when reading certain other assertions of his. For example, if one were to pluck out of the context of the system as a whole the claims that 'Man consists of mind and body' or 'the human mind is united to the body' (*Ethics*, p. 47), then these might be misunderstood as a version of Cartesian dualism. Spinoza rejects dualism. When he says that a person has a mind and a body, he means that we each have the attributes of thought and extension, but he utterly repudiates the Cartesian view that we are each made up of two substances, one called 'mind' and the other called 'body'. When he says the human body and mind are united, he means they are two aspects or attributes of the human being. He takes it to be a tremendous merit of his monism that any problem about the causal interaction between mental and physical is wholly bypassed. If there are not two substances, then there cannot possibly be any problem about how they are 'united' in the Cartesian sense, or how they may interact causally. If we accept the premiss that causal relations may obtain only between distinct items, then, on the Spinozistic view, mind and body do not interact causally.

God or Nature

What does it mean to say that we are aspects of God? To decide this, we need to know more about what Spinoza thinks God is. God, for Spinoza, possesses the traditional attributes of being infinite, spiritual, omnipotent and benevolent, and everything which happens follows necessarily from His nature. Indeed,

Spinoza thinks that the logical order of a rational and deductive understanding of the world is exactly the same order as the causal ordering of events in the world. His writing follows a 'geometrical' or logically deductive style to try to do justice to this fact, but we need not pursue this aspect of his work here.

Spinoza breaks with the traditional Judaeo-Christian conception of God in one all-important respect: God is the one substance. God is identical with the totality of what exists. God is not the transcendent cause of what is. He is what is. This means that Spinoza is a special sort of theist: he is a pantheist. Theism is the view that God exists. Pantheism includes theism but asserts further that there is nothing that is not God. God is equivalent to reality as a whole.

Why does Spinoza think pantheism is true? The reasons are many and complex, but, principally, he believes it makes sense to ascribe characteristics like 'infinite' and 'omnipotent' only to the whole of existence. For example, if God were not everything, then there would be something which was not God. Spinoza would regard this as a limitation on God's infinity. God would not be infinite in the sense of being limited, by there being something he was not. Similarly, if God is whatever does, or can do, everything, then God must be all of existence, or the system of existence as a whole. It could not be that something less than the whole did everything which happens.

Because everything which happens follows necessarily from the nature of God, Spinoza thinks that the nature of human beings also follows inevitably from God's essence. As he puts it: 'the essence of man is constituted by certain modes of attributes of God' (Ethics, pp. 45–6). An attribute is a property or characteristic which belongs essentially to something. Attributes are unchanging, and something's having the attributes it has makes it the thing it is. Modes are also properties or characteristics, but they are not essential to a thing's being the thing it is, and they change. 'Mode' is an abbreviation of 'modification', and this helps us remember that a thing's changing qualities are its modes. For example, if thinking is an attribute, then having some thought or other is a mode; and, if being extended is an attribute, then having some particular size or shape is a mode. We are now in a position to understand more precisely the relation between mental and physical on Spinoza's account. He says: 'By "body" [corpus] I understand that mode which expresses in a certain determined manner the essence of God in so far as he is considered as an extended thing' (Ethics, p. 37). So, extension is an attribute of God and one's body is a particular mode of that attribute. Despite the appearance of individuality which one's body has, it is in fact properly understood as a part of nature – as a component of the complete system of what exists – which is also known as 'God'. One's body is 'determined' in this way because its being what it is is a necessary consequence of what God is.

Conversely: 'the human mind is a part of the infinite intellect of God' (Ethics, p. 46). One's own mental life is a mode of one of the two attributes of God: thinking. Despite the appearance of individuality one's own mind has, it is in fact properly understood as part of the divine mind known as 'God' – as a component of the complete system of what exists, which is also known as 'Nature' in so far as it is extended.

People, then, are not substances, and their minds and bodies are not substances. They are modes of the two attributes of God, and He is the only substance. So when Spinoza says 'thinking substance and extended substance are one and the same thing' (Ethics, p. 41), he is talking about God, or Nature. If we wished to talk about the individual person, we could say: the individual who thinks is the individual who has a body, and the individual who has a body is the individual who thinks, so long as we remember that the individual is those mental and physical properties, and they are really parts of God or Nature.

Should we believe any of this? It is a consequence of Spinoza's metaphysics that it is not strictly correct to talk of oneself – that individual who one is – as moving one's body or thinking one's thoughts. God moves your body and God thinks your thoughts. For example:

When we say that the human mind perceives this or that, we say nothing else than that God, not in so far as He is infinite, but in so far as He is explained through the nature of the human mind, or in so far as He constitutes the essence of the human mind, has this or that idea. (Ethics, p. 46)

So when you are thinking, it is really God or the whole of existence which is thinking. We human beings have no free will because our actions are really God's actions, or causal and logical consequences of the whole called 'Nature'.

Finitude

If we are to accept Spinoza's metaphysics, and the place he has allotted to us within it, a great deal more explanation is required. Perhaps most manifestly, Spinoza needs to explain why the appearance of one's own and other people's individuality is so compelling. We each are or have a mind and a body, and yours is not mine and mine is not yours. Why should there be this appearance of individuality and separateness if in fact we are each parts of a single substance of infinite size and infinite intellect? Why, to put it metaphorically, do we not dissolve into the divine mind or infinite space? Spinoza has the makings of an answer to these objections in his definition of 'individual'. He says: 'By "individual things" [res singulares] I understand things which are finite and have a determined existence' (Ethics, p. 38). Human beings are individual things, so if individual things are finite, human beings are finite. Our minds and bodies are in fact finite modes of God's infinite attributes. I take it that it is in our finitude that our individuality and uniqueness consist. Near the beginning of the Ethics Spinoza offers us a definition of 'finite':

That thing is said to be 'finite in its kind' [in suo genere finata] which can be limited by another thing of the same kind. E.g. a body is said to be finite because we can conceive another larger than it. Thus a thought is limited by another thought. But a body cannot be limited by a thought, nor a thought by a body. (Ethics, p. 1)

It follows that we human beings may be limited by other things of the same sort. One's mind is limited by other minds. One's body is limited by other bodies. If we reflect upon what God's infinity consists in for Spinoza, we may recall that not only does God have an infinitely powerful intellect, and not only is God infinitely spatially extended, but God is infinite in the sense that He is all that there is. This is certainly not true of the individual human being. Although God's intellect exhausts or includes ours, ours does not include God's. Although God's extension exhausts or includes ours, ours does not include God's. Indeed, it is the finitude of our intellects – the fact that they are only a part of God's – which prevents them from perceiving clearly that this is what they are.

I have tried not to play down the metaphysical aspects of Spinoza's system or to make it sound more commonsensical than it is. Spinoza is a rationalist, not an empiricist, so he thinks it is by the exercise of pure reason that we may obtain the correct view of the world and our place in it, not just by observation. Despite the importance of pantheism in his system, I think there is much to commend it to someone who wishes to reconcile the reality of human mentality, subjectivity and individuality with the picture of the universe given by modern physics and biology. After all, we are a part of Nature for Spinoza, and, in his theory of the physical world, Spinoza anticipates several tenets of modern physics. He thinks for example that the amount of motion or rest in the universe is always constant, which is close to asserting the law of the conservation of energy. He also thinks physical objects are composed of imperceptible particles, which is not only consistent with, but is also implied by, our sub-atomic physics. The more metaphysical dimensions to his philosophy are likely to appeal more to those who think modern physics cannot give a complete picture of reality and who think that there remain problems about our own conscious existence and our relation to the rest of what exists.

Some theists think Spinoza is an atheist because he denies the existence of a transcendent deity. This, however, is a mistake, if we allow that pantheism is a kind of theism. Atheists may perceive his system as depending on God more than it really does. It seems much less dependent on God if we stress that 'Nature' is another word for God in Spinoza's thinking. This makes Spinoza into a kind of naturalistic philosopher who takes seriously the existence of consciousness in the world and whose doctrines can perhaps even be made consistent with a biological account of the origin of consciousness. Idealists may try to make Spinoza one of their own by emphasizing the attribute of the one substance called 'thought'. Materialists may try to enlist him by stressing the attribute called 'extension'. All of these are however distortions of the whole Spinoza. I call Spinoza a 'neutral monist' because he eschews these extremes and tries to produce a

philosophy by positing a substance which is 'neutral' between
its mental and physical descriptions. I leave the reader with two
of Spinoza's propositions (for 'God' we should perhaps read
'what is'): 'Thought [cogitatio] is an attribute of God, or God is a
thinking thing' (Ethics, p. 38); 'Extension [extensio] is an attribute
of God, or God is an extended thing' (Ethics, p. 39). For Spinoza,
so are we.

RUSSELL

It is Russell's view that ultimately or fundamentally the universe
is composed of events – spatio-temporal items with specific dura-
tions and extensions. Events, in the language of physics, occupy
portions of space–time. Some of these events are describable in
one of two ways, as either mental or physical. Under a physical
description, an event is an object of study for physics. Under a
mental description, an event is an object of study for psychology.

Neutral Monism

Clearly, Russell's theory has something in common with Spinoza's, in that mind and matter are held to be two aspects of some
more fundamental, underlying reality. Like Spinoza, Russell
rejects materialism, idealism and dualism but wishes to preserve
the truths which give plausibility to each of those positions. He
calls his theory 'neutral monism'; it finds a clear expression in his
book, An Outline of Philosophy, and is developed more fully in
his two books, The Analysis of Mind and The Analysis of Matter.
I shall begin by explaining Russell's views in An Outline of
Philosophy and then make some remarks about the other two
books. Here is Russell's own definition of 'neutral monism', in
which he contrasts it with materialism and idealism:

Popular metaphysics divides the world into mind and matter, and a
human being into soul and body. Some – the materialists – have said
that matter alone is real and mind is an illusion. Many – the idealists –
... have taken the opposite view, that mind alone is real and that matter
is an illusion. The view which I have suggested is that both mind and
matter are structures composed of a more primitive stuff which is neither
mental nor material. This view, called 'neutral Monism' is suggested in
Mach's Analysis of Sensations, developed in William James's Essays in

Radical Empiricism, and advocated by John Dewey, as well as by Professor R. B. Perry and other American Realists. The use of the word 'neutral' in this way is due to Dr. H. M. Scheffer of Harvard, who is one of the ablest logicians of our time. (*An Outline of Philosophy*, p. 303)

Philosophically, Plato and Descartes have bequeathed to us a strong distinction between mind and matter – the view that reality is divided in two, and that each of us comprises a mental and a physical substance. Materialists and idealists may be seen as attacking this tendency but, ironically, they do so within a fundamentally Cartesian conceptual framework. Russell is trying to undermine the framework itself and substitute instead his event ontology, based on modern physics. We need not take too seriously Russell's talk of primitive 'stuff' in this passage, because, as we shall see, he thinks it is a mistake to think of the universe as ultimately composed of any kind of substance at all. In fact, his thesis that 'everything in the world is composed of events' (*An Outline of Philosophy*, p. 287) is a premiss in his attack on the traditional notions of mind and matter. This is of considerable importance for the philosophy of mind because, if his criticisms are correct, then idealists and materialists alike are using mistaken notions of mind and matter and their positions are severely compromised. I shall examine Russell's criticisms of the concept of matter first, then turn to the concept of mind.

Matter

The essential sentence in Russell's account of matter is 'A piece of matter, like a space–time point, is to be constructed out of events' (*An Outline of Philosophy*, p. 289). What does this mean? Something is a logical construction out of something if it can be reduced to that thing. In general, if As are logical constructions out of Bs, or if As may be reduced to Bs, then any sentence or set of sentences about As may be translated into a sentence or set of sentences about Bs without loss of meaning. So, Russell is saying that matter is a logical construction out of events, and by this he means that what matter is may be totally explained using the vocabulary of events. We may compare, at one level, this strategy with that of the logical behaviourist and the phenomenalist (see page 117 above). The logical behaviourist maintains that mental events are logical constructions out of dispositions to behave.

The phenomenalist thinks that physical objects are logical constructions out of sense contents. Russell thinks that physical objects are logical constructions out of events. As we shall see, Russell's philosophy of mind is incompatible with logical behaviourism but consistent with a kind of phenomenalism. It has it in common with both these theories to be a kind of reductionism. Matter and mind will be reduced to events neutral between mental and physical descriptions of them.

What is the relationship between the reduction of matter to events and the theories of modern physics? In keeping with his concern to make his philosophy of mind consistent with physics, this is a question Russell is keen to address. Russell is well aware that the physicist uses rather different conceptions of matter for different explanatory purposes; for example, one is used in conjunction with the general theory of relativity to explain gravitation, and there are two possible theories used to explain atomic structure. It is these latter two that Russell concentrates on, as they come closest to the physicist's account of what matter is intrinsically. The first is due to the German physicist Heisenberg, the second emanates from the French physicist De Broglie and the Austrian physicist Schrödinger. The two theories are 'mathematically equivalent' (*An Outline of Philosophy*, p. 289). This means that, when expressed in mathematical language, all the sentences of the one theory are true if and only if all the sentences of the other theory are true. The truth of Heisenberg's theory is necessary for the truth of the De Broglie–Schrödinger theory and vice versa. They logically imply one another, so there is no contradiction between them. The differences between them do not arise at the mathematical level, so, for purposes of explanation within physics, those differences are irrelevant. A choice between them needs to be made only when they are translated into natural language. It then becomes apparent that they imply rather different ontologies – different accounts of what there is.

On the Heisenberg account, a piece of matter is a centre for the emission of radiations – for example, radiations of the energy which makes up light waves. The essential point is however that, although the radiations really exist (they are radiations of energy), what they radiate from does not exist. Rather like a mathematical point, the source of the radiations has no real existence; it is merely postulated for explanatory convenience, like the centre of a geometrician's circle. It follows that matter is just as fictitious as the ideal constructs of the mathematician.

Two other points are worth making about Heisenberg's theory, which are directly relevant to Russell. We have travelled a long way from the idea of matter as a kind of 'stuff' or 'substance' out of which the universe is 'made' or 'composed'. Instead, with the concept of radiating energy, we have adopted an event ontology, so if we ask: what exists?, the most fundamental answer we may provide is 'events'.

On the other theory used to explain atomic structure, the De Broglie–Schrödinger system, matter is analysed as wave motions. Here matter is nothing over and above a changing state of energy, nothing except the motion of energy waves themselves. Russell makes a significant point about this theory. If we ask what the wave motions are motions of, one answer is specifically excluded. We cannot correctly say that they are wave motions of matter. This is on pain of circularity. It we are using the concept of wave-motion to explain what matter is, it would be vacuously circular to try to use the notion of matter to explain what a wave motion is.

Clearly, wave motions are as much events as radiations are, so, whether we choose the Heisenberg theory or the De Broglie–Schrödinger system, Russell's event ontology finds scientific substantiation. As Russell puts it: 'We are led to construct matter out of systems of events, which just happen, and do not happen "to" matter or "to" anything else' (An Outline of Philosophy, p. 289). Russell uses this finding to mount a devastating attack upon the traditional concept of matter. Matter is usually thought of as an impenetrable substance, the external cause of our sensations, and as entering into relations, for example, gravitational fields.

So far as gravity is concerned, the general theory of relativity reduces it to '"crinkles" in space–time' (An Outline of Philosophy, p. 290), so gravity is itself a logical construction out of events, out of what happens. Gravity has no reality independent of certain space–time structures, that is, events.

Nor is matter absolutely permanent. Although it is the third law of thermo-dynamics that the amount of energy in the universe remains constant through all space–time changes, it is now believed that sub-atomic particles may annihilate one another and so utterly cease to exist; for example, under certain conditions an electron and a proton may collide and mutually destruct. If we cling to the idea that electrons and protons are in the traditional sense 'material', then we have to give up one of the traditional properties of matter: indestructibility. If we substitute Russell's view that even these sub-atomic particles are logical constructions out of events, then we may account for such annihilations of them by saying that certain processes or events have ceased.

Nor is matter the cause of our sensations – or, at least, it is extremely misleading to claim this. Russell has an interesting observation on Dr Johnson's attempt to refute Berkeley's idealism in this connection:

Dr Johnson 'disproved' Berkeley's denial of matter by kicking a stone. If he had known that his foot never touched the stone, and that both were only complicated systems of wave motions, he might have been less satisfied with his refutation. (*An Outline of Philosophy*, p. 290)

Berkeley's opponents thought that material substance was the cause of our sensations. Although Russell is not an idealist, he has it in common with Berkeley to deny this. If Russell's ontology is truly scientific, then it follows that Berkeley anticipated the findings of modern physics much more nearly than his materialist critics. Russell does not much mind our calling the causes of our sensations 'material' if this just means they are the events studied by physicists. That is, after all, true. What certainly has to be abandoned is the concept of a physical substance. It will be recalled that, on the Aristotelian account, a substance does not depend upon the existence of anything else for its own existence (see page 22, above). Russell has destroyed the idea that matter is a substance because he has shown that matter depends on events, and depends very closely. The existence of matter depends logically on the existence of events: 'Matter has ceased to be a "thing" and has become merely a mathematical characteristic of the relations between complicated logical structures composed of events' (*An Outline of Philosophy*, p. 290). If these arguments are successful, then we have to give up the idea that matter is an indestructible, permanent and substantial cause of our sensations. It is not even quite right that matter is impenetrable, according to

Russell. Although, clearly and commonsensically, two physical objects cannot occupy each other's spatio-temporal locations, events can, in Russell's words, 'overlap in space–time' (*An Outline of Philosophy*, p. 291). The idea of a spatio-temporal location is itself a construction out of events. Suddenly, in a sense, the world has become a less substantial place.

Mind

If what exists is not fundamentally material, then, on Russell's view, nor is it fundamentally mental either. The concept of mind is subjected to a critique every bit as devastating as that directed against 'matter'. To begin with, Russell points out that the concept of mind is terribly unclear. It does not seem to admit of any precise definition. However, the mental has traditionally been distinguished by a set of characteristics all of which, according to Russell, are defective. The supposed defining characteristics of mind which he criticizes rely on the concepts of perception, introspection, memory and knowledge.

In a sense it is uncontroversial that perceptions (or 'percepts', as Russell calls them) are mental, but he has a special account of what their mentality consists in. It turns out, in fact, that their being mental is their capability of entering into causal relations of the sort which may be studied by psychologists as opposed to physicists. But even if we concede that perceptions are mental, it remains unclear what else is to be subsumed under that concept and what excluded. This in turn is because we do not possess a clear definition of 'mental'. It may be noted, even at this stage of Russell's exposition, that, whatever else percepts are, for Russell they are events, and this is fully consistent with his ontology as outlined so far.

Perhaps memories are mental and the existence of memory is in some way bound up essentially in what minds are. Russell rejects this suggestion because, on his view, it is possible to explain what memory is in largely physical terms, in terms of the theory of conditioned reflexes (*An Outline of Philosophy*, p. 291). Clearly, Russell's neutral monism does not preclude something's being both mental and physical; indeed, it entails it. But it will hardly do to take some faculty or feature which is both physiological and psychological as the hallmark of the mental *qua* mental –

as the mental. Indeed, on Russell's view, 'memory' is really a biological concept which may be correctly used to characterize certain living systems, including some that are not minds. He is perhaps right in this view, if we are entitled to use the word to denote the retention and transmission of, for example, genetic information.

Introspection, on Russell's account, collapses into a sort of knowledge. It is a kind of knowledge by acquaintance or by direct perception and so is best treated as such. I have the impression that Russell is not intellectually happy with this account, but he adopts a view of the mental which employs the concept of direct introspective knowledge. Suppose we are perceiving a physical object; then, on Russell's view, what is really or directly perceived is the sound, colour, shape and size which we attribute to the object. These contents of perception are called by Russell 'sense data'. He is quite clear in his writing that sense data are neither mental nor physical. However, in so far as a person may introspectively know what he or she is perceiving, he or she is directly acquainted with sense data, and this is a kind of knowing. Anything which is a possible item of knowledge by introspection counts as mental for Russell. We need to be clear that sense data are not mental in themselves. They count as mental only because a certain kind of knowledge is possible of them: introspective knowledge by acquaintance. Russell calls the event which is the act of acquaintance itself a 'knowledge reaction' (*An Outline of Philosophy*, p. 291) and concludes, 'events to which a knowledge reaction of this sort occurs are "mental"' (ibid.).

Russell supplements this account with another which is also designed to distinguish the mental from the non-mental. He says 'mental events are events in a living brain' (*An Outline of Philosophy*, p. 292). As it stands, this is not a tremendously helpful definition even if in the end it turns out to be correct. It precludes two possibilities: it rules out the possibility that there should be mental events in things that are not brains, for example Cartesian minds and electronic computers; and it does not allow for the possibility that there might be events in brains that are not mental events (at least if the claim is intended as a definition of 'mental'). It may be that Russell, and perhaps the reader, would like to rule out at least the first two possibilities – about Cartesian

minds and computers – but, if so, some arguments need to be
produced; it is not enough to make certain things impossible just
as a matter of definition.

Russell is, I think, quite aware of these difficulties, and he
supplements his account accordingly. It is his view that the knowledge reaction and its objects are events in brains; in addition, in
explaining what sort of thing a brain is, we have to remember that
Russell has a special account of what it is for something to be
physical.

On the second of these points he says 'events in the brain are
nu` to be regarded as motions of bits of matter' (*An Outline of
Philosophy*, p. 292). On the contrary, the very idea of matter in
motion depends upon the prior concept of an event. So we should
understand the brain in terms of events, and not ask the question,
whether those events are merely or intrinsically mental or physical. They can be both or either, depending on their causal relations.

On the earlier point, about mental events being in the brain,
certain brain events count as mental just because the introspective knowledge reaction is possible towards them. This
leads to the commonsensically paradoxical but, for Russell, true
conclusion that:

When we have a percept, just what we perceive . . . is an event occupying
part of the region which, for physics, is occupied by the brain . . . what
we perceive is part of the stuff of our brains, not part of the stuff of
tables, chairs, sun, moon and stars. (*An Outline of Philosophy*, p. 292)

Notice that Russell is not merely claiming that our perceptions
are parts of our brains but that those things we directly perceive
are parts of our brains. He is led to this view by the claim that
the objects of the knowledge reaction are mental, and mental
events are events in the brain.

In understanding Russell's neutral monism we need to keep
firmly in mind that any of the events we are calling 'mental' may
also be given a physical description. They may be described
either in terms of psychology or in terms of physics. To make this
clearer I shall conclude this section on Russell by saying a little
more about his concept of a 'sense datum'.

Sense Data

A sense datum (plural: 'sense data') is anything with which we may be directly acquainted in perception: a colour, a shape, a smell and so on. Russell says about the sense datum: 'It is neither mental nor physical' (*An Outline of Philosophy*, p. 217). He means that sense data are not intrinsically mental or physical. They may be either mental or physical, depending on the sorts of relations they enter into with other events. He says 'the datum is a datum equally for physics and for psychology' (*An Outline of Philosophy*, p. 217). This means that one and the same event, a sense datum, may be studied by both disciplines. For example, a colour may be studied by a psychologist in so far as it is an object of perception. That very same colour may be studied by a physicist in terms, for example, of the length of its light waves. Similarly, a smell may be studied by a psychologist as smelled, but by the physicist as a collection of atoms and molecules. The sense datum is 'neutral' between mental and physical descriptions. It is described by Russell as the meeting point' of physics and psychology (*An Outline of Philosophy*, p. 217). Just as a name on a list is not intrinsically in alphabetical order or in some other order of precedence, so a sense datum is not intrinsically mental or physical. Names on lists are in alphabetical order only through their relations with other names. Similarly, events are mental or physical only in relation to other events. More precisely, events count as physical in so far as physicists subsume them under causal laws for the purposes of explanations in physics. Events count as mental in so far as psychologists subsume them under psychological laws for purposes of explanation in psychology. In themselves the events are neither mental nor physical:

> 'Mind' and 'mental' are merely approximate concepts, giving a convenient shorthand for certain approximate causal laws. In a completed science, the word 'mind' and the word 'matter' would both disappear, and would be replaced by causal laws concerning events. (*An Outline of Philosophy*, p. 292)

What are we to say about Russell's neutral monism? It is not too wide of the mark to say it is Spinozism with theology replaced by physics. If we are to criticize this theory, then the following might be adduced. Does it really make sense to claim that there are events – happenings – but nothing that these happen to (see page 164, above)? It seems counter-intuitive in the extreme to maintain that things happen but not to anything, or that events exist but they are not made out of any kind of substance, material or mental. By 'counter-intuitive' I mean that it does not accord with our pre-philosophical or pre-scientific beliefs. Russell might well counter this by saying that, from the fact that something does not accord with common sense, it does not follow that it is false.

An objection might be brought against the suggestion that what we perceive in the ordinary course of our waking lives is really a part of our own brain. Again, this seems extremely counter-intuitive. If Russell is to convince us of these controversial conclusions, then he needs to account for our commonsensical view that the world is composed of some sort of substance and that we perceive things in the external world directly – not merely portions of our own brains. Indeed, he needs to show that common sense is grossly mistaken.

In favour of Russell's neutral monism, it can be said that it eschews the extremes of idealism and materialism without commitment to mind–body dualism. At least someone who finds those three theories defective will find that a merit of neutral monism. Also, it is arguably to Russell's credit that he takes such pains to keep abreast of the complexities of recent science and tries not to make claims which are grossly inconsistent with modern physics. This will be perceived as a merit by those readers who share Russell's respect for the sciences and his ideal of a unified science. Materialists may be disconcerted by Russell's thesis that materialism is to be rejected because it is incompatible with science.

STRAWSON

The philosophy of mind of Sir Peter Strawson is not usually called 'neutral monism', but I think it warrants that title because it includes the view that our use of the two concepts, 'mental' and 'physical', depends upon our being able to use the more primitive or fundamental concept of a 'person'. Strawson aims to produce a position which casts doubt on mind–body dualism, yet which recognizes that persons have both mental and physical properties. What is precluded is any starting point in philosophy, which explains what a person is, using 'mental' and 'physical'. Rather, the philosophical priorities are reversed. We already have to possess the concept of a person – the concept of oneself and other persons – in order to make sense of the distinction between mental and physical. In this way the Cartesian ontology of the person is undermined using linguistic premises; premises about the parts of our conceptual scheme which include 'person', 'mind' and 'material object'.

Strawson's account of how our thinking about mental and physical is possible is chapter three of his book *Individuals: An Essay in Descriptive Metaphysics*. Descriptive metaphysics describes the functioning of our conceptual scheme as it is. Strawson contrasts this with 'revisionary' metaphysics, which recommends we alter our conceptual scheme. On this view, Berkeley and Plato would arguably come out as revisionary metaphysicians, Ryle and Wittgenstein as descriptive. The distinction is rather tendentious in that it is possible for most philosophers to be ascribed either status, pejoratively or not. Strawson, as the sub-title of his book suggests, conceives of himself as a descriptive not a revisionary metaphysician. We should bear in mind this claim in what follows and try to decide whether Strawson is in fact altering and revising our concept of a person, or whether he is merely making explicit the logic of the concept of a person which we actually possess. An important problem I shall not address is the sociological scope of 'we' here.

Material Particulars

A central contention of *Individuals* is that, unless we could identify physical objects, we could not identify anything else. For example, unless we had the concept of a physical object, we could not have the concept of any property of a physical object, and we could not have the concept of any mental state. Of course we do have the concepts of the various properties of a physical object, and we are able to identify mental states. But this feature of our conceptual scheme is logically parasitic, according to Strawson, on our being able to identify and re-identify physical objects (or 'material particulars', as he calls them). I shall not examine Strawson's arguments for this rather materialistic thesis. I refer the interested reader to the first two chapters of Strawson's book; I mention it here because it features as a premiss in Strawson's arguments about persons.

The account of persons proper begins with the making of a fundamental self/not-self distinction. Each of us distinguishes the world into two mutually exclusive and collectively exhaustive portions: the part that one is and the remainder which one is not. The philosophical problems are how the making of this distinction is possible, what the grounds are for maintaining it and for our drawing it in just the way we do. Indeed, there is a difficulty about how we can have a concept of self at all. If we reflect for a moment upon the nature of our experience, it is noticeable that lots of different sorts of items fall within it. We perceive physical objects and other people, and we have various moods, thoughts and emotions. The question is, how one can come to have an idea of oneself as the 'owner' of all those experiences, as opposed to being simply another object which is to be met with within one's experience. How can a person have the idea of himself or herself as the subject of experience? As Strawson puts it: 'If it is just an item within his experience of which he has this idea, how can it be the idea of that which has all of his experiences?' (*Individuals*, p. 89).

That is the question about the existence of the subject. There is in addition a question about the nature of the subject. Strawson notes that we talk about persons in radically different sorts of ways. We talk about ourselves as, for example, weighing so many kilograms, being in the drawing-room, lying on the sofa, but also as thinking, remembering or feeling such and such. This generates the question as to why we ascribe states of consciousness to the very same thing as we ascribe physical characteristics. So now we have a number of questions; but the two Strawson concentrates upon are: 'Why are one's states of consciousness ascribed to anything at all?' (*Individuals*, p. 90) (that is the question about the existence of the subject) and 'Why are they ascribed to the very same thing as certain corporeal characteristics ...?' (*Individuals*, p. 90) (that is the question about the nature of the subject).

It is interesting to note that Strawson thinks questions about subjectivity and objectivity are in a sense prior to the mind–body problem: the problem of what the relation is between mental and

physical. In this (if in little else) he has something in common
with Hegel, Sartre and Merleau-Ponty and, as we have seen, the
view may be strongly discerned in the writings of William James.
Strawson's project is to answer the two questions he has set
himself in a way that does not commit us to mind–body dualism
but which, indeed, provides us with a clear and non-dualistic
understanding of what a person is or, at least, how the concept,
'person', functions in our conceptual scheme.

Strawson considers three accounts of the self that might be
thought to provide answers to his questions, and he repudiates
each in turn. They are the view that one has a necessary relation
to one's body, the view that one's body is conjoined with a
Cartesian mind or soul, and the view that, in a sense, there is no
self or 'owner' of experience. We examine them next in that
order.

Three Theories of the Self

The view that one is one's body, or at least that one body in
particular has a necessary and unique role to play as the subject
of one's experiences, is criticized by way of a thought experiment.
Strawson invites us to note that the ways in which one's experiences depend upon one's body are many and complex; for
example, empirical facts about one's anatomical make-up, the
functioning of one's sense organs, and the location of one's body
all determine the nature of one's experience. Indeed, in principle
(and this is the thought experiment) the experience of a single
subject could be determined by facts about more than one body.
For example, what a subject sees could, logically, be the joint
result of facts about, say, three separate bodies: where one of
them is, whether the eyes of another are open, and the direction
in which yet another is orientated. Of course Strawson is not
claiming that our actual experience is like this, nor is he claiming
that it is empirically possible that it should be. All he needs is
this logical possibility to point out that it is a contingent fact that
one has just the body one has: a fact that could without contradiction be maintained to be otherwise.

Although one could in principle have had a body which is not
the one one in fact has, it remains true for Strawson that just one
body plays a unique role in determining the course of each

person's experience. For example, for each person there is just one body such that if that body is injured then that body, and only that body, feels pain. A person is causally dependent upon one body in particular for the experiences he or she has, and that person may experience just that body in ways which are impossible for that person to experience other bodies. So each person's body is a unique sort of object of experience for that person.

By describing the relation between oneself and one's body in these ways, Strawson achieves two important philosophical objectives. By making the relation between experience and a particular body a causal one rather than a logical one, Strawson gives a reason for his view that the relation between a particular person and a particular body is a contingent one, not a necessary one. Also, Strawson has so far deliberately eschewed two customary ways of speaking about a person's relation to his or her body. He has not talked about a person being his or her body, and he has not talked about a person 'having' or 'owning' his or her body. There is some merit in this philosophical restraint, because it is not clear what 'I am my body' and 'I have a body' may mean. They are blanket claims which hide philosophical complexities, and it is part of Strawson's purpose in the remainder of his chapter to decide the meaning and plausibility of these claims.

First, however, it has to be decided whether drawing attention to the uniqueness of each person's body to that person helps resolve the two philosophical questions, about how we may have the concept of a subject, and of a subject which is both mental and physical. Strawson decides absolutely that it does not. Although facts about the relationship between oneself and one's body may help to explicate what it means for one to call a body 'mine', it does not go any way to showing how I can have a concept of 'myself'. Indeed, the concept of self would seem to be presupposed in any talk of some body's being mine. Nor do the remarks of a person's relation to his or her body go any way towards explaining why states of consciousness are ascribed to the very same thing as physical characteristics.

We may turn now to the other two conceptions of the self which Strawson considers. The first of these is the Cartesian view that, in a sense, there are two subjects: a mental one and a physical one. As we saw in Chapter 1, the Cartesian view is that a person comprises two and only two distinct substances. One is the bearer of mental properties and the other is the bearer of physical properties, and no property of one is a property of the other. The second is the so called 'no-ownership' view of the self. It is possible that Ludwig Wittgenstein and the logical positivist Moritz Schlick were no-ownership theorists, at least for a time. It is the thesis that it is a mistake to think that one's states of consciousness are 'ascribed' to anything at all – with, perhaps, the possible exception of one's body. This is partly because it is an illusion that there is an irreducibly subjective and mental 'owner' of mental states, partly because it makes sense to speak of 'owning' or 'possessing' only when it makes sense to speak of 'losing' or 'ceasing to own'. On this view, it just about makes sense to ascribe mental states to a body because such a body might in principle not have had those states, but it does not make sense to ascribe such states to any subject such that it is logically or necessarily true that that subject has those states.

The difficulty with the no-ownership theory is that it makes use of the very notion of ownership it seeks to deny. It can be formulated only by saying all 'one's' experiences are really states of a certain body, or 'my' experiences are owned by a pure subject, or by using similarly possessive expressions. The theory is therefore self-refuting. The difficulty with the Cartesian view is how we are ever able to ascribe states of consciousness to other persons if they have private Cartesian minds. On the Cartesian view, one's states of consciousness are not ascribed to the very same thing as certain physical properties, but to Cartesian minds. But if that is the case, it seems impossible that we should be able to identify and re-identify such minds in order to ascribe properties to them at all. It follows that the no-ownership theorist and the Cartesian are equally unable to explain how we can have a concept of self at all, and how we may have the concept of a single subject with both mental and physical characteristics.

Persons

We may turn now to Strawson's own positive account of what a person is, and the ways in which he overcomes the shortcomings he perceives in the rival theories. A central part of his explanation of how it is possible to have a concept of oneself as a subject of experience is this:

> It is a necessary condition of one's ascribing states of consciousness, experiences, to oneself, in the way one does, that one should also ascribe them, or be prepared to ascribe them to others who are not oneself. (*Individuals*, p. 99)

A necessary condition is a prerequisite, or something that has to be the case in order for something else to be possible; so Strawson is saying, unless one were able to ascribe mental states to others, one would not be able to ascribe them to oneself. Notice that this is in a sense a reversal of the Cartesian order of priorities. A Cartesian would argue that one learns the meanings of mental concepts like 'pain' and 'thinking' from one's own case and extrapolates to third-person cases from one's own example. Strawson is saying that the opposite is the case. Unless we could use psychological concepts to mention the mental states of others, we could not use them to mention our own mental states.

Why does Strawson hold this view? The answer lies in the concept of a concept. Someone has the concept of something – call it X – if they are able to identify and re-identify Xs, or cases of X. They must be able to distinguish Xs from non-Xs and recognize Xs as Xs. If someone cannot do this, then they cannot truly be said to have the concept of X. If this is what a concept is, then there cannot be a concept which in principle applies to only one thing. It must be logically possible to apply the concept to more than one thing, to the range of things which fall under that concept.

It follows that the concept of a state of consciousness must be applicable to more than one thing and, if that is right, states of consciousness cannot be applicable just to oneself. There must be a range of things to which we apply states of consciousness. This is why the possibility of third-person ascriptions makes possible first-person ascriptions, and why Strawson feels entitled to the first two parts of this conclusion:

> One can ascribe states of consciousness to oneself only if one can ascribe them to others. One can ascribe them to others only if one can identify other subjects of experience. And one cannot identify them only as

subjects of experience, possessors of states of consciousness. (*Individuals*, p. 100)

The last part of this conclusion, that we cannot identify subjects of experience only as subjects of experience, is consistent with two important Strawsonian theses. First, it will be recalled that Strawson thinks we may identify anything which is not a material particular only if we are able to identify material particulars. Subjects of experience, considered as such, are not material particulars, and states of consciousness are not material particulars. It follows that we may identify subjects of experience and states of consciousness only if we may identify material particulars. This is consistent with the view that we may identify persons as subjects of mental states because we may identify and re-identify their bodies. This is a highly anti-Cartesian train of thought and leaves open Strawson's view of the person as that to which both mental and physical characteristics are ascribable. The Cartesian cannot cogently concede this while maintaining a substance dualism, because the Cartesian is committed to the view that one has the concept of oneself as a subject of experience only from one's own example; but that is ruled out if the first part of Strawson's conclusion is correct.

We are now in a position to appreciate the next stage of Strawson's account. He says the concept of a person is 'logically primitive'. Being logically primitive is a relation, and Strawson means that the concept of a person is logically primitive with regard to the concept of the individual consciousness. It follows that we could not identify individual consciousness unless we already had the prior notion of the whole person as that which possesses both mental and physical properties. Mind–body dualism is thinkable, but this is only because it is false. The thought of oneself as comprised of a mental and a physical substance is parasitic upon the thought of oneself as a whole person with both mental and physical attributes.

This thesis enables Strawson to re-examine the two questions about the subject. He claims that we may have a concept of the subject only if we have the concept of a person:

A necessary condition of states of consciousness being ascribed at all is that they should be ascribed to the very same things as certain corporeal characteristics, a certain physical situation etc. (*Individuals*, p. 102)

Now at this point it might be thought that Strawson is a kind of materialist. We might call him a 'conceptual materialist' because we may have the concepts of subjectivity and mentality only if we have the concept of a material particular. He certainly has it in common with the materialists to reject Cartesian dualism. However, we need to take seriously the role of the person in Strawson's claims. He defines 'person' in this way:

What I mean by the concept of a person is the concept of a type of entity such that both predicates ascribing states of consciousness and predicates ascribing corporeal characteristics, a physical situation etc. are equally applicable to a single individual of that single type. (*Individuals*, p. 102)

We have to distinguish the question, what a person is for Strawson, from the question, how we may identify persons and their mental states. These questions are interrelated but they are by no means the same question. We may identify persons only if we may identify their bodies. We may distinguish one person as a subject of experience from another only because we may distinguish their bodies by their physical locations and characteristics. However, if we ask what a person is for Strawson, then it is clear that there is a symmetry between the mental and physical characteristics. The symmetry is as follows. He says that physical and mental characteristics are equally applicable to persons. He does not allocate any ontological priority to the physical over mental or mental over physical in the explanation of what a person is. This makes Strawson much more of a neutral monist than a materialist. A person is that to which both mental and physical concepts apply, rather as Spinoza's one substance could be subsumed under both mental and physical concepts, or Russell's events could be described as either mental or physical, depending on their causal relations. All three think there is something which it makes sense to call both mental and physical.

So if we ask what the subject of consciousness is, then Strawson's answer is: the whole person. If we ask how it can be that mental and physical characteristics may be ascribed to one and the same entity, then his reply is that a person is precisely that to which both mental and physical terms apply. In particular it is a mistake to think that there is a pure consciousness or ego as subject of consciousness, and it is a mistake to think that there is no subject of consciousness at all.

Two Kinds of Predicate

Strawson's concept of a person is in fact richer than the one described so far. To appreciate it, we have to understand a distinction he makes between two kinds of predicate. A predicate is a word or string of words used to ascribe a property or characteristic to something. Predicates are adjectival expressions. Strawson claims that commonsensically the predicates we use to ascribe properties to persons fall into two broad categories. First, there are those we ascribe to ordinary physical objects, the ones we use to say that an object has a particular weight, a certain spatial location, and so on. Strawson calls these 'M predicates'. (Perhaps 'M' is an abbreviation of 'material'.) Secondly, there are those predicates we use to ascribe properties only to persons, such as 'is smiling', 'is going for a walk' and so on (*Individuals*, p. 104). These are called 'P predicates' (where perhaps 'P' abbreviates 'person'). M predicates would seem comparatively straightforward. But what are P predicates? The answer is that, if a P predicate applies to something, then that thing is conscious. Some P predicates, like 'is in pain', directly ascribe states of consciousness, but others, like 'is smiling', do not; but in both cases, if the predicate truly applies, then it logically follows that what it is ascribed to is capable of consciousness. P predicates imply the possession of consciousness (*Individuals*, p. 105).

If we conjoin the distinction between P predicates and M predicates with Strawson's thesis that it is a necessary condition of ascribing states of consciousness to oneself that one be prepared to ascribe them to others, then the way is open for a new line of attack on Cartesianism. It cannot be that we learn how to ascribe P predicates only from our own case, otherwise that would violate Strawson's thesis. But that means we must be able to use P predicates to make third-person ascriptions; but if that is right, then that use of P predicates depends upon observing other persons' behaviour. This is in fact Strawson's view. He uses

Wittgenstein's word 'criterion' to describe the conditions under which it is appropriate to employ a certain predicate. In the case of third-person ascriptions using P predicates, the criteria are behavioural. To make this clearer, take, for example, 'is in pain', which is a P predicate. According to Strawson, it is impossible to acquire the use of this expression from one's own case. One needs in addition acquaintance with the pain behaviour of others; this provides criteria for the use of 'is in pain'. Of course Strawson is not denying that in certain cases there might be pains but no pain behaviour or pain behaviour but no pains; but it could not always be like that, otherwise the predicate could have no meaning. It is not as though pain behaviour is a mere sign of pain. It is largely constitutive of the conditions under which 'is in pain' may have a use.

This train of thought is deeply anti-Cartesian because it makes third-person ascriptions conditions for first-person ascriptions. Descartes' philosophy, as we have seen, is intensely first-personal. It is the Cartesian view that psychological concepts primarily take on meaning from one's own case, and are then extrapolated to third-person cases. For Strawson, the extrapolation is in the other direction. The logical order of priorities is reversed.

There is a milder reading of Strawson which understands him as establishing a kind of symmetry between first- and third-person uses of psychological concepts. It is partly his view – surely correct – that when you say you are depressed or in pain, and when I say these things, we do not use the words in different senses (even though the reference is clearly different between the two cases). It is also his view, however, that depression and pain are partly felt and partly shown, partly undergone and partly exhibited in behaviour:

To put the point – with a certain unavoidable crudity – in terms of one particular concept of this class, say, that of depression. We speak of behaving in a depressed way (of depressed behaviour) and we also speak of feeling depressed (of a feeling of depression). One is inclined to argue that feelings can be felt but not observed, and behaviour can be observed but not felt, and that therefore there must be room to drive in a logical wedge. But the concept of depression spans the place where one wants to drive it in. (*Individuals*, p. 108)

This passage is interesting and important because it strongly implies a repudiation of not only Cartesianism but also of logical behaviourism. Strawson is suggesting, not only could there not be depression if depression was never shown, but there could not be depression if depression was never felt. It is as though both first-person experience and the third-person behavioural criteria are necessary for the concept of depression to have a use. If this is right, then Strawson has done something to adjudicate between the Cartesian and the logical behaviourist. He allows the logical behaviourist behavioural criteria and the Cartesian the contents of consciousness, but does not allow either to diminish the importance of the other's contribution. Hence: 'X's depression is something, one and the same thing, which is felt, but not observed, by X, and observed but not felt by others than X' (*Individuals*, p. 109). The Cartesian implies a certain autonomy for self-ascriptive uses of what Strawson is calling 'P predicates'. The logical behaviourist implies a similar autonomy for third-person uses of the same sort of predicate. In fact each type of use depends upon the other, so there is no room for scepticism about other minds or for the reduction of minds to behaviour:

It is not seen that these predicates could not have either aspect of their use, the self-ascriptive or the non-self-ascriptive, without having the other aspect. Instead, one aspect of their use is taken as self-sufficient, which it could not be, and then the other aspect appears problematical. So we oscillate between philosophical scepticism and philosophical behaviourism. (*Individuals*, p. 109)

If such is the force of Strawson's theory for Cartesianism and logical behaviourism, what is its importance for dualism specifically, and the possibility of disembodied existence?

How is Dualism Thinkable?

The problem for dualism, according to Strawson's theory, is that, if we were Cartesian minds, our existences would be utterly private to one another. We would have no way of identifying one another as minds or subjects of consciousness. Strawson concedes that we may think dualism, but that is only because we are equipped with the concept of the person as a whole. It is that which enables us to individuate or pick out subjects of consciousness. It seems then that mind–body dualism is conceivable only because it is not true.

So far as disembodied existence is concerned, this is not absolutely or logically impossible on Strawson's account – although the final two pages of the chapter on persons in *Individuals* have, I suspect, more than a touch of irony. His point is that it is not difficult to conceive of oneself as disembodied – and I think Strawson is right about that. You have to imagine experiences, just like the ones you are having now, continuing – except there is no experience of your body: your body, for example, does not feature in your visual field. Also, you have no power to initiate changes in the world around you.

However, such a disembodied existence is thinkable only because we are persons: entities to which both mental and physical predicates apply. The conceptual apparatus used to imagine disembodied existence is drawn from, is parasitic upon, its ordinary use as described by Strawson. It is just about intelligible to say that a person who was embodied may become disembodied; but, again, this kind of talk depends upon our being persons in Strawson's sense. But, according to Strawson, a disembodied being would soon lose any sense of self, being unable to engage with the physical world; and so the sense of 'person' in that context would soon be lost; it was, after all, dependent upon the fact that we are persons.

7

THE PHENOMENOLOGICAL VIEW

Phenomenology is the attempt to produce presuppositionless descriptions of the contents of experience, without any prior commitment to the objective reality of those contents. This procedure has two goals. It is hoped to exhibit the perennial features of human thought and perception – their 'essences' – and it is hoped to 'ground' all other kinds of inquiry. Phenomenologists frequently maintain that phenomenology is prior to any other kind of inquiry. It demonstrates the possibility of other inquiries, including philosophy, by showing how all knowledge is made possible by experience. Thus phenomenology may be correctly viewed as an extreme form of empiricism, because empiricism is the doctrine that all knowledge is derived from experience; but it may also be viewed as a kind of Cartesianism, because it tries to place the whole of our knowledge upon secure, indubitable foundations; and it may be viewed as a kind of Kantianism, because it is partly an attempt to show how knowledge is possible. Because of this feature it is sometimes called a kind of 'transcendental' philosophy. These three ways of thinking of phenomenology are complementary, not mutually inconsistent, and I think each provides a strong strain in the movement.

It will be apparent that phenomenology is not straightforwardly an ontology of the mind in the sense in which, say, materialism and idealism are. Nor is phenomenology in any interesting sense a 'theory'; rather, it is a practice. It is the practice of observing and characterizing the contents of experience just as they appear to consciousness, with a view to capturing their essential features. Thus, although phenomenologists usually aspire to a rigour of expression in philosophical language, it is fair to say that doing phenomenology requires an almost aesthetic or artistic ability to contemplate the qualities of one's experience.

Phenomenology is primarily a German- and French-speaking movement in modern philosophy. Its principal exponents have been the German philosopher and psychologist, Franz Brentano, whose most important work *Psychology From an Empirical Standpoint* was published in 1874, the German philosopher, Edmund Husserl, whose phenomenological writings are voluminous and include *Logical Investigations* (1900–1), *Ideas* (1913) and *Cartesian Meditations* (1929), and the most profound thinker of the three Germans (and, some would say, of the twentieth century) the philosopher Martin Heidegger. Heidegger was Husserl's most brilliant student, but his celebrated 1927 work *Being and Time* exhibits such originality as to constitute the break with Husserl's phenomenology that Heidegger intended it to be. Heidegger replaced that phenomenology with what he calls 'fundamental ontology': a philosophical inquiry into the meaning of being, a study of what it is to be.

The salient French exponents of phenomenology are Jean-Paul Sartre and Maurice Merleau-Ponty. Sartre is as well known as a novelist, playwright and left-wing political polemicist as he is as a philosopher. Merleau-Ponty too was on the Left in politics and shared with Sartre a version of existentialism: a radical and practical brand of philosophizing which gave priority to questions of human existence such as anxiety, relations with others, death and political commitment, over questions of epistemology and metaphysics. In its obsession with action over cognition, existentialism is a partial reaction against phenomenology which incorporates many of the fundamental ontological insights of *Being and Time*. The two French works which are classics of the phenomenological movement are Sartre's *Being and Nothingness* (1943) and Merleau-Ponty's *Phenomenology of Perception* (1945). These works are syntheses of phenomenological and existentialist thinking.

The two phenomenologists I have selected for study in this chapter are Brentano and Husserl. I shall concern myself with their work only in so far as it bears on the mind–body problem, but before turning to that I shall say something about the central concepts of Husserl's phenomenology. When people think of phenomenology, it is paradigmatically Husserl's brand of it they have in mind.

The most important distinction for understanding Husserl's phenomenology is that between the so-called natural attitude and transcendental subjectivity. The world of the natural attitude is the everyday, common-sense world which we inhabit when we are not practising phenomenology. It is full of physical objects and other people, and I am one of those people. The world of transcendental subjectivity is that same world, but viewed phenomenologically. It is the world as I directly experience it when I have suspended all belief in the objective reality or causal relations of the objects of my awareness. Husserl calls this suspension of belief the 'transcendental reduction' or sometimes the 'epoche' ('*epoche*' is the Greek for 'suspension of belief'). It is important to note that Husserl is not committing himself to a Berkeley-style idealism by the imposition of the epoche. Husserl does not deny that the external world of physical objects and other minds in causal interaction exists; he merely suspends this belief to do phenomenology. We can understand this by making a distinction between disbelieving something and not believing something. For phenomenological purposes, Husserl does not believe in the external world, but he does not disbelieve in the external world either. He leaves the question open.

The result of the epoche is the phenomenological presentation of the ego and the life of consciousness. Rather like Descartes, Husserl endorses the view that I could in principle continue to exist even if there were no external world. Clearly, however, 'I' can no longer denote a thinking, living human being with a body. I too have been transformed by the phenomenological reduction. I exist as a bare, subjective precondition for experience. Phenomenologically I am a transcendental ego.

From the phenomenological standpoint, certain fundamental structures of consciousness are exposed. Perhaps the most important of these is the distinction between a mental act and its content, or the 'noesis' and the 'noema'. The noema is what is perceived, what is remembered, and so on; but the noesis is the actual act of perceiving or the actual act of remembering. This distinction is not revealed within the natural attitude. It is available only to phenomenological reflection. Once the phenomenological reduction is carried out, the essential structures of consciousness may be discerned a priori by such reflection.

In what follows, considerable emphasis is given to the doctrine of intentionality. The intentionality of the mental is its alleged property of being directed towards some object or some content. Thus, all perception is perception of something or other, all hating is hating something, all fearing is fearing something, and similarly for all the other possible kinds of mental state. What is thought, feared or perceived is the intentional object of the mental act. Such intentional objects do not have to exist mind-independently in order for mental acts to exhibit this alleged feature. The idea of intentionality is not original to the phenomenologists; it is to be found in the writings of the medieval scholastics. However, it is of central importance for the way in which Brentano thinks the distinction is drawn between mental phenomena and physical phenomena. It is to Brentano that we should now turn.

BRENTANO

The interest of Brentano's work for the mind–body problem lies largely in his attempt to find a clear line of demarcation between the mental and the physical. His sharpest and most sustained treatment of this problem is in Chapter 1, Book 2, of his work *Psychology From an Empirical Standpoint*, called 'The distinction between mental and physical phenomena'. Brentano examines several definitions of 'mental' which, in differing degrees, he finds deficient, before deciding upon a solution he finds wholly satisfactory. We may follow the course of Brentano's arguments in this chapter and so trace the trains of reasoning which lead him to his own solution to the problem.

Brentano begins by noting that we possess an intuitive or pre-philosophical distinction between mental and physical phenomena but that this is not drawn in a precise way. We are in some sense aware of both the mental and the physical: 'All the data of our consciousness are divided into two great classes – the class of the physical and the class of mental phenomena' (*Psychology From an Empirical Standpoint*, p. 77). The problem is that the meanings of the two words, 'mental' and 'physical', are not clear, so we do not possess a strict criterion for distinguishing mental and physical. He describes his project as follows: 'Our aim is to clarify the meaning of the two terms "physical phenomenon" and "mental phenomenon"' (*Psychology From an Empirical Standpoint*, p. 78). In what follows we should try to decide whether he succeeds.

Mental and Physical Phenomena

Brentano's first attempt at marking the mental/physical distinction is the amassing of examples of mental and physical phenomena. It might be thought that this is a question-begging procedure because, surely, Brentano must already be in possession of a mental/physical distinction to decide which examples belong to which class. In fact the procedure is less question-begging than it sounds. He has already conceded that we mark the distinction commonsensically, and Brentano may be thought of as making more precise a distinction we already have. In any case, there is a difference between, on the one hand, possessing the ability to distinguish As from Bs and, on the other hand, being able to state explicitly what the difference is between an A and a B. Brentano's view is that we can, by and large, distinguish mental from physical phenomena, but we are as yet unable to formulate precisely what this distinction consists in.

Brentano provides us with the following examples of mental phenomena: 'hearing a sound', 'seeing a coloured object', 'feeling warmth or cold', 'the thinking of a general concept' (*Psychology From an Empirical Standpoint*, p. 79) and he claims that all the 'states of imagination' are mental phenomena (ibid.). On top of this:

Every judgement, every recollection, every expectation, every inference, every conviction or opinion is a mental phenomenon. Also to be included under this term is every emotion: joy, sorrow, fear, hope, courage, despair, act of will, intention, astonishment, admiration, contempt etc. (*Psychology From an Empirical Standpoint*, p. 79)

These examples are contrasted by Brentano with the following physical phenomena:

A colour, a figure, a landscape which I see, a chord which I hear, warmth, cold, odour which I sense; as well as similar images which appear in the imagination. (*Psychology From an Empirical Standpoint*, p. 80)

It is worth pointing out that Brentano's choice of examples perhaps accords more with his own developed idea of the mental/physical distinction than it does with common sense. For example, it is not clear that images which appear in the imagination would count as physical to the person who had not reflected philosophically (or, indeed, to many who had). It is also notable that the examples of physical phenomena are colour as seen, a chord as heard, and so on. Brentano speaks in this way because he is distinguishing different sorts of phenomena, that is, appearances; but it is clear that the demarcation between mental and physical is already roughly between an act of consciousness and the object towards which that act is directed. The act of awareness is a mental phenomenon but the content or the object of the act is physical. It is because this criterion is implicitly already at work here that the images in our imaginations are classified as physical.

Presentations

Brentano realizes that an inventory of examples does not amount to a definition, and he makes an attempt to make explicit the criterion for distinguishing mental from physical presupposed by his choice of examples. He decides on this: 'The term "mental phenomenon" applies to presentations, as well as to all the phenomena which are based on presentations' (*Psychology From an Empirical Standpoint*, p. 80). We need to know now exactly what Brentano means by 'presentation , since this term is working as the name of the hallmark of the mental at this point in the text. A clue is given when he says: 'Every idea or presentation which we acquire either through sense perception or imagination is an example of a mental phenomenon' (*Psychology From an Empirical Standpoint*, pp. 78–9). There are at least two ways of reading this. Brentano could be using the terms 'idea' and 'presentation' interchangeably so that, if something is acquired by sensation or imagination, then that could be called by two names, 'idea' or 'presentation'. Or, on the other reading, there are two sorts of acquisition possible through sense and imagination: ideas and presentations. Whichever account is intended, this much is clear: 'By presentation, I do not mean that which is presented, but rather the act of presentation' (*Psychology From an Empirical*

Standpoint, p. 79). Brentano is making a distinction between a mental act and its content; for example, if you hear a sound, then two components are to be distinguished: the sound and your hearing of it. The sound is the object of your awareness, but the hearing is your awareness of it. If you are seeing a colour or a shape, the colour or the shape is the object or content of your awareness; but this is not the same as your seeing, which is the awareness of the colour or shape. Brentano reserves the term 'presentation' to denote the awareness of an object, and excludes its use to denote the object of awareness. An object of awareness is not the same as the awareness of it or, alternatively, presented objects are not the presentations of them.

It is clear then that a presentation is an act of consciousness. There are different kinds of presentation; for example, an object might be presented by seeing it, by imagining it, by thinking of it, by smelling it, and so on. Each of these is a different kind of act of presentation (*Psychology From an Empirical Standpoint*, p. 80). So acts of presentation (presentations) are mental phenomena; but Brentano says phenomena 'based on' presentations also count as mental (*Psychology From an Empirical Standpoint*, p. 80). What does he mean by 'based on' here? It is, after all, a spatial metaphor.

The expression may be unpacked in the following way. Some phenomena are presented, and the presentation of them is a mental phenomenon. Some phenomena are not directly presented in this way, but nevertheless they count as mental because they could not have occurred unless a certain presentation had occurred. To put it another way, not only are all presentations mental phenomena but further mental phenomena count as such because they have presentations as necessary conditions for their own existence. This is consistent with the examples Brentano gives: 'Nothing can be judged, desired, hoped, or feared unless one has a presentation of that thing' (*Psychology From an Empirical Standpoint*, p. 80). Unless one has been presented with an object of hope or fear, one cannot hope for or fear that thing; so hope and fear count as mental phenomena because they are 'based on' presentations. I take it that this point is supposed to hold, quite independently of the fact that a particular fear or hope might count as mental because it is itself a presentation.

For this reason Brentano feels entitled to conclude about mental phenomena that 'they are either presentations or they are based on presentations' (*Psychology From an Empirical Standpoint*, p. 85).

One final clarification of the concept of presentation is this. Brentano says: 'As we use the verb "to present", "to be presented" means the same as "to appear"' (*Psychology From an Empirical Standpoint*, p. 85). This is fully consistent with his insistence that the presentation of an object is to be distinguished from the object itself, but it adds the refinement that, if an object is presented to someone, then it appears to him or her. It follows that, for Brentano, the appearing of an object is not the object itself, even though the object itself does genuinely appear. Its appearing is its being presented.

Brentano expresses some satisfaction with his use of the notion of presentation to differentiate mental from physical phenomena. Speaking of the claim that only mental phenomena are either presentations or are based on presentations he says: 'The definition given includes all the examples of mental phenomena which we listed above, and in general all the phenomena belonging to this domain' (*Psychology From an Empirical Standpoint*, p. 80). Despite Brentano's satisfaction, a problem seems to arise for the account so far. Suppose we accept that there are presentations in Brentano's sense; suppose further that all his examples of mental phenomena are either presentations or are based on presentations. The possibility would seem to remain that there are mental phenomena, in some pre-philosophical sense, which are not presentations nor are based on them. Indeed, arguably, some mental phenomena are presented (even though Brentano is at pains to maintain that this is not what being a presentation consists in). In the examples he has given, the things that are presented fall squarely on the physical side of the list; but moods, images, emotions, pleasures and pains are all commonsensically mental, yet they are arguably presented and are not themselves presentations in Brentano's sense. If this is right, then, although Brentano has produced a sufficient condition for a phenomenon's being mental, he has not produced a necessary condition. This is because it can plausibly be maintained that there are at least some mental phenomena which do not fulfil his requirements. It would

need further argument and a further clarification of 'based on' to
show that images, moods and emotions count as mental because
they are based on presentations. Nor has the possibility been
definitely excluded that there could be physical phenomena based
on presentations, in some sense of 'based on'.

Outside Space

So far we have seen that Brentano tries to demarcate the mental
by means of examples of mental and physical phenomena, and by
a definition which employs the concept of 'presentation'. We
should turn now to a third method of marking the mental/physical
distinction, a method Brentano rejects. It is straightforwardly the
view that physical phenomena are spatio-temporal but mental
phenomena are merely temporal. He formulates the distinction in
this way:

All physical phenomena . . . have extension and spatial location, whether
they are phenomena of vision or of some other sense, or products of the
imagination . . . The opposite, however, is true of mental phenomena:
thinking, willing and the like appear without extension and without
spatial location. (*Psychology From an Empirical Standpoint*, p. 85)

Brentano ascribes this view (correctly) to Descartes, (incorrectly)
to Spinoza, and (correctly) to Kant. It has the merit of yielding
this simple distinction: physical phenomena are 'those phenomena
which appear extended and located in space' (*Psychology From
an Empirical Standpoint*, p. 85) and mental phenomena are 'those
phenomena which do not have extension or spatial location'
(ibid.). To put the point more precisely, all and only those phenomena which are both extended and spatially located are physical,
and all and only those phenomena which are only temporal are
mental.

   Brentano's attack on this traditional formulation of the mental/
physical distinction is two-pronged. He seeks to demonstrate that
some mental events are spatio-temporal, and that it is at least
possible that some physical events are not straightforwardly
spatial.

   This perhaps surprising possibility is explained in the following way. In certain idealist traditions the spatiality of physical
phenomena is held to be a psychological achievement. The raw

data the subject receives as sensory input, the phenomenal sounds, smells, colours, and so on, are not themselves located in space but are spatially organized by the perceiver: 'They are originally without spatial location, and we subsequently localise them' (*Psychology From an Empirical Standpoint*, p. 86), as Brentano puts it. To see the plausibility of this, remember that Brentano is still speaking of physical phenomena/physical appearances to us, and accept that it is at least possible that the world as we perceive it is partially mentally constructed.

The converse possibility, that mental events should be spatial, is more commonsensical. It is for example possible to feel pains and pleasures in parts of the body so that one's pains and pleasures are spatially located at the parts of the body where they are felt. Arguably a person's thoughts are where that person is and an emotion is in the being undergoing it: 'We locate a phenomenon of anger in the irritated lion, and our own thoughts in the space which we occupy' (*Psychology From an Empirical Standpoint*, p. 87). This is not a very precise notion of physical location. We may still ask, where exactly in me are my thoughts and emotions; but it is sufficient for Brentano's purposes that they may be given some spatial location – even a vague one – to refute the thesis that all mental events are merely temporal. Notice that Brentano is not claiming that materialism or neutral monism are true by this argument, although it is an interesting consequence of those theories that mental events may be given reasonably precise spatial locations. They are where the physical events are, with which they are identical.

If Brentano's objections to this distinction are decisive, then it is not a sufficient condition of some phenomenon's being physical that it be spatio-temporal because that phenomenon might be mental. It is not a necessary condition of a phenomenon's being physical that it be spatio-temporal because it might be physical yet intrinsically only temporal. It is not a sufficient condition of a phenomenon's being mental that it be merely temporal because it might be physical, and it is not a necessary condition of an event's being mental that it be only temporal because it might be spatio-temporal.

Brentano claims that 'certain mental phenomena also appear to be extended' (*Psychology From an Empirical Standpoint*, p. 87). If something is extended, then it has size. Brentano is committed to the view that it is those phenomena which have spatio-temporal location that are extended, and this is, in general, a plausible view. If something is located in, above, or below something else, then it stands in some spatial relation to that thing, and it is hard to see how this would be possible unless it occupied space itself. If that is right, then it follows that it has size or is extended, because that is part of what is meant by occupying space. It could be objected that it does not logically follow from 'X is spatially located' that 'X has size' because an abstract object, for example a mathematical point in geometry, could be determined spatially yet not itself occupy any space. Phenomena like pain, however, would seem to have size: a pain might extend half-way down someone's leg for example, even though there is a peculiarity in saying 'my pain is thirty centimetres long'. Perhaps pains are like the visual field, in being spatially extended yet without well-defined borders. In any case it is sufficient for Brentano's argument against the distinction that some mental phenomena be extended in some sense, because it is part of the distinction that mental phenomena are only temporal.

Brentano is prepared to allow that there may be counter-arguments to the various objections he has considered, but he maintains none the less that a fresh way of marking the mental/ physical distinction is required. After all, there is something inadequate about defining the mental as that which lacks a certain property, spatiality. This gives us only a negative definition of 'mental' – tells us what the mental is not, not what it is. A positive definition is needed, one which will tell us what the mental is.

Interestingly, Brentano momentarily considers the possibility that there can be no clear-cut definition of 'mental'. Perhaps there just is not any set of properties which all and only mental phenomena possess. This is one of the few points where Brentano seems to allow that there may be no sharp mental/physical distinction. However, he quickly abandons this thought in favour of his own positive theory of the mental, to which we may now turn.

Intentionality

The central concept of Brentano's philosophy of mind is intentionality. 'Intentionality' is a technical philosophical term which means being directed towards an object. It should not be confused with the ordinary English word 'intention' and is best introduced in Brentano's own words:

Every mental phenomenon is characterized by what the scholastics of the Middle Ages called the intentional (or mental) inexistence of an object, and what we might call, though not wholly unambiguously, reference to a content, direction toward an object (which is not to be understood here as meaning a thing) or immanent objectivity. (*Psychology From an Empirical Standpoint*, p. 88)

This passage requires clarification. The scholastics were the medieval schoolmen who produced Catholic philosophy within an essentially Aristotelian framework of thinking. By the 'inexistence' of the object Brentano means that the object of our thought or perception may not actually exist independently of that thought or perception. He is not committing himself to the view that what our experience is of exists independently of that experience. It might be dependent on the act of awareness of its own existence. By 'immanent objectivity' Brentano means existing as an object of awareness. What one's experience is of is not identical with one's experience, even if it could not exist in the absence of that experience. The whole doctrine that all and only mental phenomena are directed towards an object is the doctrine of intentionality. Intentionality is the property or characteristic of the mental of being 'of' or 'about' something. For example, it does not make much sense to say there is perception but not perception of something or other (even if the perception is of an illusion or hallucination). It does not make much sense to talk about there being thinking without there being thinking about something or other (even if what is thought about is something imaginary). These mental phenomena, like all others, are intentional or exhibit intentionality. The objects of the various mental acts are their content: what is perceived, what is desired, and so on:

Every mental phenomenon includes something as object within itself, although they do not all do so in the same way. In presentation something is presented, in judgement something is affirmed or denied, in love loved, in hate hated, in desire desired and so on. (*Psychology From an Empirical Standpoint*, p. 88)

Brentano feels that at last he has come upon a foolproof criterion for drawing the mental/physical distinction:

This intentional inexistence is characteristic exclusively of mental phenomena. No physical phenomenon exhibits anything like it. We can therefore define mental phenomena by saying that they are those phenomena which contain an object intentionally within themselves. (*Psychology From an Empirical Standpoint*, p. 89)

If this is correct, then Brentano has after all found the positive definition of 'mental'. He has said what the mental really is.

There are two obvious ways of attacking the definition, and Brentano is aware of both. First, it may be maintained that there are mental phenomena which are not intentional, and, secondly, it may be maintained that there are phenomena which are not mental but intentional. It might, for example, turn out that there are physical phenomena which are intentional. We should examine each of these in turn.

Certain of Brentano's contemporaries objected that, although it is acceptable that thoughts and desires take intentional objects, feelings such as pleasure and pain do not. You can feel a pleasure or a pain and that is all there is to your state. Your pain is not directed towards an object as a perception is. To understand this objection we need to make a clear distinction which Brentano accepts. This is between the object of a mental state and the cause of a mental state. For example, the cause of one's depression might be a state of the brain, but the object of one's depression might be the need to perform certain tasks. Clearly, in this case what one is depressed about is not a state of one's brain, even if that is the cause of one's depression, so cause and intentional object may be distinct. So when it is objected that phenomena of pleasure and pain are not intentional, it is not at all being claimed that they do not have causes.

Brentano's reply to this objection is that more feelings are intentional than we might be prepared to recognize: 'certain feelings undeniably refer to objects' (*Psychology From an Empirical Standpoint*, p. 90). He has in mind those cases where we are pleased with X, sorry about Y, grieve about Z. As he says, 'our language itself indicates this through the expressions it employs' (*Psychology From an Empirical Standpoint*, p. 90). However, he is forced to concede that certain phenomena, for example moods, do not seem to be straightforwardly intentional. Imagine a case where you are depressed or exhilarated but where there is nothing in particular that you are depressed or exhilarated about (although, no doubt, there will be a cause of your condition). Brentano's solution to this problem is to say that such mental phenomena in a sense refer to themselves. The phenomenon itself is its own intentional object. This solution seems to me rather contrived and probably false. For example, if you are depressed, you are not depressed about being depressed. If you feel joy, your joy is not directed at itself. It does not take itself as its intentional object. However, Brentano is satisfied with this reply and says: 'We may, therefore, consider the intentional inexistence of an object to be a general characteristic of mental phenomena which distinguishes this class of phenomena from the class of physical phenomena' (*Psychology From an Empirical Standpoint*, p. 91).

Might there be physical phenomena which exhibit intentionality? It seems to me that there might. In a clear sense, many physical events are directed at objects. A person fires a rifle at a target, throws a punch at a punch-bag, points at a tree. Also, many biological mechanisms are functional, in the sense of 'goal-directed'. The plant leans towards the path to be in the light. Being object-directed is constitutive of these physical events as I have described them. If this is right, then 'being directed towards an object' is not something truly predicable uniquely of mental phenomena. Nor, I think, is the 'inexistence of the object' uniquely mental: a mechanical robot will continue to make arm movements appropriate for stacking objects when there are no more objects to be stacked. More needs to be built into the mental if mental and physical are to be distinguished in the 'all or nothing' way that Brentano desires.

Brentano pursues the discussion of the mental/physical distinction beyond his own solution. He discusses three further apparent rivals: the view that only mental phenomena may be perceived by inner consciousness, the view that our knowledge of our own mental states is peculiarly incorrigible or infallible, and the view that the mental is in some sense private. In terms of his own theory of intentionality he accepts the first of these, rejects the second outright, and accepts the third with some reservations.

Inner Consciousness

The 'inner consciousness' criterion is expressed in this way: 'Another characteristic which all mental phenomena have in common is the fact that they are only perceived in inner consciousness; while in the case of physical phenomena only external perception is possible' (*Psychology From an Empirical Standpoint*, p. 91). This demarcation makes the mental/physical distinction rest on an inner/outer or internal/external distinction, which is not entirely clear. It corresponds roughly to the difference between the exercise of the five senses and the exercise of introspection, and the difference between experience which is not sense experience and experience which is. There is a problem about formulating the inner/outer distinction without recourse to the concepts of mental and physical themselves, and hence begging the question. For example, it will not do to say that physical objects are the objects of outer perception but mental objects are the objects of inner perception if we are to use that distinction to define 'mental' and 'physical'. However, philosophers have formulated an inner/outer distinction without recourse to 'mental' and 'physical'. Kant thought that 'inner sense' is only temporal but 'outer sense' is spatio-temporal, for example. Brentano himself says the 'definition is not very meaningful' (*Psychology From an Empirical Standpoint*, p. 91), presumably because the inner/outer distinction is not clear.

He attempts to clarify the definition in such a way that he can accept it. He takes the step of asserting that 'mental phenomena are those phenomena which alone can be perceived in the strictest sense of the word' (*Psychology From an Empirical Standpoint*, p. 92). He does not have an argument for this conclusion, but one might be suggested along the following lines. Inner experience is a kind of condition of outer experience so that there could not be any outer experience that is not mediated by inner experience. This means that there is no object of outer experience which is not made intelligible in terms of our own mental state. It is not clear that Brentano subscribes explicitly to such a thesis, but some such claim is at work as a suppressed premiss in his view that any object of perception is, strictly speaking, mental. One might feel that Brentano's claims are rather exaggerated at this point. The view that not only our mental states but all phenomena which may be perceived are really mental is perhaps rather reminiscent of Russell's view that not only are our mental states states of our brain but what we perceive is, strictly speaking, a part of our brain (see page 166 above).

Brentano has yet a further claim. He says that mental phenomena 'are those phenomena which alone possess real existence as well as intentional inexistence' (*Psychology From an Empirical Standpoint*, p. 92). It will be recalled that if something possesses intentional inexistence then it is quite possible that it does not exist independently of a mental state; it is not a mental state but the object of a mental state. So now Brentano is saying that mental phenomena really exist, but we cannot conclude that physical phenomena have anything more than an intentional or mind-dependent existence. What sense can be made of this? I think the doctrine may be rendered meaningful, and even plausible, by drawing a distinction between, on the one hand, being or existing and, on the other hand, being perceived to be or being perceived to exist. If something exists, then it exits *tout court*; but if something is perceived to exist, then it may or may not exist when not perceived. In Brentano's view being perceived to be is a kind of secondary or derivative state and being is a primary or underivative state. This is because putatively mind-independent objects, paradigmatically physical objects, are (strictly speaking) only perceived to be and so depend upon mental phenomena, for example perceptions, in order to exist, so far as we know.

This doctrine sounds like idealism. The reader may be reminded of Berkeley's immaterialism, discussed in Chapter 2. However, Brentano is not an idealist, and there is one all-important difference between his philosophy of mind and Berkeley's. Berkeley thought it was definitely false that physical objects exist unperceived. Brentano, in contrast, thinks that is quite possible. He wishes to leave room for the logical possibility that the objects of perception – things we perceive – exist unperceived. This is not something we can know or prove conclusively, according to Brentano, but it cannot be ruled out either. He provides us with the example of colours: 'A colour appears to us only when we have a perception of it' (*Psychology From an Empirical Standpoint*, pp. 92–3) but 'we cannot conclude from this, however, that a colour cannot exist without being perceived' (ibid., p. 93). Brentano sounds a note of caution when he allocates only intentional existence to the physical. As we shall see, he anticipates an important tenet of Husserl's phenomenology when he refuses dogmatically to allocate perception-independent existence to the physical, without dogmatically denying it either: 'We will ... make no mistake if in general we deny to physical phenomena any existence other than intentional existence' (*Psychology From an Empirical Standpoint*, p. 94). He means 'deny for the purposes of his theory', not absolutely. His view is the cautious one that physical objects have at least intentional existence.

Knowledge, Privacy and Time

Closely related to the idea that mental phenomena are the objects of inner consciousness is the incorrigibility thesis. As we saw in Chapter 1, incorrigibility in connection with the mental is the view that, if you believe you are in a mental state, that belief cannot be false. Often the thesis is conjoined with the view that, if you are in a mental state, then you know you are in that state. This is the Cartesian view that the mind is, so to speak, transparent to itself. As Brentano puts it: 'inner perception possesses another distinguishing characteristic: its immediate, infallible, self-evidence' (*Psychology From an Empirical Standpoint*, p. 91). This is not the view that, if you are in a mental state, then you are aware of that state (though it is consistent with that). It is the view that, if you are aware of your mental state, you cannot be mistaken about the existence and nature of that state.

Brentano rejects the incorrigibility thesis as a criterion for demarcating the mental from the physical. He accepts that we do have incorrigible access to our own mental states, but not only to our own mental states; we also have it with regard to the physical world. For example, if something appears coloured, there is a sense in which it is coloured. It is clear that, by this stage of his argument, inner consciousness is the only kind of perception Brentano thinks really exists: 'It is the only perception in the strictest sense of the word' (*Psychology From an Empirical*

Standpoint, p. 91), so, 'strictly speaking so-called external perception is not perception' (ibid.). It follows, he thinks, that, strictly speaking, mental phenomena are the only phenomena which are directly perceived. This seems to me inconsistent with his incorrigibility thesis about the mental.

Brentano accepts that the mental is in a sense 'private'. This word has several senses in the philosophy of mind, but Brentano uses it in this sense: 'No mental phenomenon is perceived by more than one individual' (*Psychology From an Empirical Standpoint*, p. 92), so it is quite legitimate to define the mental as the 'realm of inner perception' (ibid.).

It is true that physical objects are in a sense public. You, I and others may simultaneously or successively perceive the same physical object. But you, I and others cannot have one another's perceptions of that object, any more than we can feel each other's depression or have each other's pains. Your perception is your perception and my perception is my perception. Why this should be so, in a non-tautological and non-trivial sense, is a fundamental question in the philosophy of mind. Brentano does not pursue it.

Finally, Brentano examines the concept of time for a way of marking the mental/physical distinction. This is not the temporal/spatio-temporal distinction but a fresh one. The point is 'mental phenomena always manifest themselves serially, while many physical phenomena manifest themselves simultaneously' (*Psychology From an Empirical Standpoint*, p. 94). What Brentano is considering is the possibility that one's thoughts and emotions follow one another chronologically and do not exist simultaneously in one's consciousness. For example, a person does not feel two sorts of depression at once or introspect two emotions at once. In contrast, physical events may occur simultaneously or successively.

Brentano rejects both these claims. As an example of simultaneous but distinct mental events he gives: 'frequently we think of something and at the same time make a judgement about it or desire it' (*Psychology From an Empirical Standpoint*, p. 96). This seems relatively uncontroversial, so perhaps Brentano is entitled to conclude that 'very often many mental phenomena are present in consciousness simultaneously' (*Psychology From an Empirical Standpoint*, p. 96), but it seems much less clear that 'there can never be more than one physical phenomenon at a time' (ibid.).

(Notice, if this is right, that Brentano could adopt a criterion the very opposite of that which he criticizes. Brentano does not see this.) I find it hard to believe that Brentano's last claim is true. I can see a colour and hear a sound simultaneously, and both of these count as physical by Brentano's criteria, so it is just false that I can perceive only one physical phenomenon at a time. Brentano does not have a satisfactory argument for this claim, but two possibilities come to mind. One is that he thinks we can pay attention to only one physical phenomenon at a time. One's attention is, so to speak, 'absorbed' in the object. This is, I think, dubitable, and if it is true it is arguably also true of inner consciousness of mental events. Alternatively, he is just counting all the physical phenomena falling within the scope of one's awareness as one phenomenon. If this is his position, it comes out as stipulatively true but rather vacuous.

HUSSERL

Edmund Husserl was Brentano's most brilliant student and the real initiator of that movement in modern continental philosophy called 'phenomenology'. As we noted above (see pages 86, 181), phenomenology is the careful description of what is given directly to consciousness, without any preconception as to the objective reality or causal relations of the objects of consciousness. The aim of Husserl's phenomenology is to demonstrate the foundations of all knowledge, including all science and philosophy, within experience and, hopefully, to detect certain a priori structures of consciousness common to all human beings. To achieve this, a distinction is drawn between the so-called 'natural attitude', which is our ordinary, pre-phenomenological awareness of objects and other people around us located in 'the world', and, on the other hand, the 'reduced' world of the so-called 'epoche' or phenomenological reduction. As will be recalled, 'epoche' is the Greek word meaning 'suspension of belief', so for phenomenological purposes the objective reality of the world we believe in is 'bracketed' or 'reduced' to what we literally think and perceive in the present. It is hoped to show how the richness of the ordinary world is a kind of achievement of consciousness in the sense that it is constructed out of the series of experiences we actually have.

Husserl's thinking progressed through different phases, from an early psychologism – the attempt to understand the certain and a priori nature of logic and mathematics in terms of psychology – to a complete repudiation of psychologism: from a grounding of experience in the existence of 'the world' to a rejection of this and a grounding of experience and the world in an utterly subjective self called the 'transcendental ego'. A landmark in the repudiation of psychologism is the *Logical Investigations* and the most important text for the epoche, the structures of consciousness and the transcendental ego is the *Ideas*. It is impossible to do justice to the richness and complexity of Husserl's phenomenology within this short compass – it runs to many volumes – so what I intend to do is examine just two topics: his adaptation of his teacher's concept of intentionality and, more briefly, his account of the transcendental ego. This corresponds to two important questions in the philosophy of mind: what is consciousness? and what is conscious?

Intentionality

Husserl discusses intentionality in many places in his corpus, but a sustained treatment of the topic in relation to Brentano is to be found in Investigation V, chapter 2, of the *Logical Investigations* (pp. 552 ff.). Husserl thinks that two of the criteria Brentano uses to demarcate the mental from the physical are particularly valuable: the doctrine of intentionality and the thesis that a mental phenomenon is either a presentation or is based on a presentation; yet he has strong reservations about both criteria. Husserl thinks it is undeniable that: 'In perception something is perceived, in imagination something imagined, in a statement, something stated, in love, something loved, in hate hated, in desire desired etc.' (*Logical Investigations*, p. 554), and it is a large part of his own project to isolate in greater and greater detail the different sorts of intentional acts he thinks exist. It is clear however that Husserl does not think the possession of the characteristic of intentionality is a necessary condition for a phenomenon's counting as mental, even though a large number of mental acts do exhibit this feature. Husserl thinks that there are some mental acts which are not intentional, and that Brentano has allowed certain phenomena which are in fact mental to be classed as

physical. Husserl quite possibly has in mind here Brentano's
classification of images – the contents of the imagination – as
physical. Indeed, Husserl thinks a proper psychology might well
not have to confine itself to mental phenomena in Brentano's
sense:

> It can be shown that not all 'mental phenomena' in the sense of a
> possible definition of psychology, are mental phenomena (i.e. mental
> acts) in Brentano's sense, and that, on the other hand, many genuine
> 'mental phenomena' fall under Brentano's rubric of 'physical phenomena'.
> (*Logical Investigations*, p. 553)

For example, Husserl thinks that sensations are mental phenomena but do not typically or paradigmatically exhibit intentionality,
so in this respect Husserl is in agreement with certain psychologists who were critical of Brentano. At this point Husserl
does not have an argument that sensations are not intentional.
He thinks it is self-evident, or simply given in the nature of
certain sensations, not to be intentional, that is, not to be 'of' or
'about' anything: 'That not all experiences are intentional is
proved by sensations and sensational complexes' (*Logical Investigations*, p. 556). It is clear that there is a sharp disagreement
between Husserl and his teacher on this point, because Husserl
gives as an example of an experience that is not intentional 'any
piece of a sensed visual field' (*Logical Investigations*, p. 556).
Brentano would have rejected the view that the content of the
visual field is any kind of experience, even though a colour, for
example, might be the object of an experience. On this, it seems
to me that Husserl is right in saying phenomenal colours – or
colour sensations – are not intentional, but Brentano might have
been right in classifying them as physical rather than mental.
Notice too that Brentano was never committed to the view that
the contents of the visual field do exhibit intentionality because
he does not think they are mental phenomena. However, Husserl
could have chosen other examples (pain, pleasure and mood, for
example) which would have shown a clear divergence between
his views and Brentano's. Brentano thinks all sensations are
intentional; Husserl thinks some are not. Brentano thinks all
mental phenomena are intentional; Husserl thinks some are not.
  Husserl prefers the intentionality criterion to Brentano's thesis

about presentations to mark the mental/physical distinction because it is not question-begging. The trouble with using the concept of presentation to explain what the mental really is is that it
is itself a psychological concept. We already have to possess a
concept of the mental to understand what presentations are, so, if
we employ it as a criterion for 'mental', we do so on pain of
circularity. According to Husserl, the idea of a presentation is a
useful one for phenomenology but it cannot be taken as a starting
point. It has to be explained in terms of his own concept of an
'act'.

Husserl also thinks that Brentano's use of the term 'phenomenon' is severely defective. Husserl prefers the term 'experience'
(*Logical Investigations*, p. 557) because that does not carry the
implication that everything mental is a phenomenon. Here Husserl
is trying to leave room for the possibility that there may be
mental states which do not appear to the person having them:

As 'phenomenon' in its dominant use (which is also Brentano's) means
an appearing object as such, this implies that each intentional experience
is not only directed upon objects, but is itself the object of certain
intentional experiences. (*Logical Investigations*, p. 557)

Clearly, Husserl does not wish to be committed to the view which
Brentano accepts, that every mental event is an object for inner
consciousness. Husserl thinks it quite possible that there may be
mental states which are not available to inner consciousness at
all. Despite his expressed preference for 'experience' over 'phenomenon', Husserl frequently uses the latter term to denote experiences within his own phenomenology.

Further criticisms of Brentano lead Husserl to develop his own
refinement of the doctrine of intentionality; but it is worth noting
at this point two separate conceptions Husserl has of his phenomenological method. The first of these employs the notion of content,
the second the notion of essence. He says; 'the discussions which
follow will give precision and clarity to the fundamentally different
uses of the word "content"' (*Logical Investigations*, p. 556). He
means 'content' in the broadcast psychological sense, so there is
a content to what one perceives in the sense of what is perceived,
a content to what one thinks in the sense of what one thinks, a
content to what one says in the sense of what one says. Clearly,

then, there will exist different kinds of perceptual, imaginative and linguistic content, and the notion of an intentional object will have to be broadened to take account of these contents.

Secondly, Husserl claims that 'the phenomenological assertions we aim at are all meant by us ... as assertions of essence' (*Logical Investigations*, p. 556). As we noted in Chapter 1 (see page 17 above), the essence of something is what that thing really is. It is an important part of Husserl's project to determine the essences of various mental acts – to discover exactly what it consists in to think, to perceive, to imagine, and so on. In claiming to be discovering essences, Husserl believes he is discovering perennial truths about any conscious being, not just truths about his own psychology. If he has genuinely found out what thought, perception and imagination are, then his conclusions will hold good for all thought and all perception.

Act and Object

Husserl's account of intentionality begins with two important revisions of Brentano's account. Husserl thinks it is potentially extremely misleading to say that mental phenomena are related to an intentional object, because that suggests a question about the nature of this relationship. It is as though we have three things: the mental act, the intentional object, and the relationship between the two. Husserl thinks it is harmless to retain the intentionality terminology, so long as we do not reify or hypostatize the relationship between, on the one hand, consciousness (or the ego) and, on the other hand, the intentional object of consciousness:

If talk of a relation is here inescapable, we must avoid expressions which tempt us to regard such a relation as having psychological reality [*Realität*], as belonging to the real [*reell*] content of an experience. (*Logical Investigations*, p. 558)

What does Husserl mean by 'real' here? He means phenomenologically real. He is trying to describe the essential nature of mental acts as they appear to consciousness, and this leads us to the other important revision of Brentano's account. Husserl accepts that 'intentional experiences have the peculiarity of directing themselves in varying fashion to presented objects' (*Logical*

Investigations, p. 558) but he insists that 'they do so in an intentional sense' (ibid.) and 'This means no more than that certain experiences are present, intentional in character and more specifically, presentatively, judgingly, desiringly, or otherwise intentional' (ibid). In particular, Husserl thinks that typically, or in most cases, if a person is aware of something, then he or she is not thereby aware of two things: the object and the awareness of it. For example, suppose you are looking at a colour, what you are aware of is the colour. You are not aware both of the colour and of your awareness of the colour. There are not two items present to your consciousness, but only one: 'There are (to ignore certain exceptions) not two things present in experience, we do not experience the object and beside it the intentional experience directed upon it' (*Logical Investigations*, p. 558).

We may appreciate now why Husserl wishes to substitute the notion of a mental act for that of a mental phenomenon. In the sort of example cited above there exists an intentional and so mental act – the awareness of a colour – but there is no mental phenomenon, because the awareness itself does not appear to consciousness, and appearing to consciousness is what it consists in to be a phenomenon. For this reason, Husserl gives Brentano's intentionality terminology a special reading. He says, for example, 'the intentional "relation" to an object is achieved' means exactly the same as 'an object is "intentionally present"' (*Logical Investigations*, p. 558).

Husserl is in agreement with Brentano that the intentional object need not have objective or mind-independent reality. He has a reservation about calling this the 'immanent objectivity' of the object, because this phrase too, according to Husserl, tempts us into a reification of the relations between consciousness and its contents. Husserl gives the example of the god Jupiter, who (it is assumed) does not exist mind-independently yet may exist as an object of thought: 'I have an idea of the god Jupiter; this means that I have a certain presentative experience, the presentation-of-the-god-Jupiter is realized in my consciousness' (*Logical Investigations*, p. 558). Husserl notes that the god Jupiter is not to be found as any component part of his intentional experience: 'it is in truth not really immanent or mental' (*Logical Investigations*, p. 559). But Husserl notes too that the god Jupiter has no objective or mind-independent existence either: 'But it also does not exist extra-mentally, it does not exist at all' (*Logical Investigations*, p. 559) So the god Jupiter does not exist mentally or physically. In fact, the god Jupiter does not exist at all; yet this does not prevent the god Jupiter from 'being actual', being 'our idea' and 'being a particular mode of mindedness' (*Logical Investigations*, p. 559). To make this consistent, we must not take 'at all' in 'does not exist at all' too literally. We have to read it as 'does not exist mentally or physically'. Then we can read Husserl as allowing a class of entities which are not mental acts, and not physical objects, but only intentional objects. They are neither mental nor physical but provide the content for certain of our mental acts.

However, Husserl also recognizes that the objects of our mental acts may exist mind-independently. The god Jupiter is not an example but Cologne Cathedral is (*Logical Investigations*, p. 559). Nevertheless from a phenomenological point of view, the existence or non-existence of the intentional object is irrelevant. According to Husserl, there is nothing intrinsic to a particular act of consciousness which reveals the existence or non-existence of the content of that consciousness. Hence 'It makes no essential difference to an object presented and given to consciousness whether it exists or is fictitious, or is perhaps completely absurd' (*Logical Investigations*, p. 559). So a fictitious or absurd object is presented phenomenologically in the same way as an object which exists objectively or mind-independently. That this may be so is an important phenomenological tenet. It is implied by the exercise of the epoche: the suspension of belief in the objective reality of the objects of consciousness to facilitate the description of their given or purely phenomenological properties. Husserl naturally accepts that pre-phenomenologically we hear music and see physical objects and do not hear and see phenomena: 'I do not see colour sensations but coloured things, I do not hear tone sensations but the singer's song etc.' (*Logical Investigations*, p. 559).

Consciousness and the Ego

Husserl is aware that he has been employing the concept of consciousness in a rather unanalysed way, in his use, for example of Brentano's expression 'given to consciousness'. I do not think this is particularly damaging to his exposition, because it is clear that he thinks being intentional is a sufficient condition for being mental, even if it is not necessary. If we accept his view that certain mental happenings are not phenomena yet still directed towards objects, then there seems little harm in his calling these 'acts'. Husserl also operates with the idea of a unity of consciousness, or the idea of one's consciousness as a whole. This needs to be distinguished (conceptually) from the various mental acts which make it up: 'Our first concept of consciousness, given an empirical psychological slant, covers the whole stream of experience which makes up the individual mind's real unity, together with all aspects that enter into the constitution of this stream' (*Logical Investigations*, p. 560). But this use of 'consciousness' has to be distinguished from consciousness in the sense of 'inner perception' or the 'intentional relation' (*Logical Investigations*, p. 560). These are both types of mental act which are parts of consciousness in the first sense.

If we ask what consciousness is for Husserl, it is essentially a series of intentional acts and non-intentional experiences called 'sensations'. In a sense, the structure of the intentional act is tripartite: what experiences, the experience itself, and what the experience is of; or, to put it another way, the ego, the experience and the intentional object. We have seen that Husserl thinks the description of intentional experience and intentional content as related to be phenomenologically misleading, because typically no such relation appears to consciousness: only the intentional object thus appears. We should turn now to the other component of the triumvirate, or the other of the two related by intentional experiences – the ego, or that which is conscious.

Husserl contrasts this whole picture of the structures of consciousness with the cases in which we do not reflect on experience but:

We simply 'live' in the act in question, become absorbed, e.g. in the perceptual 'taking in' of some event happening before us, in some play of fancy, in reading a story, in carrying out a mathematical proof etc. (*Logical Investigations*, p. 561)

Husserl's point is that, in this everyday, unreflective sort of consciousness, no ego appears to consciousness. As he puts it, 'the ego as relational centre of our performances becomes quite elusive' (*Logical Investigations*, p. 561). So, frequently, from a phenomenological point of view, the ego does not appear. The ego is not a phenomenon even if 'the idea of the ego may be specially ready to come to the fore' (*Logical Investigations*, p. 561).

There is a tension, then, or at least a difference, between the findings of natural reflection and the findings of phenomenology. Husserl decides that objectively there must in some sense exist an ego. Even if the ego does not appear it must still in some sense exist even when it does not appear: 'From an objective standpoint (and so too from the standpoint of natural reflection) it is doubtless the case that in each act the ego is intentionally directed towards some object' (*Logical Investigations*, p. 561). If this is so, at least from an 'objective' point of view, the question arises, what is the ego? Husserl considers two possibilities. The ego is 'either no more than the "conscious unity" or "bundle" of experiences' or the ego is 'the continuous thing-like unity, the personal subject of our experiences' (*Logical Investigations*, p. 561). So, the ego is either the unity of my experiences – my consciousness as a whole – or else it is the irreducibly subjective and most personal self that I am. The ego is what I am, and I am whatever has my experiences.

Husserl never really solves the problem of the status of the ego. He calls it the 'transcendental' ego because it does not appear within ordinary experience but is a condition for that experience. The ego transcends experience. It is that which has experience. It is not either experience or the intentional object of experience. It is left to Husserl's critic, the French philosopher Jean-Paul Sartre, to untangle the intricacies of Husserl on the transcendental ego; but a discussion of that issue would require a book in itself.

8

CONCLUSION:

How to Solve the Mind–Body Problem

The mind–body problem is the problem of stating correctly the relation between the mind and the body. Its solution depends on discussion of several questions which are logically related: What are minds? What does it mean to say something is 'mental' or 'physical'? What is thinking? What is consciousness? What is subjectivity? What is individuality? What is the self? and What is matter?

What are Minds?

To say that something is a mind is to say that it has a capacity to think. Having a capacity to think is both logically necessary and logically sufficient for being a mind, so, if there exists a thing, x, and x has the capacity to think, it logically follows that there exists at least one mind. If there exists a thing, x, and x has no capacity to think, then it logically follows that x is not a mind. I allow that both 'x is a mind' and 'x has a mind' have sense, but they have the same sense. To say 'x is a mind' is to say that x has a capacity to think, and to say 'x has a mind' is to say that x has a capacity to think.

If something thinks, then it logically follows that it is a mind, because it would be contradictory to assert that something thinks but has no capacity to think. However, it is not necessary that something should think or be thinking in order to be a mind, because there is no contradiction in the conjunction of the claims that something has a capacity to think, yet does not.

It follows that something is a mind if it has a capacity to think, whatever it is. It may be, then, that many different sorts of things are able to think. If God can think, then God is a mind; if computers can think, then computers are minds; if souls can think, then souls are minds.

In the case of humans – and, no doubt, higher animals – the answer to the question, what is the mind? is: *the mind is the brain*. This, I maintain, is an empirical and contingent truth, not an a priori and necessary truth.

It is an empirical truth that in our case the mind is the brain, because this may be decided by experience. If part of a person's brain is damaged, then part of that person's capacity to think may be damaged. (For example, some kinds of brain damage result in amnesia; a diminution of a person's capacity to remember.) This diminution in capacity to think may be known to exist empirically in two ways, by the first-person introspections of the subject and by the third-person behavioural observations (including experimental observations) of another.

In so far as 'the mind is the brain' is subject to empirical falsification, for example by replacement of brain tissue by non-organic materials, or by genuine out-of-body experience, I am prepared to give it up. Prima facie, however, the mind is the brain.

It is not an a priori truth that the mind is the brain, because what it is that has a capacity to think cannot be discovered by purely intellectual means. (Indeed, it cannot be established a priori that any brains exist. A priori, our skulls could be empty.) It is an empirical truth that at least some minds are brains, but it cannot be ruled out a priori that some items other than brains are minds.

Nor is it a necessary truth that the mind is the brain. It is a necessary truth that a mind is whatever it is that has a capacity to think, but it is not a necessary truth that it is the brain that has that capacity. It follows that it is not necessarily true that the mind is the brain, even though it is true that our minds are brains.

My view that the mind is the brain must not be confused with materialism. Materialism, as we shall see, is a false doctrine.

Strictly speaking, the answer to the mind–body problem is that the mind is a part of the body, just because the mind is the brain. Clearly, however, 'mind–body problem' is a misnomer for the philosophically interesting questions: what are the relations between thinking and the brain and between consciousness and the brain? Before answering those questions I shall clarify 'mental' and 'physical'.

What are Mental and Physical?

I shall provide two lists of predicates in two columns. Many of the predicates in the left-hand column are tacitly implied in calling something 'mental', and most of the predicates in the right-hand column are tacitly implied in calling something 'physical'. I do not mean to suggest that they are all correctly implied or that all of them are implied in all people's usage, only that many are implied in many people's usage. (When I say a predicate is 'implied', I mean someone's assertion that 'x is mental' or 'x is physical' conceptually implies 'x is F', where 'F' is the place-holder for some predicate listed below.)

MENTAL	PHYSICAL
temporal	spatio-temporal
private	public
incorrigible	corrigible
internal	external
one	many
free	determined
active	passive
I	other
sacred	profane
indivisible	divisible
unextended	extended
without shape	with shape
invisible	visible
intentional	non-intentional
subjective	objective

Many attempts to solve the mind–body problem take the mistaken form of trying to reduce the concepts in one of these lists to the other. In fact, each predicate is semantically irreducible to its opposite and impoverished ontologies are generated by denying the predicates in either list a genuine application. My view is the pre-philosophical and empirically compelling one that both mental and physical are real. Also, nothing is mental in the respect in which it is physical, and nothing is physical in the respect in which it is mental. The denial of either of these conjuncts is, or entails, a contradiction.

What is Thinking?

The variety of activities called 'thinking' is extremely large but includes at least: reflecting, anticipating, deciding, imagining, remembering, wondering, pondering, intending, believing, disbelieving, meditating, understanding, inferring, predicting and introspecting.

Thinking may take place in language, in an ordinary language such as English, or in an artificial language such as a logical notation. Some thinking also takes place in neither of those media but in mental images – pictures in the mind's eye.

'Thought' is ambiguous between 'what is thought' and 'the thinking of what is thought'. Thoughts may be true or false in the sense that what is thought may be true or false; so, if a person thinks that p, and p is true, then the thought that p is true; and if a person thinks that p, and p is false, then the thought that p is false. Also, there may obtain logical relations between thoughts because, for example, one thought may follow logically from another and contradict yet another.

All thinking has some subject matter. It does not make sense to say there is thinking that is not about anything. If there is thinking, there is something that is thought, some content, even if the thought is not truth-valued but, say, interrogative or subjunctive.

Thinking may be conscious or unconscious. If thinking is unconscious, then the mind thinking either does not know that it is thinking or, if it does know that, then it does not know what it is thinking. If thinking is conscious, then the thinking mind knows both that it is thinking and what it is thinking. Also, thinking may or may not have a phenomenology. Thinking has a phenomenology if and only if that thinking includes events which are experiences.

Thinking is a completely mental activity. I mean by this that no mental event is identical with any physical event and no mental event has any (intrinsic) physical properties. It logically follows from this that materialism is false because that is the conjunction of 'putatively mental events are physical' with 'only physical events exist'. I hold it to be self-contradictory to affirm that any mental event is a physical event, because mental and physical events are truly characterized by mutually exclusive predicates, for example, every physical event has size and no mental event has size; and it logically follows from those two premises alone that no mental event is a physical event. It logically follows from that in turn that the first conjunct of materialism is false, because that is the claim that mental events are physical. It also follows that it is false that only physical events exist from the premises that there exist mental events and that no mental event is identical with any physical event. It logically follows that the second conjunct of materialism is also false.

Materialism is a self-contradictory theory of the mind because it includes the claim that the mental is physical; but being mental partly consists in having no physical properties and being physical partly consists in having no mental properties. Being self-contradictory is a logically sufficient condition for being false, so it follows that materialism is false.

The relation between thinking and the brain is this: *thinking is the mental activity of the brain*. Crucially, there is no interface problem between things and their activities. There is no ontological or metaphysical problem about what the relation is between something and what it does. It is what I am calling the 'interface problem' that has proved most intractable in solving the mind–body problem: stating the nature of the interface between a mental event and a physical event. Materialists incoherently maintain that mental events are physical. Idealists incoherently maintain that physical events are mental. Dualists correctly maintain that no mental event is physical and that no physical event is mental but falsely believe in the interface problem.

To believe in the interface problem is to be in the grip of a metaphysical illusion, a powerful one which governs our self-conception. To help dispel the illusion, I provide a number of analogies. They are designed to show there is no ontological problem about something and its activities, or about a thing and what it does.

A light-bulb increases and diminishes in brightness, but there is no 'light-bulb-brightness' problem. Note that, were we to break the bulb or cut off the electrical supply, or if the filament were to wear out, the emission of light would cease. In the Lewis Carroll story *Alice in Wonderland* the speculative metaphysical possibility is imaginatively entertained of a 'grin without a cat'. Clearly, however, in empirical reality there may exist a cat without a grin but not a grin without a cat (or something that grins). This is because grinning is something the cat does. A chameleon is a lizard that can change its colour. Suppose the chameleon changes from blue to red. There is not thereby created a 'chameleon-colour-change problem', not just because secondary qualities logically depend upon primary qualities but also because changes logically depend upon things that change. If a bus is moving down the street, there is no 'bus-motion problem'. It is not as though the motion of the bus could exist as a ghostly see-through residue, were the bus to be dismantled. This is not just because primary qualities logically depend upon the physical objects they are properties of but also because moving is something the bus does and doings are impossible without the things that do them.

Nothing hinges, in any of these cases, on whether the things done are physical or mental or neither. It is because things done logically depend on things that do them that there is no interface problem.

In a similar way there need no longer be a mind–body problem. We, logically, could never be in a position to inspect the 'interface' between thinking and the brain. We could never, so to speak, peel thinking off the brain and discover metaphysical cement, cement that is not quite mental and not quite physical. To believe in the interface problem is to confuse an empirical possibility with a logical impossibility.

I call this solution to the mind–body problem 'Empiricism' even though, as a general thesis about thinking, it is analytic: 'thinking is the mental activity of minds'. As a particular truth about human beings and higher animals, it is empirical and contingent: 'thinking is the mental activity of the brain'. It is an important tenet of this empiricist theory of the mind that little sense may be attached to the metaphysical notion of a 'relation' between a thing and its activities. Something's activities are just what it does, whatever it is and whatever it does. All the facts about a thing's relation to what it does are empirical facts; none of them is metaphysical.

Notably there are no causal relations between things and their activities other than those to be mentioned in explaining how or why they engage in those activities. If we persist in thinking of thinking as a thing or substance, we will continue to ask about causal connections between thinking and the brain, instead of correctly regarding thinking as the mental activity of the brain. It is an empirical question, which parts of the brain are required for which kinds of thinking. There is no non-empirical causal question about thinking and the brain.

It is an empirical truth that the brain is necessary for thinking in humans and higher animals, and it is an empirical truth that thinking is an activity, or something that is done. The empiricist theory of the mind is the identification of the brain with that which engages in the activity of thinking. This identification is itself empirical.

What is Consciousness?

'Consciousness' is notoriously difficult to define verbally, and later I shall make a suggestion as to why this should be so. However, something like an ostensive definition is possible for the term.

Suppose you are looking at something, for example at this page of *Theories of the Mind* open in front of you. Uncontroversially, certain things are thereby true of you. You exist, your eyes are open and orientated towards this page. You have a brain connected to the back of your eyeballs by the optic nerves. Light waves leaving the page contact your retinas and an electronic signal is transmitted along them to your brain. The page of the book in front of you also exists and it is presented as an oblong-shaped expanse of white-coloured surface with black marks on it we call 'letters'.

Now, this account of seeing the page would seem to be incomplete, not just in its physiological details but in a way that makes it radically defective. I have missed out of the account your *awareness* of the page. Even if I described in extraordinary detail all the physiological facts and in equal detail all the perceptible variations in the colour of the page and the shapes of the letters, the central feature of the situation still seems to be missing: your seeing of the page.

The missing component is consciousness. Seeing something involves being conscious of it or being aware of it. The physiological input to the eyeballs is passively received; it runs in the direction object–eyeball. However, one's awareness of an object runs in the opposite direction: eyeball–object. You see the page. You are conscious of it.

This active relation is not physical. Your awareness has no size or shape or hardness. It is an ethereal, invisible, ultimately ineffable relation between you and the page. It is consciousness.

More generally, there exist not only sounds but the hearing of them, not only smells and tastes but the smelling and tasting of them, not only sensations of touch or pain but the feeling of them. In each case 'the . . . of them' denotes some act of pure awareness.

Notice that the existence and nature of consciousness cannot be captured by any physical description of the world. Suppose there existed a set of sentences which mentioned only physical facts about the world. Suppose *per impossible* such a set were complete. It would still not be possible logically to derive any further sentence from this set asserting the existence of consciousness or characterizing its nature. Such a putative derivation could only be a *non sequitur*.

I wish now to make a radical suggestion: *consciousness does not exist*. Of course experiences exist, but, once we have itemized all the experiences a person is having, there is absolutely nothing at all to be captured by 'consciousness'. Consciousness is nothing over and above experience. I have three grounds for this. First, empirical parsimony: all the familiar phenomenological facts about us can be captured adequately by mentioning only experiences. Secondly, the onus is on the advocate of consciousness to prove that it exists. Thirdly, on my view two famous facts about consciousness may be explained; these facts are its ethereal and invisible nature and the ineffability of the concept. Both these are explained by the fact that there is no such thing as consciousness. It logically follows there need no longer be any philosophical problem about the relation between consciousness and the brain. That version of the mind–body problem is solved.

There remains the question of the relation between experiences and the brain, and the rest of the physical world. The solution is that the brain, and the rest of the nervous system and the sense organs, jointly comprise what I call an *environment transformer*. I mean, the brain transforms a physiological sensory input into sensations and secondary qualities. Sensations and secondary qualities are what I call 'brain transformations'.

Sensations and secondary qualities logically depend on primary qualities though they cannot be reduced to them. I mean, it would be ultimately self-contradictory to affirm that at least one secondary quality exists but to deny the existence of all primary qualities but, nevertheless, it does not logically follow from the fact that all the primary qualities exist that any secondary quality exists. Similarly, all sensations have spatio-temporal locations, but the phenomenology of any sensation could never be captured by any sentence or set of sentences mentioning only primary qualities. Nor is there anything mysterious about this phenomenology. It is something most of us are more familiar with than physiology.

Environmental transformation is something the brain does, and this activity depends on the well-working of the nervous system and sense organs; for example, the activity called 'seeing' is no longer possible if the eyes are destroyed. This is true in two senses of 'possible': seeing is an activity so it logically depends on whatever sees, and in our case seeing empirically depends on the physical sense organs called 'eyes'. I think the brain is an environment transformer for evolutionary reasons: (a) phenomenology is a simplification of physiological sensory input and so is part of what I call 'environment management'; (b) environment management has proved conducive to survival. Brain transformations are *qualitative* phenomenological results of *quantitative* physiological sensory inputs and neurological activity (rather as a photograph may be, among other things, the product of a large quantity of small dots).

There is no interface problem about the relation between the brain and brain transformations because they are activities of the brain. Also, to think that there is an interface problem about sensations and secondary qualities, on the one hand, and the physical objects they are transformation-states of is to be in the grip of a metaphysical illusion. We could not peel the colour off a physical object in the way we could peel the paint off a physical object. The metaphysical illusion of the interface is an empirical image whose application lies elsewhere.

What is Subjectivity?

Being a subject is being capable of having experiences. Being capable of experience is both necessary and sufficient for being a subject; so, if there exists something, x, and x is capable of experience, it logically follows that there exists at least one subject. If there exists something, x, and x has no capacity for experience, then it logically follows that x is not a subject. I allow that 'x is a subject' and 'x possesses subjectivity' both have a sense, but they have the same sense. 'x is a subject' means that x is capable of experience and 'x posseses subjectivity' means that x is capable of experience.

If something experiences, than it logically follows that it is a subject, because it would be contradictory to assert that something experiences but has no capacity for experience. However, it is not necessary that something should experience or be experiencing in order to be a subject, because there is no contradiction in the conjunction of the claims that something is capable of experiencing yet does not.

The subject of an experience is that which has that experience, and the object of an experience is what the experience is of. For example, the subject of a perception is a perceiver or that which perceives, but the object of a perception is a perceived or that which is perceived.

In the case of a human being, such as you or I, subjectivity is partly revealed in the fact that we each have a peculiarly partial visual perception of our own body. For example, your eyes, now, are open and seeing, but (and this is the crucial point) they do not see themselves. In a similar way, your own head does not fall within your own visual field (except, sometimes, the tip of your nose) and you cannot see the back of your own head. Your body is visually presented to you from the shoulders and chest downwards. You do not see your back or the top of your head. These facts are not to be explained entirely by the biological contingency of the location of the eyeballs at the front of the head. There is a more profound reason for them. They are partially constitutive of being a subject, being the subject that one is. I mean, such perceptual peculiarities do not obtain in one's visual perception of another person – a person other than oneself – they obtain only in the case of oneself, the person who one is, whoever one is.

It is a startling and philosophically puzzling fact about us that we are subjective or possess subjectivity. It is not possible to notice one's subjectivity by thinking of oneself as just one person among others. Others, for you, exist only as objects – objects of your experience – and you, for others, may exist only as an object – the object of their experiences. You experience yourself partly as subject, partly as object. For example, you experience yourself as partially looking out of your body, but you may look at your body. Such subjective facts are quite neutral as to whether you are your body, or whether you have a body, or whether you are inside your body. They depend partly on *observing* the person who you are and partly on *being* the person who you are.

The existence of subjective facts, of which there are many, is logically consistent with my view that thinking is a mental activity of the brain, and at least some subjective facts are logically implied by the existence of brain transformations.

What is Individuality?

By 'individuality' I mean 'being an individual', or that, in virtue of which one is an individual. By being an individual I mean being the one that one is.

To see that there is a philosophical problem about individuality, consider the following. There exist billions of people on planet earth; there have, in the past, existed billions of people on planet earth; and presumably there will exist billions more in the future. Consider all the people of the past (if you like, in a long line), add to that all present and future people (again, if you wish, in a line). Now consider yourself. It is a striking and puzzling fact that out of all the people there have been, are and will be, you yourself are one of them. You are, so to speak, inserted into history. Why should this be so? How come? Why should it be that, out of all these people, you are one of them? In asking these questions I am in full agreement with Thomas Nagel's claim that there is a genuine philosophical problem about 'being someone' (*The View from Nowhere*, pp. 54ff.).

The problem of individuality is the problem of one's own existence. Notice that it cannot possibly have any scientific (for example, biological) explanation. From the fact, for example, that two specific parents had a child, it does not logically follow that that child is or became you. Nor is the problem a trivial modal issue. It is necessary that everything is self-identical. I mean, it is a necessary truth that each thing is the thing it is and not another thing. This holds of anything, whatever it is. The modal point does not capture the insight that something is oneself.

The question 'Why are we here?' is a profound metaphysical question not to be dismissed on linguistic grounds. It seems to me that one's own existence is, in a fairly precise sense, a 'miracle'. It does not violate any laws of nature, but it is not to be explained in terms of them. We do not need God and the soul to solve the mind–body problem – it is the brain that thinks – but we may well need them to explain why each of us exists and what it is for us to be who we are.

What Is the Self?

A self is an individual that is conscious of itself. 'Itself' is not used question-begging here. I mean that a self is an individual that is conscious of the individual that it is. This is a necessary but not a sufficient condition for being a self, because an individual could in principle be conscious of itself but not be conscious that it is what it is conscious of. However, an individual that is not conscious of itself is not a self (even though it is itself). It is sufficient for being a self that an individual be conscious of the individual that it is and be conscious that it is the individual it is conscious of.

That is what a self is, whatever it is. In our case it may be that the self is nothing over and above the brain, its thoughts and its experiences. To see this, consider the subjective self: the self as the unperceived perceiving subject – the self that never perceives itself. A clear but neglected candidate for this is the brain: the brain perceives but is not perceived. You have, for example, never perceived your brain. This is to be partly explained by the biological contingency of the arrangement of your sense organs, but it is also explicable if your brain is what you are. What is looking out of your eyes at this page now? Arguably, your brain is. This is an empiricist answer to the question 'what am I?' It is not an answer to the question 'who am I?' That is a version of the metaphysical problem of individuality.

Also, there need be no psychic self as a subjective centre of consciousness over and above sets of experiences: just as there is no such thing as a hole in the ground over and above the sides and the base.

What is Matter?

Matter is the material substance that physical objects are composed of. Anything spatio-temporal is composed of matter, and matter has an atomic and sub-atomic constitution. Physicists tell us more and more about this constitution, discovering smaller and smaller particles and constituents of particles which do not seem themselves to be straightforwardly particles.

Like consciousness, *matter does not exist*. I have three grounds for this. First, everything that can be said about the physical world can be said in terms of physical objects or space–time events, their structures, and the relations between them. 'Matter' is redundant. Secondly, the onus is on the proponent of matter to prove that it exists. Thirdly, the empirical inaccessibility of matter and the ineffability of the concept are accounted for at a stroke by my view: there is no such thing as matter.

In conclusion, the solution to the mind–body problem is that thinking is the mental activity of the brain and experience is a phenomenological transformation of the physical environment. This leaves many metaphysical problems unsolved, but the mind–body problem is not one of them.

FURTHER READING

Anthologies and General Works

Ned Block (ed.) *Readings in Philosophy of Psychology* (London, 1980) 2 vols.

Paul Feyerabend and G. Maxwell (eds) *Mind, Matter and Method* (Minneapolis, 1966).

Anthony Flew (ed.) *Body, Mind and Death* (London 1977).

Douglas R. Hofstadter and Daniel C. Dennett (eds) *The Mind's I: Fantasies and Reflections on Self and Soul* (Sussex, 1981).

S. Hook (ed.) *Dimensions of Mind* (New York, 1960).

Colin McGinn *The Character of Mind* (Oxford, 1982).

Hilary Putnam (ed.) *Mind, Language and Reality: Philosophical Papers Volume Two* (Cambridge, 1980).

Jenny Teichman *Philosophy and the Mind* (Oxford, 1988).

G. N. Vesey (ed.) *Body and Mind* (London, 1970).

Dualism

René Descartes *Discourse on Method* and *The Meditations* (trans. F. E. Sutcliffe (Harmondsworth, 1974).

Anthony Kenny *Descartes* (New York, 1968).

Anthony Kenny (ed.) *Descartes: Philosophical Letters* (Oxford, 1970).

G. W. Leibniz *Philosophical Writings* edited by G. H. R. Parkinson (London, 1984).

John Locke *An Essay Concerning Human Understanding* (Oxford, 1950).

Nicolas de Malebranche *Dialogues on Metaphysics and Religion* trans. M. Ginsberg (London, 1923).

Plato *The Phaedo* trans D. Gallup (Oxford, 1975).

Karl Popper and John Eccles *The Self and Its Brain* (London, 1977).
Howard Robinson *Matter and Sense* (Cambridge, 1982).
Richard Swinburne *The Evolution of the Soul* (Oxford, 1986).
Bernard Williams *Descartes: The Project of Pure Enquiry* (Harmondsworth, 1978).

Logical Behaviourism

Carl G. Hempel 'The logical analysis of psychology', in Block (1980).
Anthony Kenny *Wittgenstein* (Harmondsworth, 1975).
Hilary Putnam 'Brains and behaviour', in Block (1980).
Gilbert Ryle *The Concept of Mind* (London, 1949).
Ludwig Wittgenstein *Philosophical Investigations* (Oxford, 1958).

Idealism

George Berkeley *Principles of Human Knowledge With Other Writings* edited and introduced by G. J. Warnock (London, 1977).
John Foster *The Case for Idealism* (London 1982).
John Foster and Howard Robinson (eds) *Essays on Berkeley* (Oxford, 1988).
G. W. F. Hegel *The Phenomenology of Spirit* trans. A. V. Miller (Oxford, 1977).
—— *The Philosophy of Mind* trans. W. Wallace and A. V. Miller (Oxford, 1971).
Stephen Priest *The British Empiricists: Hobbes to Ayer* (London, 1990) ch. 3.
—— (ed.) *Hegel's Critique of Kant* (Oxford, 1987).
Timothy Sprigge *The Vindication of Absolute Idealism* (Edinburgh, 1983).
J. O. Urmson *Berkeley* (Oxford, 1982).

Materialism

D. M. Armstrong *A Materialist Theory of the Mind* (London, 1968).
C. Borst (ed.) *The Mind–Brain Identity Theory* (London, 1970).
Donald Davidson *Essays on Actions and Events* (Oxford, 1980).
Ted Honderich *A Theory of Determinism: The Mind, Neuroscience and Life-Hopes* (Oxford, 1988).

Michael E. Levin *Metaphysics and the Mind–Body Problem* (Oxford, 1979).

Colin McGinn 'Philosophical materialism', *Synthese* 44, June 1980.

John Mepham and D.-H. Ruben (eds) *Issues in Marxist Philosophy: Vol. II Materialism* (Sussex, 1979).

U. T. Place 'Is consciousness a brain process?', in Borst (1970).

J. J. C. Smart 'Sensations and brain processes', in Borst (1970).

—— *Philosophy and Scientific Realism* (London, 1969).

David-Hillel Ruben *Marxism and Materialism* (Sussex/New Jersey, 1977).

Edgar Wilson *The Mental as Physical* (London, 1979).

Functionalism

David Armstrong 'The nature of mind', in Block (1980).

Ned Block 'Problems with functionalism', in Block (1980).

David Lewis 'Mad pain and Martian pain', in Block (1980).

Hilary Putnam 'The mental life of some machines', in Putnam (1980).

—— 'The nature of mental states', in Putnam (1980.

John Searle 'Minds, brains and programs', in Hofstadter and Dennett (1981).

Alan Turing 'Computing machinery and intelligence', in *Mind* (1950).

—— 'Intelligent machinery', in B. Melzer and D. Michie (eds) *Machine Intelligence* (Edinburgh, 1969).

Double Aspect Theory

Thomas Nagel *The View From Nowhere* (Oxford, 1986).

Bertrand Russell *An Outline of Philosophy* (London, 1970).

Benedictus de Spinoza *Ethics* trans. A. Boyle (London, 1977).

Peter Strawson *Individuals: An Essay in Descriptive Metaphysics* (London, 1959).

The Phenomenological View

Franz Brentano *Psychology From an Empirical Standpoint* trans. A. C. Rancurello, D. B. Terrell and L. L. McAlister (London, 1973).

Edmund Husserl *Cartesian Meditations* trans. D. Cairns (The Hague, 1960).

—— *Ideas Pertaining to a Pure Phenomenology and to a Phenomenological Philosophy First Book* trans. F. Kersten (The Hague, 1983).

—— *Logical Investigations* trans. J. N. Findlay, 2 vols. (New York, 1970).

—— *The Paris Lectures* trans. P. Koestenbaum (The Hague, 1964).

Maurice Merleau-Ponty *The Phenomenology of Perception* trans. Colin Smith (London, 1962).

—— *The Structure of Behaviour* trans. A. Fisher (Boston, 1963).

—— *The Visible and the Invisible* trans. H. F. and P. A. Dreyfus (Evaston, 1968).

Jean-Paul Sartre *Being and Nothingness* trans. Hazel Barnes (London, 1957).

—— *The Transcendence of the Ego* trans. F. Williams and R. Kirkpatrick (New York, date unknown).

INDEX

THEORIES OF THE MIND

Stephen Priest was born in Oxford, England. He studied philosophy at the University of Cambridge and is a lecturer in the Department of Philosophy at the University of Edinburgh. During 1977 he worked in the Press and Information Department of the Council of Europe, Strasbourg, covering the European Parliament and the European Court of Human Rights. During 1986 he was a Fellow in Philosophy and Public Affairs at the Salzburg Seminar in American Studies. He has held lectureships in philosophy at the universities of Manchester, Bradford and Leeds and is Visiting Professor in Philosophy at Fort Lewis College, Colorado.

Stephen Priest is the editor of *Hegel's Critique of Kant* (1987) and author of *The British Empiricists: Hobbes to Ayer* (Penguin, 1990). His *French Philosophy Since 1945* is forthcoming from Penguin and he is presently writing a book about the French philosopher, Maurice Merleau-Ponty. His articles and reviews have appeared in many journals, including *The Philosophical Quarterly* and *The Times Higher Education Supplement*.

Stephen Priest has given radio broadcasts, public lectures and newspaper interviews on philosophical and political subjects in the United States and has read papers at many universities, including Oxford, Cambridge and Edinburgh. During 1990–91 he is Convenor of the Oxford Political Thought Group at New College, Oxford.

Stephen Priest's major interest outside philosophy is archaeology. He has dug in the English Lake District, in the Loire Valley with teams from the Sorbonne and the University of Caen, and in Cambridgeshire for the British Museum. Most recently he has explored Mayan and Toltec sites in the Yucatan peninsula of Mexico.

Stephen Priest lives and writes in Edinburgh.